A MODEST THEORY OF CIVILIZATION: WIN-WIN OR LOSE

How Cooperation Leads Society, Economics, and History Forward

+ + + + +

WILLIAM BONNER

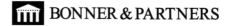

About Bonner & Partners

Over time, the patterns of history tend to repeat themselves. Our goal is to put our subscribers on the right side of history, even if it should take years before it becomes obvious.
– Bill Bonner

BONNER & PARTNERS is a financial publishing group based in Delray Beach, Florida. It was founded by Bill Bonner and his son Will in 2009 as the culmination of Bill's decades in the financial research business.

Bill founded the worldwide research network, The Agora, in 1979. Analysts at the group, including Bill himself, have exposed and predicted some of the world's biggest shifts since that time, starting with the fall of the Soviet Union back in the late 1980s, and more recently, the election of President Trump.

Bonner & Partners focuses on noticing what the mainstream media ignores. Its everyday mission is to help you look behind the curtain of Wall Street and Big Government and prepare you for big changes before they happen.

Since its founding, Bonner & Partners has recruited a group of all-star analysts, including a former corporate banker who outperformed Warren Buffett and Carl Icahn over a 10-year period, as well as a former tech CEO turned active angel investor. Bonner & Partners serves more than 500,000 readers, including almost 100,000 paying private subscribers.

Table of Contents

Introduction

"It is forbidden to kill; therefore all murderers are punished unless they kill in large numbers and to the sound of trumpets."
– Voltaire

┿┈┿┈┿┈┿

HISTORY DOESN'T TELL US who made the first falafel… or how Cleopatra felt when Marc Antony kissed her on the lips. But it does tell us that the Elamites slew the people of Uruk and the Amorites slew the Sumerians. Then, the people of Uruk slew the people of Kish. Or was it the other way around? In any case, at least the Bible is clear about it: Cain slew Abel.

And take a look at the Kennewick Man, a human skeleton discovered in Washington State in 1996. He lived around 9400 B.C. He died when another human shot him with an arrow.

The royal tomb at Ur, one of the oldest cities in the world, shows the pattern was already well developed in 2600 B.C.

Discovered at that site during the original excavation in 1922 was a wooden box with a frieze carved into it. This "Standard of Ur" depicts an army of soldiers, horses, and war chariots attacking an unidentified enemy. Soldiers are run down by the chariots. Others are led before the king to be sent into slavery, tortured, or executed.

On a stone stele discovered not far away in southern Iraq, it is recorded that Eannatum, king of Lagash, conquered the city of Umma.

On this "Stele of the Vultures," as it is called, we see the victorious phalanx marching over the bodies of the defeated enemies… with buzzards picking at the severed heads underfoot. That was in 2450 B.C. By then, this sort of thing had already been going on for at least a thousand years… and it was just beginning.

Another stele from 200 years later shows the victory of Naram-Sin, an Akkadian monarch and the grandson of King Sargon of Akkad. He fought the Lullubi, a people with an unknown language, thought to be pre-Iranian, who had come down from the Zagros mountains. He won, of course. Otherwise, the stele would be dedicated to the Lullubi king. There he is, Naram-Sin, larger than life, leading his warriors to victory… with the enemy pleading for mercy.

These are among the first records of civilized warfare. Alert readers will be quick to notice that "civilized warfare" is oxymoronic. That contradiction is at the heart of the present work.

When you set out to write a book, you know where you begin. But you don't know where you will end up. As you think and study, your ideas evolve. As the philosopher Yogi Berra put it: "You've got to be very careful if you don't know where you are going, because you might not get there." Sometimes, you end up somewhere you hadn't intended to go. But often, it is where you ought to be.

My goal was to attack the crooked timber of mankind with a chainsaw. I intended to write a book called "The Public Spectacle." In it, I would cut into the lurid and fantastic space where public life takes place.

We all spend a good deal of our lives there… Newspapers and TV shows are devoted to it… It controls many of our thoughts… It takes up our time and money… It kills millions, imprisons millions, and shackles hundreds of millions to the toxic illusions of public life. But few people have done much careful thinking about it.

Not that I was going to approach the subject in a serious or academic way; that was far more work than I was prepared to undertake. But at least I could make the chips fly and have a few laughs.

The resulting book is not the product of diligent scholarship or even careful study. Don't be surprised to find loose ends and contradictions. And don't hold your breath for precision, either. As you get deeper into the book, you will find out why.

Besides, more serious books on similar subjects, with similar conclusions, are available. Steven Pinker has a masterful tome, *The Better Angels of our Nature: Why Violence Has Declined*, with a much more thorough treatment of the origins and decline of violence in human life. William von Hippel takes up the subject of cooperation in his marvelous book, *The Social Leap*. Robert Wright's *Nonzero* does a better job of describing the evolution of a win-win society. And John Gray has thought much more deeply about the philosophical implications in his book, *The Silence of Animals*. All deserve a careful reading.

This book was supposed to be merely a collection of insights, observations, and playful guesses from someone who is trying to connect the dots – sometimes right, sometimes wrong… and always in doubt.

But what has emerged is something that has turned out to be more serious, and less funny, than I expected. The comedy is there. But there is something else, too. The same capacity for myth-making that makes public life such a hoot is also what makes civilization possible.

As we will see together, the public space – where civilization takes place – is a world that can only exist if people are willing and able to imagine things that don't exist, believe things that aren't provably true, and do things that don't really make sense for them, individually, in any conscious, immediate, or logical way.

Why else, in 1812, would 700,000 Frenchmen and their allies give up their wine and sausages, forego the warm, late-summer sun on the Seine and Rhine… and say goodbye to the coquettish smiles of their *filles* and *fräulein*… so they could join Emperor Napoléon's war, tromp 1,000 miles across the barren Steppe to freeze their *derrières* off in a fight to the death with barbarous Cossacks?

Why else would Americans spend $7 trillion to fight a "War on Terror" when there is statistically less chance of coming to grief at the hands of a terrorist than of choking to death on a filet mignon?

Why else would people believe that Pharaoh was a god... that alcohol should be outlawed in twentieth-century America... or that educated Cambodians should be forced to move to rural villages, where they could learn to be subsistence farmers?

These ideas are called "memes" by technologically inclined authors. Richard Dawkins, for example, suggests that they are very much like viruses that seek only to replicate themselves in the fertile mush of our minds. Once there, they direct our thoughts and behavior.

Given that I have trouble turning on a television, I prefer to call them "myths"; an older word that fits more elegantly into my more literary approach. As we go on, we will also see that Dawkins' "meme" concept is not really suited to our hypothesis anyway. Our desire to do win-win deals with one another doesn't come from a "meme" that has somehow found a home in our brains. More likely, the success of win-win deals caused the brain to invent a myth... or a meme... to help make sense of it.

This is not meant to diminish the power of the idea, of course. Wherever it comes from, once an idea is anchored in the public space, it tends to shape our other ideas, and our conduct, too.

Many people, for example, think "democracy is the worst form of government, except for all the others." This could be the result of observation. Or a successful meme. Or a myth, invented to protect us from other, less successful forms of government.

But we don't know whether a democracy is better. Its virtues cannot be tested. No one even knows what it means. "Better" can mean almost anything. For the concept to have any meaning at all, you have to know what "democratic government" is, too. And that is another compound abstraction given life by our imaginations.

In other words, government, along with every other thing of "importance" in the public space, is dependent on shared myths. Not necessarily true or false... good or bad, these myths are multilayered, complex, and fluid. They give rise not merely to the form of government you choose, but – at some level – to the existence of government itself.

You can find many proofs of "government" – in elections, police, wars, taxes. You can go to Washington and see government buildings… and meet people who are paid to work for "the government." You can get a check from "the government." You can get very mad at "the government." You can get put in jail by "the government"… or killed by it. But governments would disappear immediately if we stopped believing in them.

And you can't see "the government." You see people. You see uniforms (actually, what you see are colors… and things you interpret as fabrics, worn by moving things you interpret to be people). You see things going on… which you believe – in an elaborate confection of fraud, fantasy, and fact – are connected in some way to "the government."

The government is untouchable, intangible, and abstract. From its parts… its effects… and its works, you can infer that there is something going on, which you can call a "government."

But there could be other explanations for the phenomena you experience. You might just as well believe that all the things you see – thought to be related to "government" – are actually the paraphernalia of a giant film or stage production, like *The Truman Show*, where "government" employees and politicians are being portrayed by actors working in a huge set. Or it could be a red-pill dream world, like *The Matrix*, where all the sensations and thoughts arise in your own drug-fueled imagination.

Proof that government exists usually comes from its actions. "German Army Attacks Poland," said *The New York Times'* headline on September 1, 1939. The sentence would be meaningless without the existence of governments. But while reality can give a sentence meaning, a sentence cannot create reality.

Unless you believe it. Then, it brings forth a reality of its own. In this case, it suggests the existence of a "government" that organizes events and directs the movement of people and inanimate objects.

That also requires that you believe in the existence of a "country" – whatever that is – known as "Poland," which has some connection to a specific parcel of ground. But the Bavarian Alps did not attack the Polish Tatras. The Rhine did not assault the Warta. In other words, the "government" and "country" inferences are just interpretations; they are explanations for phenomena that may, or may not, be related.

If you wanted to see what really happened, you would strip away the inferences and look at it as a chipmunk might have seen it. A group of people did something. These people were dressed in similar get-ups, suggesting some sort of group allegiance. They carried objects… and traveled in other objects.

Most of the people on both sides of the action – in the "countries" we know as Poland and Germany, neither of which would exist without the imaginations of many of the people in them – probably had no idea what was going on. When informed, most were probably puzzled… appalled… excited… or indifferent. Certainly, the chipmunks were indifferent. The weather and growing seasons went on as before. The beer still fermented at the same rate. The nuts still fell from the trees.

As near as we can tell, everything continued as before… except where people did something different because they believed they were "at war" with people they had never met. Being "at war," too, required a whole panoply of ideas, none of which could be tested or proven. Some, at least on the surface, were outrageous and preposterous.

What did the typical German have against the typical Pole? Why would he want to kill him… or risk being killed by him? There was no easy answer. Instead, a person in favor of the "at war" hypothesis needed to come up with evermore incredible explanations, dipping deeper and deeper into the magic well.

He might, for example, make reference to Germany's need for "living space" to justify a "Drang nach Osten" policy. But why would the well-fed *bürger* from Köln believe such an amazing claim? How much "living space" did the typical German need? Where was he living now? Where was the evidence that more living space was needed? Why didn't he simply rent or buy, like every other honest citizen?

Adolf Hitler, a self-taught, quack economist, thought Germany couldn't feed itself. He proposed a solution: stealing underused land from the Poles. He even compared it to the Americans' taking of North America from the natives.

But had Adolf verified any of his suppositions – that the land mass of Germany was insufficient for its population… that additional output couldn't be had by further investment in agricultural modernization… that the Poles' land could be brought into cultivation economically… that Germans would want to farm in Poland… that they couldn't buy the land they wanted, or simply buy food grown by others… that food grown in Poland could be brought to market in Germany… and so on?

Of course not. And even if all these things were indisputably true, why was it a concern of the government? German families wanted automobiles, too. Was the government to begin manufacturing them? Since when was the government – which had never produced a single grain of wheat or raised a single hog – in the business of directing German agricultural output?

Or perhaps, in his search for an explanation, an observer might draw on Nietzsche's idea of the "superman." He might claim that Germans were *übermenschen*, who were not bound by the normal constraints of polite, civilized society. Like celebrities today, as current U.S. President Donald J. Trump might put it, they could do whatever they want.

There was certainly no evidence for this claim, however. It could not be tested. It could not be proven. Nietzsche himself denied it. He despised the common German *volk* and claimed that he was actually Polish!

Poor Nietzsche. He saw the limitations of the tribal "us"… the deceit that runs through much of modern public life. He knew that only a few – the natural elite – could be supermen. "Us" had nothing to do with it.

The individual had to rise above the herd... He had to avoid groupthink... He had to stand out by thinking more clearly – especially by seeing through the lurid fantasies of tabloid patriotism. Few individuals, and only the most courageous, could make the grade. Otherwise, mediocrity, swinish instincts, and cheap, me-too morality would drag him down to the level of the masses.

How it must have troubled Nietzsche's eternal rest when crackpots like Hitler, and his own sister, Elisabeth, took up the idea – and applied it to the lumpen! It was the exact opposite of what he had preached. And yet, there was the Führer himself, visiting Nietzsche's public archives in Weimar – not once, but several times. And there was Nietzsche's own sister, recruited by rascals and used to promote a woebegone project, setting up a super-race of scoundrels and dim-brained dupes in the Paraguayan wilderness.

And yet... there, too, on the backs of these fantasies, charged a "nation" of some 80 million people. This was extraordinary, not just because so much time, energy, and resources were committed to an absurd cause, but also because Germany had been among the most civilized of the Earth's countries, and now, it was launching itself on a thoroughly barbaric enterprise.

I set out to explore the manure-rich soil where these ideas take root. That is, I intended to map out the "public space." This space did not exist at all for most of our (humans) time on Earth. There were no newspapers. There was no TV. Public spaces – where you could encounter new people, ideas, and products – didn't appear until fairly recently. The ancient agora, the public square, of Athens is reliably dated to only 700 B.C.

Public meeting and market places are much older, of course. They arose with civilization, trade, and sedentary living arrangements. In the Greek agoras, the thoughts and concerns of publicly minded people were debated. But these discussions were probably limited to relatively few people. And you had to be physically present in the square to take part. No one tweeted the key ideas. No CNN featured the latest comments. And for the average person, the public space was still a relatively minor part of life.

It was in fifth-century Athens that Pericles made a public spectacle of himself. His funeral oration made very modern use of the public space, both physically and politically. He invoked the shared myths of the community to rally his fellow citizens to support a foolish war. When that war was over, Athens had been captured, with much of its population having been killed or sold into slavery.

Crucially, no widespread public space existed during the millions of years in which we evolved into the people we are now. So it is not at all surprising that we are not equipped to deal with it.

Instead, we tend to view this new space as though it were no different from the spaces in which we lived when we came down from the trees. Back then, we can guess – though we have no way of knowing it – a man's imagination didn't need to be so active. He lived too close to the edge; he couldn't take his eyes off the here and now. Chased by bears... or desperately searching for dried-up berries... he probably had little time to compose a sonnet or to wonder about the categorical imperative. Nor did he have any illusions about the people he lived with.

Anthropologists tell us that early tribes were rarely much bigger than 150 people. Everyone knew everyone else – personally. Election slogans were unnecessary. People surely had their delusions and myths, but they were probably not very elaborate... and much more subject to correction.

Instead, what early man knew was generally backed by personal experience or tradition. He may have had plenty of monsters, fairies, and spirits in his imaginary world. They must have entertained him, and perhaps warned him away from dangerous adventures ("Don't cross the river... there are dragons over there").

But his public space was extremely restricted. With too little surplus food... too little extra time... and too many threats to his existence, he couldn't afford too many expensive delusions.

If he had the time to think about it, he, like his descendants, may have come to think that he needed to build pyramids... sacrifice his children... worship gods... make war... or vote in elections. But these things take time and resources. And larger public spaces.

Only when there was more of a cushion between him and the rigors of everyday life could he afford these luxuries. And a surplus only appeared as he switched to new methods of earning his daily bread. Then, with crops and goats to draw on, his numbers increased, and what we know as history emerged. And it was a bloody mess.

The "cradle of civilization," the vast swaths of Mesopotamia and Ancient Egypt that constituted the Fertile Crescent, is strewn with details in bone, rock, and writing. And yet, the story is mostly about uncivilized behavior between unconsenting adults. That is, it is not a history of "what happened," for there were an infinite number of things happening. Instead, like today's newspapers and TV, even the earliest histories are accounts of the most notable events taking place in politics.

The region has been invaded countless times. Each time, heads rolled. Study it too carefully, and your head begins to wobble, too... you are soon lost in the countless details.

But what luck! Walking through the airport bookstore in Buenos Aires, we happened upon a special issue of *National Geographic* on the history of Mesopotamia – only 158 pages, including pictures.

We all know something of the history of Mesopotamia. Some of it is in the Old Testament. Slay, slew, have slain... without the Bible, we wouldn't know how to conjugate the verb. Which would be a shame; it seems to be the most important verb in the history of the entire Near East. The nouns are many, varied, and nuanced. But the verbs are nearly always the same – slay, slew, have slain.

And here, for convenience, we give you a broad-brush history of the Fertile Crescent region:

- Around 3700 B.C. – the first Sumerian civilization appears
- 2900 B.C. – the "first old dynasty" is in charge
- 2750 B.C. – the "second old dynasty"
- 2350 B.C. – the Akkadian Empire
- 2112 B.C. – the Paleo-Assyrian Empire
- 1650 B.C. – the Hittite Kingdom
- 1450 B.C. – the Hittite Empire
- 1000 B.C. – the Neo-Assyrian and Neo-Babylonian Empires.

There. Now you know less than you did before. Because history only tells part of the story. And not the important part. As Henry Ford put it, history is mostly "bunk" because the public space is full of fake news, loopy opinions, and fraudulent ideas… all of which lead to the disastrous events compiled as "history."

A person who is ignorant of history knows nothing. But at least his ignorance is unblemished. The person who knows something, on the other hand, often has negative knowledge. That is, he thinks he knows something, but what he knows is either untrue or so sketchy and misleading that he really knows less than nothing.

Reaching for a broader and more controversial point, in order to know some history, you must put into your brain a public spectacle narrative that is, in whole or in part, counterfeit. Your brain can never contain the totality of what happens. It can only grasp a piece of it… and then, only after it is shorn of the many links and connections that bind it to the real thing.

History pulls out a few details and focuses on them as if they were the only – or, at least, the most important – part of what happened. In order to "know" this history, you must ignore the many more complexities, ironies, and contradictions that cast doubt on it. So, the more you know, the more of the real past you must deny. And what you end up with is myth.

The part of history that *doesn't* get into the history books is the most interesting part. Monuments, broken bones, and carved steles tell us about the win-lose deals in the public space – the invasions, the battles, and the wars. The win-win deals – the private ones, made willingly, leaving both parties better off – are forgotten.

We are told, for example, that Tilgrath-Pileser conquered all the lands of the Amarru, Biblos, Sidon, and Arvad. He was a big winner. He said so himself. But who learned to weave? Who figured out how to irrigate fields and operate sluices and water gates? Who invented the wheel? Who did the things that really matter to us?

What a shame that history – like the daily news – is so focused on violence. It leaves the casual reader with an unbalanced and unhealthy view of life. He presumes that the important part of life is the public part... where the Russians, North Koreans, and terrorists are all out to get him!

He thinks they might slay him at any moment. Better to slay them first, he says to himself! Even in his career and personal life, he is likely to get the wrong idea. Like Donald Trump, he is likely to think that in order for him to win, someone else must lose.

Killing had been going on for a long time before the first grain of wheat was planted in Mesopotamia. Mankind previously lived in small groups and followed tribal instincts. Man's closest relative – the chimpanzee – still lives in tribes, attacks other tribes, and rips outsiders apart. It's a good guess that most of man's prehistory was similar. Groups attacked other groups when they could... and defended themselves as best they could.

But as the communities grew larger, "public life" grew, too. And with it grew new kinds of knowledge, new ideas, and new codes of conduct. In the Battle of Qadesh, two Mesopotamian invaders – Hittites and Egyptians – confronted each other. It occurred in 1284 B.C., in what is today Syria. It was a huge battle for the time, with as many as 47,500 soldiers and 3,500 war chariots.

Personal courage, charisma, and raw energy could not hold together an army so large... or keep it in the field for months at a time. It took organization, discipline, and a sense of purpose. While some of this was supplied by brute force, as we will see later, public myths played a big role. Soldiers and administrators had to believe that they were part of something larger... tolerable, if not just... and inevitable.

But as the myths that made large-scale warfare possible evolved, so did other myths of an entirely different sort. Some of them shriveled and died when daylight hit them. Others put down deep roots and bore fruit. It is these different myths that ultimately drew our attention and became the chief interest of this book.

"Thou Shalt Not Slay" was handed down by Moses as God's law, for instance. Had this restriction been taken seriously, it would have brought the history of Mesopotamia and the Levant to a halt. The wars and conquests made possible by the public myths of the first sort would have ended thanks to this myth of the second sort. But like Eros and Thanatos, love and hate, win-win versus win-lose, the two sorts of myths are in constant conflict.

Besides, the words left some room to maneuver – did Moses' new law outlaw "murder" and not "killing"? And "Why should we care what the god of the Jews has to say?" In any event, there was enough slack to keep the wars going.

The prohibition against murder – like all Moses' Commandments – is not a tribal prescription. It is directed at individuals. It is a private, moral rule. Even non-Jewish and non-Christian people now generally follow it. They believe there is a reason not to kill others that goes beyond formal, written law. At a practical level, they fear they may be arrested and put in jail. But that is only a possibility because so few people put it to the test. When the trumpets sound, and killing becomes widespread, the police join in (as we will see more clearly later). Kill one person, and it is a crime. Kill one thousand people, and it may win you a medal of honor.

Look more closely, and you see that the express law against murder is a result of a deeper prohibition. In other words, there would be no chance of getting arrested for murder unless murder were against the law. But it is only against the law because there is some mythic, deep-seated abhorrence of it.

Whence cometh this abhorrence? Was it the result of some moral awakening? Did reasoning lead us to it? Or religion? Perhaps you really do go to Hell if you murder someone. This is possible, but not provable. Some people – impressed by neither law nor religion – believe that the prohibition against murder is simply a "good idea" and a "good rule to live by"… that it represents some basic, ineluctable progress of humanity.

Does it? Again, there is no way to know. But the prohibition against killing appears to be useful. It allows people to come and go, to their work, to their schools and shops… secure in the knowledge that most, if not all, will get home safely. In short, it is one of the myths that make modern civilization possible, even if we can't prove it is true or know whence it came.

This insight – that the myths that thrive in public spaces… often dopey and absurd, but sometimes useful or essential… are worthy of further study – changed the focus of this book. Instead of mocking the public space itself, along with the myths and delusions you find there, we have directed much of our exploration to the myths that make civilization possible. How are the myths of civilization different from other myths? What is it that makes people "civilized"? What turns them into brutes?

It is easy and enjoyable to make fun of the fools and knaves you find in the public space. But the public space is also where you find civilized life. Without shared myths, civilization wouldn't be possible. Of course, neither would large-scale warfare, genocide, or the U.S. Congress.

How do you know which myths are beneficial to civilization? How do you separate the "civilized" from the "warfare"? How can you tell a useful myth from an appalling lie? What is "civilization" anyway?

Those are the questions I take up. You will have to judge how well I have succeeded in answering them.

A few final notes:

First, this book is not meant as a definitive work on civilization; I'm not that crazy or conceited. Instead, it is merely an exploration of civilization's foundations. With pick and trowel, we poke and dig... looking for broken shards and crumbled bones. We hope to find the bedrock, where the barbarous past ends and our civilized era begins.

Nor is there any illusion here about solving problems or building a better, more civilized future. It's hard enough to figure out what is going on. Improving it is expecting too much. Besides, once you begin meddling, you are no longer paying attention; you become a part of the thing you were trying to observe. Pretty soon, you're no longer seeing straight. If we can just manage to pass along a tiny, honest peek at civilized life, we will consider our mission complete and the book a success. We leave it to others to do with it as they please.

Readers will also note that we are from Baltimore, Maryland, which provides many rich examples of public space grotesquerie. And we travel frequently. That is neither here nor there, as far as our subject is concerned, but it – and our observations along the way – often provides illustration and context for our remarks.

And one final note: You'll notice that we have switched to the first-person plural. None of the ideas in this book are entirely original. Even those that are relatively novel were discussed with others – including other members of the family... or readers of our blog, *Bill Bonner's Diary* – always with much helpful or absurd feedback.

Ideas are never the product of a single mind. Nor do they have any real existence until they are out in the open, shared with others. "We" is simply a recognition of the contributions of so many people, over so many centuries... so many books and news articles... and so many conversations. Many of these ideas and contributions came from unknown sources... some alive, some dead. Some insights come unbidden in an offhand, easy manner. And some are the result of a lifetime of dreadful pain and suffering.

For all of them, "we" are grateful.

Bill Bonner

In the Beginning

...For I was hungry, and ye gave me no meat; I was thirsty, and ye gave me no drink; I was a stranger, and ye took me not in; naked, and ye clothed me not; sick, and in prison, and ye visited me not.
– Matthew 25:42-43

✛·✛·✛·✛

IN APRIL 2017 came news of the discovery in Morocco of a long-lost cousin. This was not the first, but the fifth relative to show up in the last few years. The human family, it turned out, is much bigger... and much older... than we had previously thought. The new findings are possibly 300,000 years old – about 100,000 years older than the oldest as-yet-discovered "human."

At the end of the previous century, people still believed the simple "out of Africa" story. Its hero was a single species of human... perhaps descended from a single mutant. The *Homo sapiens* tribe survived and spread all over the world, adapting to local conditions as necessary. At least the story was easy to remember.

But it wasn't true. In the last few years, anthropologists have identified several other human species. The first, already well known, was *Homo neanderthalensis*, presumed to be our closest relative. There are enough bones around, so we have a pretty good idea what he looked like – heavier than modern humans, perhaps smarter, and often depicted with red hair.

The surprise came when scientists traced a small percentage of the modern human genome to these Neanderthal ancestors. Europeans and Asians, but not Africans, all have a Neanderthal swinging from their family trees.

Then, it came out that there were several other skeletons in the closet. *Homo naledi* was discovered in South Africa in 2013. *Homo denisova* was found in Siberia in 2010. *Homo floresiensis* was uncovered in Indonesia in 2003. And the latest bones found in Morocco were very close to human, too.

If we were planning a large wedding, we would have one heck of a party! Some of these guys were… well… real animals!

All but one of the branches of the family have died out. And not all may have left us on friendly terms. Many of these relatives lived in the same place and at the same time as *Homo sapiens* – aka us. So far, the DNA record shows a connection between us and Neanderthals, as well as Denisovans. As for the others, we wouldn't be surprised to find that they got up to hanky panky from time to time, too, and that there are traces of still other human species in us all.

So what? It's none of our business who did what to whom out in the woods. But we are exploring the origins of civilization – how it came to be and what it means to our modern, civil society. What we notice first in the human record is not the Eros that brought different humans together, but the Thanatos that had them go for each other's throats.

ARGUING WITH GOD

It is one thing to kill people you don't know, simply because the *federales* command it. But what is it when you kill your own children because God tells you to do so? Yahweh, Abraham's god, told him to kill his only son, Isaac. Abraham was ready to do it, too. He had a knife in his hand when an angel told him to stop, that it was just a test. God was looking for a few good men who would do His bidding, including killing their own kin for His sake.

Arguing With God is a play written by a friend, John B. Henry. It is the story of the Jews… and their long, difficult relationship with their god. It is the theme of the Old Testament, before the coming of Christ. But it is told in contemporary language, leaving the audience to make the quick connection: "The chosen people" of antiquity become the one, "indispensable nation" – the USA – of today.

God chose the Jews to be his standard bearers – apparently because they were willing to do outrageous and appalling things in His name. He sent them off to kill and conquer. And no angel intervened. Instead, God Himself goaded on the killers and was upset when they left the job only half done.

In the book of Deuteronomy, for example, we have the story of the annihilation of the Canaanites. It was not enough to conquer territory. God ordered the Israelites to "not leave alive anything that breathes" and to "completely destroy them." And not just the fighting men. He wanted to snuff out women, children, beasts of burden… even household pets.

John B. Henry grew up the son of an Episcopalian minister in Virginia. By the time he left home, he had read the Bible cover to cover seven times. But it was only when he reread it as an adult, he says, that the violence of the Almighty came fully into focus. He was shocked.

The Old Testament recounts one act of murder and genocide after another. The Lord Jehovah was not content to shoot off a few hundred rounds in a nightclub, murder a few dozen school children, or stab a few passers-by on the street in London. He'd take out an entire town.

Here is what Genesis tells us destroyed Sodom and Gomorrah: "brimstone and fire from the Lord out of heaven." In Deuteronomy 29:23, Moses later described what it looked like:

> [23] *The whole land will be a burning waste of salt and sulfur – nothing planted, nothing sprouting, no vegetation growing on it. It will be like the destruction of Sodom and Gomorrah, Admah and Zeboyim, which the Lord overthrew in fierce anger.*

At God's suggestion, the Israelites exterminated the Amalekites, too. From book of 1 Samuel 15:8:

> *⁸ He took Agag, king of the Amalekites alive, and all his people he totally destroyed with the sword.*

The book of Ezekiel 9:4-6 further reports:

> *⁴ The Lord said to him, "Go through the midst of the city, even through the midst of Jerusalem, and put a mark on the foreheads of the men who sigh and groan over all the abominations which are being committed in its midst."*
>
> *⁵ But to the others He said in my hearing, "Go through the city after him and strike; do not let your eye have pity and do not spare. Utterly slay old men, young men, maidens, little children, and women, but do not touch any man on whom is the mark; and you shall start from My sanctuary."*
>
> *⁶ So they started with the elders who were before the temple...*

And when God was displeased with His people, He practically exterminated them, too.

"Seven days from now I will send rain on the earth for forty days and forty nights, and I will wipe from the face of the earth every living creature I have made," He says in Genesis 7:4.

Arguing With God is meant to make audiences wonder about America's place in the world and its connection to God. But it made us wonder about God Himself. What kind of god would urge his people to destroy their neighbors?

The God of the Old Testament is a tribal god in a win-lose world. His role was to assure the survival and prosperity of His chosen people.

After escaping from Egyptian captivity, the Israelites wandered in the desert for 40 years. It was during this time that Moses handed down the Ten Commandments, with "Thou Shalt Not Kill" prominent on the list.

Then, arriving in the land of milk and honey, the sons of Abraham had to take the milk and honey away from their owners, who were reluctant to give them up. Here, we quote extensively from the book of Joshua:

Joshua 6:21-24

21 And they utterly destroyed all that was in the city, both man and woman, young and old, and ox, and sheep, and ass, with the edge of the sword.

22 But Joshua had said unto the two men that had spied out the country, Go into the harlot's house, and bring out thence the woman, and all that she hath, as ye swore unto her.

23 And the young men that were spies went in, and brought out Rahab, and her father, and her mother, and her brethren, and all that she had; and they brought out all her kindred, and left them without the camp of Israel.

24 And they burnt the city with fire, and all that was therein: only the silver, and the gold, and the vessels of brass and of iron, they put into the treasury of the house of the LORD.

Joshua 8:25-29

25 And so it was, that all that fell that day, both of men and women, were twelve thousand, even all the men of Ai.

26 For Joshua drew not his hand back, wherewith he stretched out the spear, until he had utterly destroyed all the inhabitants of Ai.

27 Only the cattle and the spoil of that city Israel took for a prey unto themselves, according unto the word of the LORD which he commanded Joshua.

²⁸ And Joshua burnt Ai, and made it an heap forever, even a desolation unto this day.

²⁹ And the king of Ai he hanged on a tree until eventide: and as soon as the sun was down, Joshua commanded that they should take his carcase down from the tree, and cast it at the entering of the gate of the city, and raise thereon a great heap of stones, that remaineth unto this day.

Joshua 10:24-43

²⁴ And it came to pass, when they brought out those kings unto Joshua, that Joshua called for all the men of Israel, and said unto the captains of the men of war which went with him, Come near, put your feet upon the necks of these kings. And they came near, and put their feet upon the necks of them.

²⁵ And Joshua said unto them, Fear not, nor be dismayed, be strong and of good courage: for thus shall the LORD do to all your enemies against whom ye fight.

²⁶ And afterward Joshua smote them, and slew them, and hanged them on five trees: and they were hanging upon the trees until the evening.

²⁷ And it came to pass at the time of the going down of the sun, that Joshua commanded, and they took them down off the trees, and cast them into the cave wherein they had been hid, and laid great stones in the cave's mouth, which remain until this very day.

²⁸ And that day Joshua took Makkedah, and smote it with the edge of the sword, and the king thereof he utterly destroyed, them, and all the souls that were therein; he let none remain: and he did to the king of Makkedah as he did unto the king of Jericho.

²⁹ Then Joshua passed from Makkedah, and all Israel with him, unto Libnah, and fought against Libnah.

³⁰ And the LORD delivered it also, and the king thereof, into the hand of Israel; and he smote it with the edge of the sword, and all the souls that were therein; he let none remain in it; but did unto the king thereof as he did unto the king of Jericho.

³¹ *And Joshua passed from Libnah, and all Israel with him, unto Lachish, and encamped against it, and fought against it.*

³² *And the LORD delivered Lachish into the hand of Israel, which took it on the second day, and smote it with the edge of the sword, and all the souls that were therein, according to all that he had done to Libnah.*

³³ *Then Horam king of Gezer came up to help Lachish; and Joshua smote him and his people, until he had left him none remaining.*

³⁴ *And from Lachish Joshua passed unto Eglon, and all Israel with him; and they encamped against it, and fought against it.*

³⁵ *And they took it on that day, and smote it with the edge of the sword, and all the souls that were therein he utterly destroyed that day, according to all that he had done to Lachish.*

³⁶ *And Joshua went up from Eglon, and all Israel with him, unto Hebron; and they fought against it:*

³⁷ *And they took it, and smote it with the edge of the sword, and the king thereof, and all the cities thereof, and all the souls that were therein; he left none remaining, according to all that he had done to Eglon; but destroyed it utterly, and all the souls that were therein.*

³⁸ *And Joshua returned, and all Israel with him, to Debir; and fought against it.*

³⁹ *And he took it, and the king thereof, and all the cities thereof; and they smote them with the edge of the sword, and utterly destroyed all the souls that were therein; he left none remaining: as he had done to Hebron, so he did to Debir, and to the king thereof; as he had done also to Libnah, and to her king.*

⁴⁰ So Joshua smote all the country of the hills, and of the south, and of the vale, and of the springs, and all their kings: he left none remaining, but utterly destroyed all that breathed, as the LORD God of Israel commanded.

⁴¹ And Joshua smote them from Kadeshbarnea even unto Gaza, and all the country of Goshen, even unto Gibeon.

⁴² And all these kings and their land did Joshua take at one time, because the LORD God of Israel fought for Israel.

⁴³ And Joshua returned, and all Israel with him, unto the camp to Gilgal.

Joshua 11:9-23

⁹ And Joshua did unto them as the LORD bade him: he houghed their horses, and burnt their chariots with fire.

¹⁰ And Joshua at that time turned back, and took Hazor, and smote the king thereof with the sword: for Hazor beforetime was the head of all those kingdoms.

¹¹ And they smote all the souls that were therein with the edge of the sword, utterly destroying them: there was not any left to breathe: and he burnt Hazor with fire.

¹² And all the cities of those kings, and all the kings of them, did Joshua take, and smote them with the edge of the sword, and he utterly destroyed them, as Moses the servant of the LORD commanded.

¹³ But as for the cities that stood still in their strength, Israel burned none of them, save Hazor only; that did Joshua burn.

¹⁴ And all the spoil of these cities, and the cattle, the children of Israel took for a prey unto themselves; but every man they smote with the edge of the sword, until they had destroyed them, neither left they any to breathe.

15 As the LORD commanded Moses his servant, so did Moses command Joshua, and so did Joshua; he left nothing undone of all that the LORD commanded Moses.

16 So Joshua took all that land, the hills, and all the south country, and all the land of Goshen, and the valley, and the plain, and the mountain of Israel, and the valley of the same.

17 Even from the mount Halak, that goeth up to Seir, even unto Baalgad in the valley of Lebanon under mount Hermon: and all their kings he took, and smote them, and slew them.

18 Joshua made war a long time with all those kings.

19 There was not a city that made peace with the children of Israel, save the Hivites the inhabitants of Gibeon: all other they took in battle.

20 For it was of the LORD to harden their hearts, that they should come against Israel in battle, that he might destroy them utterly, and that they might have no favour, but that he might destroy them, as the LORD commanded Moses.

21 And at that time came Joshua, and cut off the Anakims from the mountains, from Hebron, from Debir, from Anab, and from all the mountains of Judah, and from all the mountains of Israel: Joshua destroyed them utterly with their cities.

22 There was none of the Anakims left in the land of the children of Israel: only in Gaza, in Gath, and in Ashdod, there remained.

23 So Joshua took the whole land, according to all that the LORD said unto Moses; and Joshua gave it for an inheritance unto Israel according to their divisions by their tribes. And the land rested from war.

Whew! In this section of the Bible, we also get another verb... now almost forgotten: smite, smote, have smitten. Without smiting and slaying, history would have disappeared.

But that's how you get ahead in a zero-sum game. Do unto others good and hard, before they do unto you.

Glancing ahead, the hypothesis of this book is that something big happened 3,000 to 2,000 years ago. A big change. A revolutionary change. The biggest change in history. A new god was in town. It was the change from win-lose to win-win… from theft to barter… from force to persuasion… from brute politics to civilization… from rape to seduction… from credit and gift-giving to hard money and double-entry bookkeeping… from tribalism to universalism… from forced collectivism to voluntary collectivism… and from the Old Testament to the New Testament.

Most important, it was a change in public attitudes… and myths. "Do unto others as you would have them do unto you," said Jesus of Nazareth. The Jewish prophet, Hillel, his contemporary, said almost the same thing, but in the negative: "That which you don't want someone to do to you, don't do to them." Win-win, in other words.

This was a radical innovation, perhaps the biggest and most important one ever. In evolutionary terms, it was a mutation. But it was a rare one… and a successful one. Today, with one major exception (which we will address in another chapter), and millions of minor ones, most of the world operates most of the time on win-win deals.

But let us step back further. We will see that slaying and smiting began long before Moses crossed the Red Sea. We will see also the context in which slaying and smiting made sense.

IGNOBLE SAVAGES

There are two opposing views of prehistory. In one, the noble savages lived at great remove one from another; violence was limited. In the other view, prehistoric people were drenched in each other's blood.

Man, in his present form, has been around for 200,000-300,000 years. We believe we can divide that into two parts. The first stage – prehistory – lasted many thousands of years. In that stage, the idea of "murder" didn't exist. There was no word for it. As we will see more fully later, humans are unique in the animal world in one important way: we have words. Words fill our minds and shape our world. And each word is an idea… a myth… a meme.

In the beginning, there was no murder. And no right or wrong. Killing was normal. We survived by killing animals. And before the advent of what we call "civilization," killing other humans was more often a badge of honor than a mark of shame. People took great pride in killing others, often keeping their scalps or skulls as souvenirs. In one tribe in New Guinea, for example, men wear elaborate makeup and gaudy decorations. But they are only allowed to do so after they have killed someone. Many other tribes had similar customs, where full participation in mating and other adult privileges were reserved for those who had proven themselves – by killing.

Readers will note that this point of view is unpopular with a broad swath of scholars, politicians, and the public. Since the time of the eighteenth-century philosopher Jean-Jacques Rousseau, it has been common to think of indigenous, pre-civilized, prehistoric peoples as untainted by the corruptions of modern life. They were believed to have a "purer" form of human community, unadulterated by the contrivances of civilization, including its words. And they were considered "freer," unshackled by the restraints of more-advanced societies.

According to Freud (and many others), the distinguishing feature of civilization is restraint. In the course of this little book, we will discuss the various restraints needed for civilization to take place. We will give our definition, or theory, of civilization. And we will look at why the principles, requirements, and rules of civilization are more than cultural prejudices or consciously imposed laws.

In the beginning was the word. That is, the first restraint of civilization is language. No law commands you to speak a language. But if you want to take part in civilized life, you must communicate… following the rules of language. It's no good to blab out whatever you want. You must stick to the program.

That was the first thing the ancient Greeks noticed about the people they called "Barbarians." They didn't speak a civilized language. Instead, they just seemed to be barking at each other... "bar... bar... bar..." That is, at least by some accounts, how the Barbarians got their name.

But words are not neutral, clean, information-carrying vessels. They are metaphors, images, myths, and lies. And as man furnished his mind with words, he created a world that did not – objectively – exist.

For example, as soon as you invent the word "murder," you have introduced a whole new concept, unknown in the animal world – morality. So, too, does "Thou Shalt Not Steal" suggest an idea of property rights that does not exist without human imagination and myth-making skills. The prohibitions against murder and theft require a whole, elaborate décor of right and wrong.

Human civilization requires these restraints, for reasons that will become more obvious as we continue. It also needs restraints of other sorts – money, manners, and common laws, for example. And perhaps writing. Each one of these things limits what we say and do. We are no longer wild. We are tame. Our actions are limited. And so are our thoughts, through words and myths, directed into acceptable channels. As we will see, no declaration by any king or dictator forces these rules on us. This is the "strain of civilization," as philosopher Karl Popper described it. It is a restriction on what we can and cannot do. Within these limits – as with the rules of language – we can accomplish much more than without them. They are chains, but they leave us free to operate in a much broader, more productive way. Not that we can take credit for these things, as if we invented civilization. We did not. Instead, it invented us.

And before we go further, it is only fair to stop and warn you, Dear Reader, that this next section may be more demanding than usual – of reader as well as of writer.

So, if you want to get off the bus here, there will be no hard feelings. First, because the going might be rough. And second, because you might not like it very much when we get there. And third, because once you get there, you may not be able to ever come back. This is a one-way ride.

"Oh, people are funny," said our driver, taking us from the airport in Dublin, Ireland to a hotel in County Waterford. It was a long journey, giving him plenty of opportunity to express himself.

"See that highway…" He pointed to a turn-off. "It's the road to Limerick. The engineers had all done their work. The planning was done. Contracts were let out. The bulldozers and trucks were all lined up. And then, a local farmer asked: 'What about the fairy tree?'

"Now, you ask anyone, and they'll tell you they don't believe that nonsense about fairies and the spirit world. But down deep, we all believe.

"So, they had millions of euros already set aside to build the road. But nobody would cut down the fairy tree. I can just imagine the conversation.

"'Sean…you cut it down.' 'No… Paddy, you cut it down.' 'Nooo… Ronan, you're a good man with a chainsaw… Go ahead and cut the damned tree down.' 'Look, if you want it cut down… cut it down yourself.'

"Nobody wanted to cut it down. Because there would be a curse on whoever did. In the end, they had to reroute the road.

"And probably, on some level, they don't really believe in the spirit world. But nobody wanted to put the curse to the test.

"That's the way it is with a lot of things. What we say we believe is not always what we really believe."

Whence cometh these peculiar beliefs? The hardware we know as "human" – the bones and the meat – was apparently developed by billions of years of adaptation and mutation… and perhaps divine intervention. We don't know exactly how or why it worked the way it did… but it delivered to us the wrecks we know as "human beings."

And you are perfectly within your rights to fill in the missing knowledge by saying: "God created man." And perhaps He did. If so, you can blame Him or praise Him. But the process by which He made us appears remarkably "hands off." That is, the bone record looks like a lot of fumbling and bumbling... trial and error – the same process we see in the rest of the natural world. From Lucy – the female primate who was supposed to be mother to us all – to all manner of knuckle-dragging bipeds... From monkey to man – with plenty of dead ends, false starts, and mutant ninja turtles along the way – the process can be described as "evolution," even without knowing exactly how it works.

The more interesting and controversial point is this: The human software was created in more or less the same way. Why do we think what we think? Why do we smile? Why do we shake hands, or say please and thank you? Again, there are oceans of ignorance on the subject. But on our little patch of dry land, the process that gave us our thoughts, our instincts, and our emotions looks a lot more like evolution than any other word we can think of.

When we fall in love, we don't do so because we think it would be a good idea to fall in love. We don't do it because there is a falling-in-love contest that we want to win. We don't do it because someone tells us that we should, or because we'll earn more money if we do. Instead, we do it because we're programmed to do it.

We didn't think our way to falling in love any more than we thought our way to having five fingers rather than seven, or to wanting to eat fried *foie gras* rather than raw sewage.

But we do fall in love. Our most powerful instincts and emotions are engaged in a way that has very little to do with what we think. Or, to put it another way, we think what our instincts and emotions lead us to think. We think she's pretty. We think she's smart. We think she's sexy.

But why do we bother to think any of these things? "The mind is just the heart's dupe," wrote author André Gide. Your thoughts are brought to bear as your instincts and emotions – your heart – command, not the other way around.

What you think is what your software tells you to think. Of course, there's room for "creative" thinking... or thinking "outside the box"... coming up with ideas that seem to be contrary to your basic instincts and wellbeing. And sometimes, you are faced with choices which your brain has to figure out, more or less on its own.

You may even think that falling in love is not such a good idea. You may decide not to marry and not to have children. You may come to believe you can jump off a cliff, flap your arms, and fly. You think... and therefore, you are flying! You don't do yourself any favor with this sort of fantasy. But you do the human race a useful service – you eliminate your DNA from the gene pool! That software, in other words, is taken off the shelf.

The population that exists today is the product of people whose parents probably fell in love, wanted to have children, and didn't jump off the cliff. And their software – made up of instincts, emotions, social conventions, and traditions – is our software.

The restraints of civilization are part of our software, too. But they are fairly new. They exist not because we were smart enough to invent them, but because those who couldn't, or didn't, take them on have been killed or marginalized.

Greek- and Roman-era writers had a culturally biased view of civilization, rooted in the deepest, most atavistic, and most disastrous part of our software. The difference between Barbarians and civilized people was simple: it was the difference between them and us. "We" are civilized. "They" are not. A "Barbarian," from the Greek word *barbaroi*, simply meant a non-Greek. When writers undertook to define the critical difference more carefully, they claimed the Barbarians lacked dominion over themselves. The tribes to the north and the east were ruled, they believed, by "temper and insatiable desires." That is, the Barbarians didn't submit to the fetters of civilization.

Polybius, the Greek historian who accompanied the Roman general Scipio in his conquest of the Carthaginians, described Barbarians:

They lived in unwalled villages and had no knowledge of the
refinements of civilization. As they slept on straw and leaves, ate
meat and practiced no other pursuits but war and agriculture, their
lives were very simple and they were completely unacquainted with
any art or science. Their possessions consisted of cattle and gold, since
these were the only objects which they could easily take with them
whatever the circumstances and transport whenever they chose.

It was as if, he said of the Gauls, "fortune had afflicted the whole
race… with a kind of epidemic of aggression."

Alas, the Romans of the fifth century found it impossible to stop
the Barbarians from crossing the Rhine into the empire. The best they
could hope for, they said, was to turn these new immigrants into new,
romanized men… who would reject impulsivity and instead rely on
rational thought and calm reflection. It was a tall order. And a bad bet.
You could take a Barbarian out of the forests, but you couldn't take the
forest out of a Barbarian.

Tervingians, Merovingians, Salian Franks, Rhenan Franks, Goths,
Vandals, Huns… the Veneti, the Anares, the Boii, the Lingones, the
Senones, and many other tribes too numerous to mention… turned
on their hosts, massacred and enslaved them, and laid waste to most of
Europe west of the Rhine, and much of North Africa, too.

Two steps forward. One step back. Or two. It takes thousands of
years to make a civilized man. And even then, *Homo sapiens* himself
doesn't change much. He still looks like a wild man of the forests. He
often acts like one, too.

Generally, we respect the rules of language and property, as well
as those of social and commercial intercourse. But Rome wasn't built
in a day. And civilization is not like turning on a light. It's not either
on or off. Just as there is no switch that causes a complete shift from
pre-civilized codes to those of the civilized world, nor is there anything
that prevents a little civilized behavior from creeping into otherwise

barbarian cultures. Many pioneers and captives told of being treated well by American Indians. Some captive European women married native men, had children with them, and when "rescued," refused to return to the "civilized" world.

In *Discourse on the Origin of Inequality*, Rousseau writes:

> [N]othing is so gentle as man in his primitive state, when, placed by nature at an equal distance from the stupidity of brutes and the fatal enlightenment of civil man [...] he is restrained by natural pity from needlessly harming anyone himself, even if he has been harmed.

This view is probably both correct and absurd. The savage was largely untethered by the ropes and reins of civilization. But he was far from noble. Eyewitness and expert testimonies show the indigenous peoples of whom we have historical records to be violent, brutish, and cruel. The archaeological record, too, suggests that violence was a much bigger part of life before the arrival of civilization. The records from both sources tell us that pre-civilized people were given to murder, mayhem, torture, and cannibalism. Not to mention slavery, rape, and massacre.

Even as recently as November 2018, an American missionary set out to bring the Christian faith to Sentinel Island's natives in the Bay of Bengal. They appear to have killed him soon after he set foot on the island; and we doubt that they felt they had done anything wrong.

This was hardly shocking. We have enough bones from the Late Paleolithic and Neolithic periods to see that killing was common. One ancient boneyard, Cemetery 117, on the east bank of the River Nile in northern Sudan, shows signs of a massacre 13,000-14,000 years ago. Many of the almost 60 skeletons discovered there have arrowheads embedded in them. We don't know what happened, but we can be pretty sure the damage was not self-inflicted. Half the skeletons are female; they are probably not deaths from a battle. In Turkana, Kenya, meanwhile, there are numerous 10,000-year-old human remains with evidence of major traumatic injuries, including obsidian bladelets in the ancient bones.

Californian anthropology professor Mark Allen studied the record of prehistoric hunter-gatherers in the central part of the state. Looking at fragments of bones from the last 1,000 years, he came to the conclusion that violence was a way of life. His research showed that more than one in 10 males suffered some form of violent trauma – a rate not even reached among soldiers in World War II. Among females, the rate of violent trauma, as measured by the bone records, was one in 20. In the 14th century, at Crow Creek, in what is now South Dakota, the homicide rate was up to 60%.

We turned to *North American Indigenous Warfare and Ritual Violence*, edited by Richard J. Chacon and Rubén G. Mendoza, for further illustration. We will just quote various passages, more or less at random:

> *The objective of surprise attacks and battles was to kill as many of the enemy as possible: men always, and usually women and children as well. (p. 19)*

> *Inuit warriors attacked the group of Omushkegok people, mostly women and children and the elders, while the men were hunting... the Inuit descended from their hiding place and attacked the camp, killing all the elders and the children and the women. (p. 37)*

> *The Inuit make war on all their neighbors, and when they kill or capture any of their enemies, they eat them raw and drink their blood... (p. 37)*

> *The Cree [...] when their enemies fall into their hands they scalp them. They tear off the skin which covers the skull and they put as many marks of themselves as they have taken scalps. (p. 39)*

> *Cree war parties attacked Inuit on the eastern coast of Hudson Bay: 1707, 1728, 1730, 1735, 1736, 1738, 1755, 1757, 1766, 1767, 1770, 1774, 1777, 1781, 1782, 1783, 1791, and 1793... (p. 51)*

Warfare between the Cree and the Chipewyan was intense and violent... (p. 57)

The skeletal evidence shows trauma in the form of depressed skulls, fractures from club blows, facial and anterior tooth fractures, defensive forearm and outer hand injuries, and decapitation. (p. 60)

40% of the individuals recovered in the Prince Rupert Harbour area were found to have fractures to the limbs and spine... (p. 62)

Warfare is postulated to have been endemic across the northern Southwest in the 13th century. (p. 116)

Human death is necessary to give the sun energy. (p. 120)

The archeological record indicates the pre-contact [before the arrival of Europeans] war in the northern midcontinent was a part of everyday life. (p. 130)

The pattern is consistent and clear [...] About 16% of several hundred burials showed signs of having died a violent death, with evidence of decapitation, scalping, blunt force trauma, and arrow points embedded in bone... (p. 139)

Raiders virtually decimated the population of a large fortified village [...] The mutilated bodies of nearly five hundred villagers were recovered... (p. 140)

Conflicts were not limited to particular kinds of societies, however they might be classified [...] Anybody, regardless of age or sex, could fall victim to an attack; nobody was spared [...] Weak and debilitated people who were least able to fight or flee were most likely to be killed [...] Ambushes were the most common form of attack... (p. 185)

On and on... page after page. Whenever archaeologists dig up bones in North America, they find evidence of a dog-eat-dog world inhabited by humans. If the implied murder rate in much of the past – about 10% – were today's rate, some 30 million people in the U.S. would die violent, non-accidental deaths. Even in Baltimore, one of America's most murderous cities, a 10% murder rate would be shocking and appalling. There, only about 300 of the city's 600,000 population die violently every year. Of the 6,000 deaths there last year, 5% came about violently.

Responsible scholars draw back from sweeping generalizations. No one knows what prehistoric life was like... or even if it was uniform enough, over hundreds of thousands of years and thousands of different cultures, to permit generalizations at all. But the bone records, as well as anthropological studies of primitive tribes, tell the tale: In the distant past, violence was common.

Anthropologist Margaret Mead, after a lifetime of studying primitive tribes, guessed what public life was like for most humans during the hunter-gatherer stage: If you met someone from a different tribe, your first instinct – as demonstrated by the aforementioned Sentinel Islanders – was probably to kill him. There is a good reason to think this was so: It was probably the smart thing to do. There were only so many fat birds and slow deer, and only so many women. If your tribe were to survive and prosper, it could not "create" more wealth. It had to take it away from someone else. And even if your tribe was fat and happy, with no ambition to take anything from anyone else, it was still well advised to annihilate other tribes whenever it could. Otherwise, it was just a matter of time before you were attacked.

Generally, there was no such thing as win-win, in other words, in the primitive world. Man, a part of nature, had his place. He hunted. And he was hunted. He killed animals to eat. It is not much of a leap to think that he killed humans, too.

It is indisputable that proto-*Homo sapiens* came into contact with other human species. In one cave in Siberia, for example, remains of three different human species have been found – Neanderthals, Denisovans, and *Homo sapiens*. All competed for the same game... the same hunting grounds... and, perhaps, the same shelter. The disappearance of these rival species could have "natural" causes. But what would be more natural, in the prehistoric world, than murder? And, perhaps, cannibalism. Even as late as the 16th century, when Europeans spread throughout the world, they found cannibalism was still widely practiced.

There were times, surely, when tribes could expand without eating their competitors. The movement into empty continents and islands, for example, permitted large population increases without interspecies competition. In the space of a few thousand years, however, Australia and the Americas filled up. The easily hunted megafauna – giant sloths, flightless birds, and odd creatures such as the glyptodon – were exterminated. Then, it was back to zero-sum. And that was, more or less, what the first Europeans found when they arrived in these new lands. The local tribes were in constant warfare with one another.

Within their own tribes, there is no reason to think that Native Americans, for example, were particularly bloodthirsty. But even colonial-era tribes were likely engaged, often with unbelievable ferocity, in long, protracted wars for dominance and territory.

Revenge was a powerful, and logical, motive. If you knew that another tribe would seek revenge – perhaps like Donald J. Trump vowing to hit back "ten times as hard" – you would have to think twice before attacking. And if you attacked, you would want to be sure that your target was not merely damaged, but exterminated. Typically, all males were killed – even infants. Women were taken as slaves and concubines. No one who might seek revenge should be left alive.

There were peaceful tribes in some areas, and groups of tribes that had worked out peaceful alliances with each other. But they were fleeting. As far as we know, peace was based on convenience rather than deeply held "myths" or moral values. Again, as far as we know, there was no concept of murder and no "rule" against killing someone from another tribe (though there were compensatory systems and ritualized warfare in some places to prevent excessive bloodshed). The reader will see, as we get deeper into our subject, that moral values and "myths" are more likely the product of convenience than the other way around.

The rule against murder, for example, arose after the Neolithic Age for a very simple reason: murder ceased to pay. But we'll get to that later.

The most recently inhabited large land mass – New Zealand – provides some interesting evidence. The islands were discovered and settled only about 700 years ago by a handful of Polynesians. DNA and oral traditions both suggest that these founders numbered no more than about 400 people, probably all from the same tribe, and presumably travelling in small boats.

It does not take much imagination to think these first settlers enjoyed a good romp over both islands, exterminating the large moa bird by the year 1300 or so. During the early years, we imagine that there was little reason for one group to compete with another. The "sum" was not zero... not even close. It was apparently unlimited. No group had to give up anything in order for another group to expand. But wealth, power, and status are relative, not absolute. And the history of the Spanish conquest of the New World, however, suggests that the early immigrants to New Zealand probably fought with each other anyway. Even with an entire continent to conquer, and only a handful of Spaniards to do the work, new arrivals nevertheless often found their fellow conquistadores to be their most lethal enemies.

This small group of pioneers that first encountered what is now New Zealand was able to expand to 100,000 people, as estimated by the English when they arrived in the mid-1700s. By then, the Māori – as the descendants of the first settlers came to be known – were at each other's throats. The "indigenous" people had formed into rival tribes and built extensive forts to protect themselves from each other. In 1642, Dutch explorer Abel Tasman, the first white man to see the islands, named his first port of call "Murderers' Bay" (now Golden Bay), after he was attacked there by the Māori. Early missionaries were appalled by the almost unrelenting violence – murder, rape, beatings, war, reprisals, and slavery. It must have been like Baltimore! Cannibalism was common, too – the ultimate win-lose proposition.

Europeans brought new technology, including the musket. This tipped the balance of power in favor of those locals who got their hands on them first. By 1835, a tribe of Māori armed with muskets attacked their distant cousins, the Moriori tribe on Chatham Island, and practically annihilated them. By 1901, there were only 35 Moriori left on the island.

"Thou Shalt Not Kill," proclaims the Commandment. The Māori didn't seem to get the message. Why not kill? Is it because God said so? Whose god? In the long period of human prehistory, at least after the debut of the Neolithic Age, it appears that killing others paid off. The killers gained an advantage.

If you live in a zero-sum world, there is no obvious incentive not to kill. If you kill, you are arguably better off. There's one less hunter to compete with... one less man who might kill you... and one less man to muscle out of the way so you can have access to females. Like a shareholder after a buy-back program, the sum will be shared by fewer people. But this logic probably doesn't apply within a tribe. Members of a tribe may be necessary to ensure each other's survival. The gatherers gather. The hunters hunt. The women bear children. The men fight off predators and usurpers. All share similar DNA, culture, myths, and food. The loss of a fellow tribesman may be a loss to everyone in the tribe, perhaps imperiling the entire group.

Within a tribe, there are rules and customs that help the group survive. In times of famine, for example, the old and young may be abandoned. Food may be rationed, with the biggest portions given to the young men needed for hunting or protection. Superstitions and myths may help tribe members avoid any temptation to jeopardize their survival.

Even in modern times, under stress, groups of people revert to uncivilized behavior in which the codes of acceptable action are more consistent with the barbarous past. In modern times, the hyperinflation in Germany in the 1920s, and again in the immediate aftermath of

World War II... in Nanking, when the Japanese captured the city... in Naples, after the German army left... in the prisoner of war, work, and extermination camps – extraordinarily unchristian and uncivilized things took place. In German camps, for example, starving Soviet prisoners were reported to have routinely fought over the corpses of their dying comrades, tearing the meat off the bones before the bodies were dragged away.

Back in Paleolithic or Neolithic times, the rule against murder, if there was one, probably didn't extend very far. Even today, murdering foreigners is not regarded with much revulsion. Early in Donald J. Trump's presidency, for example, a team of Navy Seals was sent into a village in Yemen at night to steal some laptop computers. A firefight broke out. Apparently, up to 30 civilians, including women and children, were shot dead... and one Navy Seal lost his life. The U.S. media focused much attention on the dead Navy Seal... and almost none on the dead foreigners. More broadly, America's wars in the Middle East are said to have caused as many as 1 million deaths in the region. Almost no one in the U.S. is even aware of this number; few care.

Economist and philosopher Adam Smith highlighted this phenomenon, suggesting that an Englishman would be more aggrieved by the loss of his little finger than by the death of 100,000 people in China. Steven Pinker, though, believes we are now a better species, and that almost no one today – if he had the choice – would consciously choose a finger over 100,000 Chinese lives. Perhaps. With the world watching and enough anesthesia, a person may surrender a finger to save the multitudes. But what if he had to cut it off himself, with no one to praise him for doing it or to criticize him for not doing it?

Strangers are not "us." They are "them." They are a different tribe. Most Americans know that more than 50,000 U.S. troops died in the Vietnam War; very few know or care that 40 times as many Vietnamese may have died. Today, murder is frowned on almost everywhere, but when foreigners are killed, there is little sense of outrage or loss.

But our guess is that Pinker is more right than wrong. Little by little, over thousands of years, the macroeconomic context changed. Returns to killers must have begun to decline. Cooperation became relatively more profitable; the sum expanded and eventually, killers could no longer compete. Today, we still have killers. But killing is prohibited by law and custom, as well as religious and social taboo. Perhaps more important, it is not profitable. The killer rarely gets to keep his victim's property... or his women. He has no need for revenge killing either; he has the government to do that for him.

Even the idea of "murder" may be more modern than we realize. Would Moses have brought down a tablet banning murder if it had already been a no-no? Which brings us back to our question: What's so bad about killing people? We kill animals. Why not humans?

MORALITY PAYS

The central idea of this book, in its crudest and simplest form, is that economics leads morality, and that the transition to a win-win world beginning about 4,000 years ago brought modern morality with it. American journalist Robert Wright probably has it backwards when he says, "memes which manage to pass through this gauntlet of cultural selection, and come to characterize whole societies, often encourage non-zero-sum interaction."

More likely, the success of win-win deals set the imagination to work to craft explanations, rules, and myths. As anthropologist Franz Boas explained, "It seems to be one of the fundamental characteristics of the development of mankind that activities which have developed unconsciously are gradually made the subject of reasoning."

This is not a new idea. Nineteenth-century philosopher Karl Marx and many others were on the case long ago. Marx thought economic changes were the real source of both political and moral developments. And American economist Mancur Olson described how morality evolved; he explained that ethical rules lagged economic developments.

"Morality is what used to pay," he wrote.

Marx and his followers then made an extraordinary and unfortunate leap. From the insight that morals are driven by circumstances (power relationships, technology, and broadly, economics), they jumped to the staggering assertion that "bourgeois" morality didn't matter, and that they could change both the economy and morals at will. Reconfiguring economic and political systems to their liking, they thought they could dispense with the process by which they had been created and the hidden insights they carried with them.

But neither the economy nor the moral system was ever fully subject to their conscious designs. They could design a new economy, but it wouldn't do what an economy should do – make it possible for people to get what they want. They could insist on a new moral structure, too – but, entirely synthetic, it would soon be shown to be immoral.

This is probably a good place to step back and look more fully at the point we are making.

To that end, we turn to one of the big bestsellers of recent years – a book by the aforementioned Steven Pinker, *The Better Angels of our Nature: Why Violence Has Declined*. Right off the bat, we know that the author thinks we have a nature, and that it has good and bad angels somehow attached to it. But the gist of the book is that violence has been in decline for a long, long time.

Pinker's contribution to this discussion is to prove it. In this, he does a masterful and thorough job. Drawing on bone records, anthropological studies, police statistics, history, folk tales, and art, he uncovers levels of past violence – as illustrated in this chapter – that modern readers will find shocking. The ancient world was unbelievably brutish and dangerous. He shows an unsteady, but unrelenting, decline in murder rates everywhere. And not just murder rates. Rape, theft, slavery – all forms of violence have become less common.

The shocking part is how common they once were. In some places, in some periods, you were more likely to be killed than to die from natural causes. Also shocking are the other forms of violence in the ancient world – tormenting animals, torture, and cruel and unusual punishments. We will not bother you, gentle reader, with the descriptions of the many torture devices used in the old days; apparently, there is a community of aficionados who collect them. And it seems that there were always people willing and ready to use them – to inflict pain... to extract confessions... or simply for amusement.

After reading a few hundred pages about the atrocities committed by our ancestors – or suffered by them – we are delighted to discover that not only are these practices in sharp decline, but the appeal of them has also mostly disappeared. That is, they've gone out of style. Somewhere along the way, man has developed a sense of empathy for his fellow human beings. Most people no longer delight in the suffering of others – nor even of animals. We no longer want to set cats on fire or cut off the noses of people who annoy us. Bull baiting, bear baiting, gladiator combats, stoning people to death, burning at the stake, breaking on the wheel, the Iron Maiden – most are not just illegal, but unimaginable. Even in the movies, if a man kicks a dog early in a film, you know he'll probably be dead by its end. Something has changed; generally, we no longer appreciate the use of violence, unless it is far away and used on strangers, out of sight. That is probably how the pilot and bombardier of the Enola Gay were able to sleep at night after incinerating 185,000 innocent people; they saw no one die.

But why has the attitude to violence changed? Pinker is an optimist who believes in the perfectibility of man. He guesses that it is a triumph of reason. He believes the Enlightenment encouraged an awareness of what we do and a consideration of the likely consequences, not just for ourselves, but for others, too. According to this line of thinking, evil is merely an error. As we become more thoughtful and more knowledgeable, it will gradually disappear. He believes, too, that governments have contributed to this decline in violence. They gradually gained a monopoly on the use of violence, and they – especially democracies – use it more sparingly.

Our own guess, which we develop more fully in a later chapter, is that government violence is a different sort of violence. It is controlled and systematic… and then episodic and horrendous. Taking on the task of punishing and deterring "bad" behavior, government has probably helped to reduce private sector violence. But while it inhibits private sector theft, for example, it institutes a system of exploitation which separates far more people from far more money than freelance thieves ever could. Today, in America, for example, the practice of civil forfeiture alone costs citizens more than private thievery.

And while the government prevents and deters people from killing one another privately with Smith and Wesson handguns, it develops nuclear bombs, tanks, artillery, and huge standing armies trained and equipped to kill millions of people as a matter of public policy.

A further guess is that civilization and the decline in violence are mutually reinforcing parts of the same phenomenon, and that both are the natural consequence of what is called "gentle commerce." Where that expression came from, we don't know. But it describes what happens when people beat their swords into plowshares. Then, rather than kill one another in a zero-sum quest for success, they find they can get ahead by producing things with which they can trade.

Producing and trading – rather than murdering and stealing – sets in motion a whole train of ideas, attitudes, and customs that are, by nature, non-violent. That is, they are perforce voluntary, as all win-win deals must be. Thus, they are "gentle" rather than brutal.

It is no coincidence that this gentleness surged over the last 4,000 years. There were probably hundreds or thousands of codes, memes, ideas, and moral recommendations available during this evolutionary period. "Do unto others…" survived; it worked.

Then, the desire to please customers, co-workers, and employers leads to much more than the division of labor, economic progress, and a greater economic surplus. First, it leads to the basic elements of civilized commerce – property rights, money, and communication. Later, it leads to the trappings we mistake for civilization itself – smiles, handshakes, art, manners, and modern morals. The earliest writing samples we have, for example, are neither poems nor government proclamations; they are sales records memorializing win-win deals.

Once win-lose deals no longer paid off as they used to, man looked for ways beyond brute force to dominate… to be cool… to feel superior. Our most fundamental drive – beyond survival itself – is not wealth; it is mating. "It is the ultimate goal of almost all human effort," wrote German philosopher Arthur Schopenhauer of sexual desire.

Sociobiologists say money is just a "status marker" and that status markers are substitutes for genetic markers, signaling suitability for parenting. In a win-lose, zero-sum world, the use of violence was relatively straightforward and conclusive. The male who was able to get in a dominant position – whether by physical strength or group manipulation – had access to the most females. Later, in the win-win, positive-sum world that arose after the agricultural revolution, he needed to develop wit as well as strength, and an elaborate system of status markers, to replace the more conclusive use of force. That is why, today, the rich movie star probably has more mistresses available to him than the poor bodybuilder.

"The tireless pursuit of social status, even of conquest," writes Robert Wright, "has ultimately elevated the human condition, allowing more and more people to live, on balance, better lives." Today, most of our efforts to gain status are focused on becoming richer, smarter, more knowledgeable about Chinese porcelains and chess champions, and so forth. But humans spin out an intricate lace of status markers. They are capable of finding status in just about everything… and often, in contradictory ways. One may feel superior because he drives a big, expensive car. Another feels superior because he doesn't. One feels superior because he is muscled-up. Another says the muscleman is a moron; he reads books instead.

All of this modern human "software" can best be understood not as the product of the Enlightenment or a moral awakening, but as the product of cultural evolution, in which social innovations adapted to the new positive-sum world. And while it would be nice to think that the death rate was in irreversible decline, thanks to the conscious efforts of enlightened governors, it may not be so. There was an explosion of state-supported violence in the early 20th century. Since then, most of the wars have been small and fake-ish. But that could change in a matter of seconds.

This is not a very popular point of view, either. Evolution has no mind, no meaning, no purpose, and no destination. What's more, cultural evolution leaves little room for human conceits. Smart people, for example, like to think they can use their brains to craft a better public life, just as they do in their private lives. If they can figure out how to make indoor plumbing work, they reason, surely, they can also fashion a better society.

Secular authorities like to see themselves as the source of wealth and power... as well as the arbiters of right and wrong. They think they are the custodians of the economy and that they are essential to the prosperity of the people under their supervision. They claim to manage it for the benefit of the public – through regulation, taxation, and fiscal and monetary policy. Meanwhile, many religious people believe that murder is immoral because God said so. They think moral rules are divinely inspired, handed down to us by prophets who had some inside track with the Almighty.

If that were so, and it might be, you still wonder why God would take so long to announce what would seem to be universal and timeless rules. Moses waited until the Egyptian *séjour* was at an end before coming down the mountain with the Ten Commandments. Was it okay to murder people before then? It doesn't seem likely, not if the rule were timeless and universal. So why didn't God say something sooner? Not that we are second-guessing God. Rather, we are second-guessing our fellow men, whose views of history, religion, economics, and morality we regard as too simplistic to be accurate... and yet, not simple enough.

"Thou Shalt Not Kill" is a simple rule. Great exceptions are made, of course, even where it is generally honored. Babies not yet born may be murdered in most places. Criminals are often put to death. And, of course, enemy soldiers, even quasi-soldiers, such as "terrorists"... who wear no uniforms, have no military training, and even, in some cases, are incapable of doing much real mischief because they are blind or confined to wheelchairs... can be killed with no due process, no declaration of war, not even a warning.

The idea of "immorality" is a recent invention. It presumes an awareness of time and of the concept of consequences. It suggests an awakening to the notion of cause and effect; what you do today may have something to do with what happens tomorrow.

There are two types of moral rules. The first is merely an observation wherein past, present, and future are connected in a disagreeable, finger-wagging kind of way. "If you don't save for your retirement, you're going to be in trouble," says the responsible spouse. "If you keep smoking like that, you're going to end up in the hospital," says the doctor.

The second type of moral rule is deeper and more abstract. It involves the idea of "right" and "wrong" in some way that goes beyond the likely, observable consequences. This is the key "consciousness" on which civilized life ultimately rests, the recognition of the connections between things that happen now and those that may, or may not, happen in the future.

The contribution of the Christian religion is largely to extend the cause and effect into the afterlife. So, even if you are not collared by the *gendarmes*, you will still pay for your crime later. Is it true that you could delight in Heaven or burn in Hell, depending on what you do on Earth? We don't know; but like so many other myths, it could be best to think so.

Even today, there are some people with little grasp of time. The

Bushmen of the Kalahari Desert, for example, reportedly have only an incipient awareness of cause and effect. They eat when they are hungry. They mate with whomever they please, whenever they please. They sleep when they are sleepy. They have no creation myth, no religion, and no sense of extended time, neither remote past nor life after death. Anthropologists who studied them were surprised. It seemed almost impossible that such people have survived so long with no progress towards civilization. They guessed that they had perhaps lost their "culture" when they were chased into the bush by other tribes or European invaders.

Even among civilized groups today, tribe-based moral systems have not been completely abandoned. In April 2018, this story appeared on the news website *Mondoweiss*:

> *Rabbi Ophir Wallas of the Bnei David Military* Mechina *was caught on video teaching young would-be soldiers that Israelis are, from the halachaic point of view, permitted to wipe out Palestinians, and that only fear of massive retaliation prevents that.*
>
> *"The laws of a* mitzvah *war, a war of occupying the Land. Even if I don't conquer Gaza right now, [conquering it] is part of my ability to settle the Land of Israel, so it is also a part of the* mitzvah *of conquering the Land. And therefore it follows, there's no other way; like, we'd have to kill them all. Because this is the difference between the Law of the Persecutor and* mitzvah *wars. [...] A* mitzvah *war of conquering the Land, which is not limited to saving the people of Israel from their enemies, according to some of the Rishonim, I could, on the face of it and by the essential law, destroy, kill and cause to perish all of them. I will not do so, because if I were to do so, and reject international treaties, then the State of Israel shall parish, unless we shall witness a miracle of miracles – and one must not trust in a miracle. And that's the only reason I won't do it." [As translated by Yossi Gurvitz.]*

A few months later, Israel's parliament passed into law a bill that defined the country as an exclusively Jewish state. It was a move right out of the Old Testament. Or 1930s Germany. The new law echoed the Nazis' 1935 "Race Laws," which were designed to protect "German blood and German honor." The Germans made citizenship the exclusive right of ethnic Germans; the new Israeli law declared the country to be the "homeland of the Jewish people" who had an "exclusive right to national self-determination in it."

This example is a modern expression of the ancient, pre-civilized myth illustrated in the Old Testament. What is especially unusual about it is that it is so obvious and unvarnished. Generally, modern governments tart up the old "us versus them" myth in the hotpants of "national security," manifest destiny, or some other claptrap.

AN INTRODUCTION TO BAD GUY THEORY

In the world of finance, abundance – not scarcity – is the bigger risk. Nothing ruins people faster than getting too much money with too little effort. Few bank robbers, lottery winners, or sports stars can resist the temptation to extravagance, luxury, and excess. In a few years, they're broke.

But if "too much" is a problem in the money world, perhaps it is a problem in the political world, too? Power corrupts. Perhaps it is true what they say about absolute power, too. By May 2018, in Israel, the rot seemed well advanced. Israeli troops fired on a crowd of demonstrators, hitting at least 1,300 of them. A few Jewish intellectuals with their sense of shame still intact thought they had gone too far: "We've gone over to the dark side," they said. "We're becoming decivilized."

Why some people are more civilized than others is a subject for debate. It may be that "civilized" people have a more developed, abstract, moral sense. More likely, what they don't do to others is, generally, what they're afraid may be done to them. It is not abstract virtue that makes us good, in other words; it is fear of jealous husbands, determined creditors, and the Huns.

But what if we knew they could do us no harm? What if you were a giant in a race of Pygmies? What if you had an AK-47... and your enemies had BB guns? What would happen to your civilized restraint then?

Going over to the dark side seems to be what people do from time to time, when the coast is clear. They get out the thumbscrews and the water boards. They slaughter without fear of retribution. They lie, cheat, and steal without worry – because they can get away with it.

Had Israelis become the bad guys? In Israel itself, some thought so. Recalling a more innocent era, writer and politician Uri Avnery wrote:

> *I was a member of the National Military Organization (the "Irgun"), an armed underground group labeled "terrorist."*
>
> *Palestine was at the time under British occupation (called "mandate"). In May 1939, the British enacted a law limiting the right of Jews to acquire land. I received an order to be at a certain time at a certain spot near the sea shore of Tel Aviv in order to take part in a demonstration. I was to wait for a trumpet signal.*
>
> *The trumpet sounded and we started the march down Allenby Road, then the city's main street. Near the main synagogue, somebody climbed the stairs and delivered an inflammatory speech. Then we marched on, to the end of the street, where the offices of the British administration were located. There we sang the national anthem, "Hatikvah," while some adult members set fire to the offices.*
>
> *Suddenly several lorries carrying British soldiers screeched to a halt, and a salvo of shots rang out. The British fired over our heads, and we ran away.*

But now, the gun is in the other hand. Palestinians demonstrate. Israeli snipers do not shoot over their heads.

Here's Jeremy Scahill, founding editor of *The Intercept*:

> *Israel has once again conducted a premeditated, full-scale massacre in broad daylight, in front of the cameras of the world. Once again, it took place in Gaza.*
>
> *On May 14, Israeli snipers and other forces gunned down more than 60 Palestinians, and wounded thousands of others, including civilians, journalists, and paramedics. [...]*
>
> *Among those killed by Israeli forces was an 8-month-old infant. Her name was Laila al-Ghandour. They also killed at least seven other children and a man in a wheelchair, and that man had lost his legs after they had to be amputated following an earlier Israeli attack.*

There is nothing, specifically, that you have to do to be civilized. But there are some things you shouldn't do. Killing people is perhaps one of them.

Among the comments arising from the Gaza incident were some pointing the finger at the USA. The U.S. president's daughter and son-in-law seemed to approve of the Israeli government. Rather than condemn the killings, the U.S. blocked an international investigation. Had Americans become "bad guys" too?

After the fall of the Berlin Wall in 1989, the U.S. stood alone. It was the "end of history," author Francis Fukuyama suggested. America was No. 1... the *ne plus ultra* of the 20th century. By comparison, the whole rest of the world was just one big "sh*thole."

America's only plausible enemy – equipped with both industrial-age factories and nuclear-age warheads – was the Soviet Union. And it gave up the competition – it even ceased to be the Soviet Union – in 1991. Still, America's military spending continued to increase, rising, by 2018, to twice its level 30 years before. By comparison, the rest of the world had beaten its swords, its BB guns, and its slingshots into plowshares. And now, with such a big difference in military spending, U.S. foreign policy could be economically and elegantly described in three words: "We're America, bitch."

Power was unbalanced and disproportionate. It was all take, with no give. It was live... but not let the other guy live. The U.S. could invade Iraq; the Iraqis couldn't invade America. The U.S. Army and the CIA could target extremists for drone assassination; but back in the homeland, Americans slept in peace.

Therein lay the fatal temptation...

Iran hasn't invaded another country since the Achaemenid dynasty went on a spree in the fourth century B.C. Since then, it's been invaded by almost everyone able to do so – Mongols, Russians, English, Muslims, and, in 1980, U.S.-backed Iraq. In the 1950s, the country also endured a *coup d'état*, organized by the U.S. Its democratically elected president was replaced by a CIA puppet.

And today, Iran is considered such a bad *hombre* that U.S. Secretary of State Mike Pompeo read it the riot act on May 21, 2018. The Associated Press followed the story:

> *The Trump administration on Monday demanded that Iran make wholesale changes in its military and regional policies or face "the strongest sanctions in history," as it sought to turn up heat on Tehran after President Donald Trump's decision to withdraw from a landmark nuclear deal. [...]*
>
> *Unless such a treaty can be reached, Pompeo warned that Iran would face tough sanctions that would leave it "battling to keep its economy alive." [...]*
>
> *"These will end up being the strongest sanctions in history by the time we are complete," Pompeo said...*

President Trump followed up in July in a tweet inspired, no doubt, by the history of the Assyrian conquest, warning that the Iranians would "suffer consequences the likes of which few throughout history have ever suffered before. We are no longer a country that will stand for your demented words of violence and death. Be cautious!"

Moses, bringing the law down from Mount Sinai, announced 10 things Jews needed to do to keep themselves in God's good graces. But Pompeo demanded 12 changes of the Iranians. We don't recall Iran ordering the U.S. to make even one change, let alone 12 of them. Is that because the U.S. is already perfect... or because the Pentagon spent an amount equal to the entire Iranian defense budget every eight days?

Power has rules of its own. Win-win reciprocity isn't one of them. When you can throw your weight around without worrying about someone else's weight being thrown at you, what's to stop you?

Nature, like civilization, needs balance. Harmony. "Too much" upsets it. Instead, it thrives on limits, restraints, and corrections. When there is "too much," something has to give. Otherwise, nature tips over into chaos and claptrap. And when a nation has too much power, like a child who has had too many desserts, it becomes insufferable.

After the Cold War ended, the U.S. was master of the field... unopposed... on top of the heap. It could have brought its troops home and cut its military spending in half... or more... restoring some measure of balance with the rest of the world. It could have taken up the America First slogan, minding its own business and being a good neighbor to other countries. It could have balanced its budget, paid off its debt, and devoted its time, money, and energy to building a great country.

Instead, with no debate in Congress, it took another path.

And now, all over the world, it bombs, sanctions, and assassinates... bullying, bossing, and bamboozling small countries that can't protect themselves. But who drones America's "extremists" in Kentucky? Who assassinates "insurgent" leaders in California? Who imposes sanctions on America?

The U.S. has invaded 84 countries since its founding. Modern Iran: zero. The U.S. has weapons of mass destruction… and has proven that it is ready to use them; it dropped an atomic bomb twice – both times on civilians. No other country has used atomic weapons in an act of war. Iran has no atomic weapons. The U.S. has troops in Afghanistan and Iraq, within easy striking distance of Iran. Iran has no troops in Mexico or Canada. So who's the bad guy?

The whole idea of "bad guys" as a focus of U.S. foreign policy came after the fall of Baghdad to U.S. troops and George W. Bush's famous "Mission Accomplished" speech on a U.S. aircraft carrier in 2003. The war was won. But it went on. And on the shifting sands of the Middle East, amid the shifting focus from one religious, tribal, sectarian, or political group to another, military spokesmen couldn't keep up. They began referring to the enemy *du jour* as simply "the bad guys."

But who, really, were the bad guys? Our myths tell us that what is good for the goose is good for the gander. But the gods know better. If the goose is big enough, and powerful enough, the gander can just watch out.

People come to think what they need to think when they need to think it. And when people have a vastly disproportionate amount of military power, they soon find reasons to use it. They begin to see bad guys everywhere. Readers of our own daily blog – *Bill Bonner's Diary* – illustrated the point. They thought they knew not only what happened in Gaza that day, but why it happened. They thought they could look into black hearts and see corrupted souls – even from thousands of miles away.

The Palestinians were fiends from Hell, said one reader:

> *When faced with a screaming horde of fanatics who want to exterminate your existence, do what it takes. Be glad that Mexico is not dominated by Islamists.*

They had blood dripping from their hands, said another:

A significant number of Palestinians killed were unquestionably identified by independent sources as terrorists.

They were mass murderers, said a third:

They intend to kill indiscriminately and create a 5th column within Israel to destroy it.

In other words, they all deserved to die. They, not the Israeli gunmen who shot them down, were the evil ones. No charges were ever filed. No evidence presented. No verdict rendered. And no sentence pronounced. But the protesters got the firing squad anyway. That's the advantage of power – you don't need to hold a trial. And you never need to say you're sorry.

Looking into their own hearts and minds, Americans see saints in the mirror and angels dancing on the White House lawn. Foreigners probably see something else. Some might look back, for example, to America's bloody campaigns against the Cherokee or the Sioux... to its invasions of Mexico or Nicaragua... or to its conquest of the Philippines. U.S. troops took over the Philippines after a fake battle with Spanish forces (the two armies agreed to a mock battle in Manila to justify the handover to Americans rather than to the natives).

"Hooray," said the Filipinos. "America is a beacon of independence. Now, we will be independent, too."

It was still very early in the 20th century. But the U.S. was already woozy; the imperial juice was going to its head. Instead of handing over the Philippines to the "brown people," the white people back in North America chose to hold onto their colonial prize.

Alas, the ungrateful inhabitants resisted. As many as 1.5 million of them – mostly civilians – died as a result of fighting, massacres, concentration camps, and disease.

American soldiers told the tale in their letters home:

The town of Titatia was surrendered to us a few days ago, and two companies occupy the same. Last night one of our boys was found shot and his stomach cut open. Immediately orders were received from General Wheaton to burn the town and kill every native in sight; which was done to a finish. About 1,000 men, women and children were reported killed. I am probably growing hard-hearted, for I am in my glory when I can sight my gun on some dark skin and pull the trigger.

Back home, Americans had little doubt who the bad guys were. They backed their boys in the field, as they always do. But a few had second thoughts. In his diary, Mark Twain referred to American soldiers as "our uniformed assassins." He described the war as:

...a long and happy picnic with nothing to do but sit in comfort and fire the Golden Rule into those people down there and imagine letters to write home to the admiring families, and pile glory upon glory.

After a week or so of this kind of thinking in our daily blog, we were set to heave it over the side, like a fish too small to meet the legal limit. Readers didn't appreciate it. But reading our mail... followed by a restless night... we decided to look further. And then, we saw it more clearly – slimy and hideous. Bad Guy Theory (BGT) is the updated version of tribe-based morality. It maintains that there are some people who are good, and others who are bad. The good ones think they can spot the bad ones... and that they have the right and duty to kill them, because... well... they're up to no good.

Many of our readers believed BGT was essentially correct; they knew damn well who the bad guys were... and thought your author was an SOB for suggesting otherwise. Wrote one, referring to Muslims, Persians, or Palestinians (we're not sure which):

If they could, they'd kill you, me and our families.

We have some personal experience. We lived in Paris for many years and knew, casually, some Iranians. We had dinner with them once or twice in their apartment in the 16th *arrondissement*. Never once did they go for our throats with a butcher knife.

Another reader thought our suggestion that even good people sometimes do bad things was out of line:

You owe all of your subscribers an apology.

This reader was particularly annoyed by our suggestion that dropping an atomic bomb on civilians was perhaps not a civilized thing to do. (We'll come back to that in a minute.)

BGT is as ancient as the Old Testament. Each generation, each culture, each tribe has had its bad guys. The neighboring village. The nation over the mountains. Spartans. Yids. Queers. Reds. Bourgeois reactionaries. Mensheviks. Kulaks. Intellectuals. Gypsies. Heretics. Papists. Prods. Huns. Gooks. Kafirs. Cathars. Sorcerers. Insurgent Filipinos. Rebel slaves. And bog-trotting, mouth-breathing Paddies. They all deserved to die... and all got the death sentence. Not that they necessarily did anything wrong. But their thoughts... their beliefs... their intentions and motivations marked them as bad guys.

But how could you know what was really in people's hearts and minds? Use the rack and thumbscrews to find out! Or don't worry about it. "Kill them all," said the Count of Citeaux before the massacre at Béziers in 1209. "God will sort them out."

As already noted, the God of the Old Testament seemed ready for any sort of mayhem. But Jesus had another idea. He didn't care what group you were part of. He didn't seem to care what you had done in the past either; it was what you did now and in the future that counted. "Go forth and sin no more," said He to the bad gal who was about to be stoned to death.

Common law also emerged gradually and organically from the

swamp and blood of prehistoric life. It, too, turned away from BGT. Justice was blind. Were you a Jew? Were you a Muslim? Were you a believer... or a sinner? It hardly mattered. Instead, the judge wanted to know where you were on the night of the 23rd... that is, he wanted to know what you had gotten up to, not who you were. You were judged on the basis of your actions.

So let us look at the action that brought our readers to grab a rail, feathers, and pitch and come looking for us.

GRAVE MISGIVINGS

On August 8, 1945, Nagasaki, Japan was still intact. Its citizens were living on short rations. They were mostly old men, women, and children – the young men had already been drafted into the army. If we had been able to look into their hearts and minds, we probably would have found that they wished the entire American nation would drop dead. It was because of it, they reasoned, that they were dying of disease and hunger, lacking food, fuel, clothing, and just about everything else.

It was onto these people that Harry Truman dropped the second atomic bomb.

They were "bad guys," said the U.S. press. They "supported the war," said God-fearing Americans. Besides, it "saved our soldiers' lives," said Truman.

Dwight Eisenhower, then supreme commander of the Allied forces in Europe, disagreed. He recalled in a 1963 interview that:

> *...it wasn't necessary to hit them with that awful thing... I voiced to him [War Secretary Henry Stimson] my grave misgivings, first on the basis of my belief that Japan was already defeated and that dropping the bomb was completely unnecessary, and secondly because I thought that our country should avoid shocking world opinion by the use of a weapon whose employment was, I thought, no longer mandatory as a measure to save American lives.*

William Leahy, the president's chief of staff, wrote in his diary:

> *It is my opinion that the use of this barbarous weapon at Hiroshima and Nagasaki was of no material assistance in our war against Japan. The Japanese were already defeated and ready to surrender... [...] My own feeling was that in being the first to use it, we had adopted an ethical standard common to the barbarians of the Dark Ages. I was not taught to make war in that fashion, and wars cannot be won by destroying women and children.*

Even the Uber Bomber himself, Major General Curtis LeMay, was against it:

> *The war would have been over in two weeks without the Russians entering and without the atomic bomb. The atomic bomb had nothing to do with the end of the war at all.*

So was Admiral Chester Nimitz, who had beaten the Japanese fleet and chased them back to the home islands:

> *The Japanese had, in fact, already sued for peace before the atomic age was announced to the world with the destruction of Hiroshima and before the Russian entry into the war... The atomic bomb played no decisive part, from a purely military standpoint, in the defeat of Japan.*

And what about America's top commander in the Pacific, General Douglas MacArthur? President Nixon recalled:

> *[General Douglas] MacArthur once spoke to me very eloquently about it, pacing the floor of his apartment in the Waldorf. He thought it a tragedy that the bomb was ever exploded. MacArthur believed*

that the same restrictions ought to apply to atomic weapons as to conventional weapons, that the military objective should always be limited damage to noncombatants... MacArthur, you see, was a soldier. He believed in using force only against military targets, and that is why the nuclear thing turned him off...

So, what to make of it? Who were the bad guys? You decide.

But keep in mind that for every person who thinks he can tell the good guys from the bad ones, there must be hundreds of broken bones... thousands of broken hearts... and a million sorry souls roasting in Hell... wishing they had never tried.

CHAPTER 2

On Cooperation and Win-Win

A physician cannot heal the sick if he is ignorant of the causes of certain conditions of the body, nor can a statesman help his fellow citizens if he cannot follow how, why or by what process each event had developed.
– Polybius

✝·✝·✝·✝

AT ONE POINT in his short life, Jesus was invited to take control of government. Political power... the power to force win-lose deals on others... was offered to Him. Luke 4:5-8:

> *⁵ And the Devil taking him up into a high mountain, showed unto him all the kingdoms of the world in a moment of time...*
>
> *⁶ And the Devil said unto him, All this power will I give thee, and the glory of them: for that is delivered unto me; and to whomsoever I will give it.*
>
> *⁷ If thou therefore wilt worship me, all shall be thine.*
>
> *⁸ And Jesus answered and said unto him, Get thee behind me, Satan: for it is written, Thou shalt worship the Lord thy God, and him only shalt thou serve.*

Who offers political power? The Devil himself! Not the voters. Not the aristocracy. Not God. Instead, the Devil says clearly that government is his to do with as he wishes. And if Jesus wants it, all He has to do is worship him who gave it to Him: Satan.

We've heard sermons of all sorts… in big cities… and in small country churches… high churches, low churches… Catholic, Baptist… and God-knows-what. Almost all the ministers, priests, and preachers we have heard from believe that God is good… and that He expects us to support good works, private and public. Often, they think they hear our political leaders speaking for God Himself. They think they hear Him telling us to back more government aid to unwed mothers, limits on carbon emissions, or more help for Native Americans. "We need to do this… or that…" they say, sounding a bit like an editorial in *The Washington Post*.

But there is no "we" in the Gospel. No appeal to special interests or to the common good… or to collective justice, shared virtue, patriotism, or social economy. No tribes. No sects. No flags. No creeds. No political parties. Neither Pharisee nor Sadducee. There is only the unique person… the individual, alone… with his God.

Only once, in a little country church in Normandy, France, did a priest take up this insight:

"God doesn't ask you to change the world," he said. "He asks you to do something much more difficult – to change yourself."

It is difficult because you are changing your own software… updating programming that has been in place for thousands of years. Of course, it is much easier to ask somebody else to change. Change his religion! Change his behavior! Change his government! Change the way he spends his money… the way he treats his wife… the way he drinks… the way he works! Make his women take off the hijab. Make his men say the Hail Mary.

But wait. What if he doesn't want to change? He'll bristle at higher taxes. He'll whine and complain about new regulations. He'll want to keep his old gods. He'll resist your grand projects for a better world. Marching to Moscow in the winter isn't in his plan. Nor is living in a godforsaken slum simply because the party bosses say so. What to do? What would Attila or Adolph do? Force him to do what you want! You know what's best for him. You know what's best for the world. Force him to do it!

Jesus knew it wouldn't work. He never suggested that the Roman rulers should take care of the poor. He never hinted that it was Pontius Pilate's responsibility to look after the cripples of Judea or to fix the price of lamb on behalf of Jewish shepherds. In his Parable of the Good Samaritan, a traveler was beaten, stripped of his clothes, and left for dead beside the road. He wasn't rescued by the army... or by the tax collectors... nor by the social welfare agencies of the time. Even the priest walked by. Instead, it was a Samaritan – a member of a group with whom Jews enjoyed a mutual contempt – who helped him.

This story was told by Jesus in response to a question. When told that one should "love thy neighbor," a lawyer asked: "But who is my neighbor?" "Who's 'we'?" he might have asked.

Jesus explained that it had nothing to do with group affiliation or group responsibility... or the "common good"... or the good that government can do with central planning and elite, expert guidance. It didn't matter what race, creed, religion, or gender box you checked.

"Loving thy neighbor" was a radical idea at the time, a major software update. It still is radical. It suggests, to many, that the whole edifice of Christian morality is built on love. Our own guess is that it stands on a more solid foundation – two sturdy pillars: fear and self-interest. But either way, the responsibility is squarely on the individual, not on the group.

This new religion did much more than announce a "moral code" or a "good idea." It also described the transactions of a modern, growth economy and anticipated the codes of modern civilization. "Do unto others..." turned out to be a capitalist manifesto.

There are only two kinds of deals: cooperative, voluntary deals... or deals made at the point of a gun. In a fixed, non-growth economy, violence is almost the only way to get ahead. This was our subject of consideration in the previous chapter; you can only get more by taking market share from someone else. That was why murder and theft were so common in the ancient world; there were few alternatives available to the ambitious person.

Back then, the idea of the "common good" made sense. Tribal life was, perforce, collective. The "common" good was the good of the tribe. Ethologist Richard Dawkins describes a human being as a "survival machine" for our genes. But it is more likely that the tribe was the survival machine. The individual was simply a detachable part. The tribe carried a group of genes. Individuals were expendable. The tribe was not.

The "common good" was not universal. That is why the Old Testament is focused on a tribe – the Jews – and its progress. The tribe could benefit, for example, by exterminating a rival tribe. It could benefit by pushing another tribe away from its prime hunting grounds, or by capturing its young women in a raid. Wealth was limited. Generally, it couldn't be increased. It could only be moved from one tribe to another.

There was little opportunity for an individual to realize any "progress" of his own or pursue happiness in his own way. He could hunt. He could gather. He could fight. He could pass along his genes to a new generation. What he thought probably didn't matter much. What he wanted probably never came up in conversation. It was probably very rare for tribe members to sit around the campfire and discuss their eating disorders, their political preferences, or their career aspirations. The individual didn't count for much.

Modern, extended societies sometimes slip back into tribal thinking. "Ein Volk, ein Reich, ein Führer," as Hitler famously put it. The idea was simple enough – he would treat the German people as though they were "we," members of the same tribe with a "common good" that could be had by following their leader.

There was one *Reich* (government), but there were many different *Volk* (people) in Germany. But while the "we" of a prehistoric tribe was natural, authentic, and could benefit from the win-lose protocols of a zero-sum world, the "we" of Nazi Germany was fake. Needless to say, not all Germans shared the same enthusiasm for the success of the master race. Eventually, almost all of them – Jews, Gypsies, and Nazi Party members, too – came to detest it, as they suffered from trying to insist on win-lose deals in what had essentially become a win-win world.

RULES OF THE ROAD

On any given work day, approximately 250 million people in the United States get up in the morning... and go somewhere. Using trains, planes, and automobiles of all sorts... flying through the air or flying down the road by the millions... coming from every point of the compass... they go places that no central authority has ever recorded or organized. And yet, by obeying a few simple "rules of the road," all but a tiny fraction of them get where they are going.

And that is just the beginning. These millions of people – short, tall, smart, dumb, educated, illiterate – then go to work in enterprises that are, mostly, organized by no central authority, serving no common goal, following no central program. They have no Führer leading them. No chief orders them forward. No master plan tells them where to go or what to do. Instead, they labor to provide some service or good to others, with no idea how it all fits together or where it leads.

And then, imagine, at lunchtime, almost every one of these 250 million Americans (not to mention the 80 million more left at home) eats lunch! How is it possible to organize so many meals... all at about the same time... for so many people? And get this – they don't all eat the same thing.

Approximately 7.5 million of them eat only vegetables. Up to 60 million are said to be lactose intolerant. And another 15 million or so are gluten intolerant. And that is just the beginning of it. The typical person has a choice of dozens of different luncheon items. Nationwide, there are thousands... maybe millions... of different selections. Big Macs, Whoppers, meatball subs, pasta, salads, steaks... hallal... kosher – you can get almost anything you want. And then, one person wants his meat well-done. Another wants it "blue." One wants fries with his burger. Another wants onion rings.

One further complication: Neither the farmers, the food preparers, nor the customers are likely to know each other. The people growing the wheat have no idea where it will go or who will eat it. The people preparing the sandwiches have no idea how or where the wheat is grown... not to mention the tomatoes and avocadoes. Many will not know whether they are grown on bushes or trees, in the tropics or in the desert. (A recent news item in France, for example, tells us that most Americans are unaware that the hamburger comes from beef cattle.) And the consumer has no idea – beyond the vaguest intuition – what is in his food, where it comes from, or how the supply chain works.

What if the kitchen is unclean? What if the clams have gone bad? What if the milk has turned?

How does the diner know the food is edible... or that he won't be put to sleep so his pockets can be picked by the restaurant crew? How does he know the mayonnaise hasn't been poisoned? How can he be sure the mushrooms aren't poisonous? And yet, except for a tiny fraction of diners, all will survive.

Commercial kitchens are routinely inspected by the government. But how often? Suppose that specific kitchen wasn't inspected on that specific morning? It is impossible for the government to guarantee the hygiene of hundreds of thousands of kitchens all across the city and the country, from 6 a.m. to midnight every day, Saturday and Sunday included. How come so few people get sick? How come so few die? If even a handful drop dead, it is a national scandal and the feds make a federal case out of it. In 2015, for example, there was an outbreak of

E. coli at a series of Chipotle restaurants. Some 55 people became ill. It was national news. But these events are extreme outliers.

It is practically a miracle. More than 300 million individualized meals, all prepared and served in the space of a few hours. And many of them hot! Thousands of different selections. Not just the food, but the drinks, too. Let's see, 300 million people… each makes three choices… among, let's say, 500 different possibilities… Run that through the calculator. We get 4.5e11… Wait… What does that mean? We don't know. But it must mean billions of different lunch combination choices. And somehow, the system matches each individual diner with exactly the food he wants. It is not random.

But wait, the complexity of it doesn't stop there. Many restaurants change their menus from day to day (See Today's Special!), so the choices are not fixed, but variable over time.

What a task, feeding such a multitude, not just with loaves and fishes, but with brie, barbecued ribs, fresh leaves that came all the way from California, and water that came all the way from Italy! And then, after the food has been consumed… the tables cleaned… the plates washed… and the diners are back at their jobs, what happens? The restaurants prepare to do it all again a couple of hours later. How is that possible? What kind of "we" could organize such a thing? What kind of tribe could pull off such a complex operation? Who could take charge? Who could decide?

Of course, it wouldn't be possible. It is only made possible by modern, post-tribal civilization. Not by conscious rules or explicit laws, which could by no means cover so many millions of unique food options. And not by inspectors and regulations; at best, they could only oversee a tiny percentage of luncheon output. It is only possible because people follow "rules of the road" that are largely unwritten, colloquial protocols, and make their decisions based on particular, private, and unrecorded knowledge.

Just as man developed language – with no central organizer to tell him how to connect subjects and predicates – so did he develop other conventions that made large-scale public life possible.

Aristotle believed that civilization could only exist in a small community. In book VII of his tome, *Politics*, Aristotle argued that, "Experience shows that a very populous city can rarely, if ever, be well governed; since all cities which have a reputation for good government have a limit of population." "Beyond the herald's cry," he said, were just barbarians. He had a point. Back then, only a smallish group could share the codes and the information needed to conduct itself in a way that seemed "civilized."

But he was wrong about civilization itself. A few universal rules – one in particular – made it possible to extend civilization far beyond any one culture, language, city, or centrally planned, well-governed community.

WIN-WIN... OR LOSE

There are only two ways to get what you want: win-lose deals or win-win deals. Win-lose deals, outside of the tribe itself, dominated prehistoric life – with widespread murder, rape, and theft. It was a zero-sum world, where win-lose was the only way to get ahead. Win-win deals arose with agriculture and animal husbandry, when it became possible to improve your status without slaughtering your neighbors.

Jesus' Sermon on the Mount described how to do cooperative, win-win deals. Those deals, as we will see more fully later, are the only way to make real progress. This is largely because of four things. First, they are more efficient, eliminating the wastes of time and resources that win-lose deals require. Second, they are initiated by people specifically to increase human satisfaction. Third, each deal adds to our knowledge of what works and what doesn't. Ultimately, what separates wealthy people from poor people is that the former have accumulated more useful knowledge. And fourth, win-win deals allow people to specialize, dividing the labor among them so that they may each learn more and become better at what they do. The result, aggregated in markets, is more wealth for everyone.

Let's look at these things a bit further. Win-win deals are voluntary. They do not need to be enforced or policed. In a slave system, a considerable amount of energy is required to keep the slaves from getting away. As economies become more sophisticated – requiring more highly skilled labor – the cost of keeping slaves on the job rises. Just try to imagine running Google, for example, with slave labor. They could easily ruin the business in minutes. And with their skills and knowledge, they could easily get away... transferring their marketable abilities to other firms, perhaps without the slave master even knowing it.

It was probably the decline in net income from slave labor that doomed slavery in the 19th century, not a sudden and worldwide rise in anti-slavery sentiments. Or, to put it differently, the high-minded sentiments of the abolitionists were much more affordable when slavery ceased to pay.

Slavery, obviously, is not win-win. It is a win-lose deal. The slave owner wins. The slave loses, with the difference equal to the market value of the slave's work minus the cost of his maintenance. As those two things converge, slavery becomes less attractive.

Theft, too, is a win-lose proposition. It becomes less appealing as alternative ways to get what you want make themselves available. In modern societies, theft is illegal – unless it is done by the legal authorities themselves or permitted by them. This alone makes stealing relatively unattractive. Stealing is a conscious decision made by the thief. He redistributes wealth. But taking a pair of sneakers from a teenager at gunpoint has very different consequences from getting the sneakers honestly – that is, by working for money and using it to buy a pair of sneakers from someone who made them. The former is a win-lose deal. The latter is win-win. In a win-win deal, both parties aim to come out ahead (though both can be disappointed). A win-lose deal aims to disappoint one of the parties. It has only one winner... and provides no net increase of goods or services to the economy.

Nor does a win-lose deal provide much useful information. How much does it cost to make a pair of sneakers? The thief doesn't find out. Do people prefer red or blue? Most likely, he has little opportunity to express a color choice. How much are consumers willing to pay for a pair of sneakers? Who knows!

Without the information and markets to express, aggregate, and mediate it, specialization is not possible. So, there is no improvement in productivity, and no generalized increase in wealth.

For all four reasons – higher enforcement costs, lack of increased output, little information gain, no elaboration of the division of labor – win-lose deals are far less likely to promote prosperity than win-win deals.

THE WINNINGEST WIN-WIN

One weekend in the summer of 2017, in France, we celebrated the oldest and greatest win-win deal in human life... the beginning of the division of labor. We drove the 10 miles or so down to a neighboring town, Le Dorat, on Saturday afternoon. The medieval town sits on a hill in the green Limousin countryside, with the remnants of a defensive wall still visible along the western side. It is on the frontier of two regions which were once distinctive, not only in the lay of the land, but in the stone underneath and the people above. East and north of Le Dorat are flattish regions of limestone, where people once spoke the "oie" form of French. To the south and west, granite is the stone at hand, and the people used the "oc" form... as in Languedoc. Both "oie" and "oc" meant "yes"... which, today, we hear in the ubiquitous "oui."

The area is also known as the "Basse Marche." It is a "march" area because it lies on the border of two different political and cultural regions – with the English in the South and the French in the North. During the Hundred Years' War, these areas saw a lot of win-lose deals, as armies and brigands marauded over the entire countryside.

But we were not going to Le Dorat to kill or plunder. No, it was not a win-lose deal that tempted us there, but a win-win deal… of its most ancient variety. So, we drove around the perimeter of the town and then turned onto one of the tiny, twisty streets to find a place to park.

The *collégiale* is a massive church, situated down the hill slightly from the center of town. Though a Catholic church, it is a monument to win-lose deals run wild. Burnt and looted in 866 by the Normans, it was rebuilt, then burnt again by attackers from a neighboring town in 1013. Rebuilt again, it was burnt again in 1080. The present large, heavy, grey-granite, Romanesque structure is the result of the 12th-century rebuild… which was more heavily fortified in the 15th century.

In the middle ages, Le Dorat combined both temporal and spiritual authority. Today, the town has little of either. But the bones of two saints – Théobald and Israël – still rest in the crypt below. Every seven years, they are brought out and paraded through the streets.

We took our places in the pews just as the organ opened up. Like the assault on Verdun, it began with all guns blazing. The stones shook. Plaster fell from the ceiling. The massive instrument looked as though it was installed about the same time as the bones below. As it gathered force, our inner organs vibrated in sympathy. The thunder probably would have awakened Théobald and Israël, too, had they not shared the deep, innocent slumber of angels.

We estimated the crowd at about 300, all dressed in their wedding finery. Chiffon dresses were popular. Hats may have been fashionable at our last wedding a month before. This time, few of the women covered their heads. The ceremony began with the grandparents and the mother of the bride being led to their seats in front. Then came the crucifer leading the priest, who was, in turn, trailed by a small group of children dressed in white and carrying candles. Finally, the bride and her father, both with an equal mixture of joy and solemnity on their faces, and with 600 eyes following them, like an incoming tide, slowly and inexorably made their way down the aisle to the groom.

"We are here today to celebrate the marriage of these two young people," the priest began. "But we celebrate much more than that. We reaffirm our own vows to each other, to the church, and to God."

We quickly lost track of what the presiding cleric had to say. So we take the liberty accorded to us – the only real *lagniappe* of our lowly trade – to tell you what we think he should have said:

"Marriage is a sacrament in the Catholic Church. But the church did not create marriage. Men and women have been getting together – for better or for worse – ever since Adam met Eve. No law requires it. No Ph.D. in sociology invented or manages it. No government program supports it. There are no manuals on how to do it, at least as far as we know. And many of those who have done it more than once – that is to say, the experts – advise against it.

"And yet, it happens. It's been happening – though in many different forms and with many different rituals and myths attached – for thousands of years. And it happens now in almost every country, nation, tribe, culture, and community – certainly the civilized ones – throughout the world.

"Why? It is not always easy. Marriages frequently fail. Even the best of them have their depressions and wars. And yet, couples keep at it.

"And most of the people at this wedding, too, have come here like the dumb beasts going up the gangway onto the Ark – two by two.

"Of course, we don't know why. All we know is that they do. We know, too, that men and women together do things than neither can do on his or her own… things the government, the church, the army, TV entertainers, and billionaires can't do. None of them can do it. Only men and women can do the one thing that we all depend on, providing the most common good of all.

"The Bible says God created men and women as separate beings. Scientists tell us that our remote ancestors were physically different… or capable of doing different kinds of things… for at least 2 million years. Males were bigger than females back then. They still are. And now, as then, they get together. Like plants, they send down their roots deep into the earth, put out branches, bring forth flowers, and later bear the fruit that is us. That is, together, in a mutually beneficial, win-win deal – each bringing what the other lacks – they create something that is more than what they are. Alone, they are just two more or less happy people. Together, they may be miserable… But who cares?"

That's the thing about win-win deals – we interrupt the sermon with our own reflection. You don't know who will win. And sometimes – as in a failed marriage – both parties may feel like losers. But in themselves, win-win deals – the joining of man and wife, the connecting of buyer with seller, the matching of investment with entrepreneur – may not be what makes the world go around; but they give it a spin!

"Maybe we have arrived at a new era when you don't need men and women to work together to have children or to raise them. And maybe the division of labor has been forever altered by new technology, so men no longer need to hunt and women no longer need to gather.

"Man's role may have changed. He may no longer be the hunter or breadwinner. But he is still a fool. And woman's role is still to let him know it. That division of labor is at the foundation of our species and our civilization.

"Statistically, people who are married live longer… and are wealthier. Whether it is worth it or not is a matter of opinion. But I'm talking about something more than happiness or opinion. The Bible scarcely ever mentions "happiness." And Jesus never promised to make people happy. If you want to be happy, you can take drugs.

"But that's not what it's all about. I'm talking about more than what you or I want. I'm talking about something so sublime and so profound, it had to be conceived in the mind of God, not man. So when we say that "God joins these two people in marriage," and "Those whom God has joined together, let no man put asunder," we're not kidding. We never created this system. We didn't invent men or women… or cause them to want to get together with each other. Instead, they follow an impulse… an instinct… that comes from somewhere outside of any of us. Beyond us. Whatever you call it, the bond between men and women goes beyond anything we humans ever created. Like the invisible hand that brings producers and consumers together, so does an invisible force... a kind of software written by God or evolution... lead them to do win-win deals in their personal lives.

"So, I am here, like the many generations of priests before me, to join these two people in the winningest win-win deal ever – marriage.

"You may now kiss the bride."

CHAPTER 3

What Civilization Is Not

To eat your own children is a barbarian act.
– Soviet poster from the 1930s

┼··┼··┼··┼

CIVILIZATION SUFFERED two huge setbacks in the 20th century. The first was World War I, which called into question all the conventions and conceits of modern society. For no apparent reason, and with nothing to gain, Europe took up its most bloody war ever. After more than two years of disastrous killing, France, England, Germany, and Russia were exhausted... and ready to call it quits. Then, the United States, equipped in equal measure with money, soldiers, and illusions, joined the fight... prolonging the misery another 19 months and costing millions more lives.

It was supposed to be the war to "make the world safe for democracy," which was never remotely plausible. It was alternatively advertised as the "war to end war," which was disproven 20 years later.

World War I shook the world's confidence. All of a sudden, social progress did not seem like such a sure thing. Things were not necessarily getting better all the time. For four years, they had gotten noticeably worse. And what could you blame if not evolved bourgeois society, with its many pretensions, rules, and manners? Surely another form of society... more consciously designed and organized... would be an improvement.

Thus emerged the second great setback – the "isms." Bolshevism and fascism, in Russia and Germany, respectively, were the primary strains of the disease; other varieties flourished in Italy, Argentina, China, and elsewhere.

In the Second World War, the "isms" went at each other's throats… western liberalism against German, Italian, and Japanese fascism… and the latter against the bolshevism of the Soviet Union. Civilized people discovered that not only could they take up another catastrophic and pointless war, but they could also engage in mass murder and acts of depravity little different, except in technique, from those of Tamerlane himself.

Readers will be quick to think of the Nazis' concentration camps, with their systematic annihilation of Europe's Jews, gypsies, communists, and political enemies. But the Soviets had their own murder machine operating at full throttle, too. Its toll was even greater than that of the Germans. And let's not forget the Allies. British and American bombers coolly exterminated hundreds of thousands of innocent lives, including women and children, in firestorms – 25,000 in Dresden, 45,000 in Hamburg, and 25,000 in Iwo Jima, for example. In fact, the single most murderous act in the war was carried out by Americans when they dropped an atomic bomb on Hiroshima; 140,000 died.

These were civilized countries – all of them. For example, Germany, a major player in both wars, was perhaps the most civilized country on Earth. It was home to the great philosophers Marx, Kant, Hegel, Schopenhauer, Leibniz, Fichte, Heidegger, and Nietzsche. And the roster of German-speaking composers is so long and heavy, it practically breaks the shelf – Mendelssohn, Brahms, Beethoven, Bach, Schumann, Handel, Wagner… the list goes on and on. And yet, civilization prevented neither the wars nor the atrocities that went with them. Thoughtful people couldn't help but notice that civilized people were often more bloodthirsty than Barbarians.

Persian conqueror Tamerlane of the 14th century annihilated the ancient city of Isfahan, murdering 70,000. He was said to have executed 100,000 prisoners before the Battle of Delhi in 1398. Altogether, his campaigns may have caused the deaths of 17 million people. But World War I and World War II, together, killed off an estimated 76 million in the space of a single generation. How could 1,000 years of civilization have failed to prevent this? asks the lead character, Paul Baumer, in *All Quiet on the Western Front*.

After a close look at the mischief and mayhem perpetrated by civilized men in World War I and World War II, it became difficult to look down on Barbarians. There was little reason to think they were less virtuous than "civilized" people. There was little evidence that they were less kind. For all anyone knew, they were as good as anyone else. But much of the reaction against "civilization" post-World War II was probably a reaction against what civilization was not. Killing people with a machine gun… or in a gas chamber… may have been efficient. But it was not civilized.

Still, in art, music, architecture, and popular culture, the distaste for bourgeois values spread. The trends were already in place, even before the Great War. They intensified later. Gone were the refinements of the Greco-Roman tradition in architecture. The evolved vernacular shapes and styles were spurned in favor of more utilitarian, often brutalist, architecture. Painting, too, ceased to be the representational art reaching for the beauty of earlier eras. Instead, it turned away from beauty to reveal darker, or more ideologically worthy, sentiments.

(Interestingly, while the art world turned away from beauty, the practical world turned toward it. Picasso and Bacon may have wanted to show how ugly things could be. But the artists at the General Motors design shop spent millions to turn out the most beautiful vehicles in history. Some day, the Citroen DS may be regarded as the greatest work of art produced in the entire 20th century.)

In the 1960s, the revulsion against "civilization" was still going strong. A "natural" aesthetic ran wild. It was the Age of Aquarius. You could be liberated from the constraints of civilization and still keep your air conditioning. Burn your bra. Don't cut your hair. Flout convention. Don't get married. Enjoy sex with whomever you want, whenever you want. Turn on. Tune in. Drop out.

Intellectuals in America and France were still largely backing the Bolshevik experiment. China was still admired as the bowsprit of a whole new era. And mainstream economists – notably Paul Samuelson – still believed the Soviet Union's centrally planned slave system would prove superior to an open, free economy.

In 1973, a friend of ours from Pennsylvania shocked us by announcing that she had joined the Communist Party in Paris and would devote her life to doing "whatever they tell me to do." And in the 1980s, another friend left house and home in New Mexico to join the Venceremos Brigade, providing the Sandinistas in Nicaragua with what they least needed – unskilled manual labor to build houses.

VIOLENCE AND PERSUASION

Human experience is marked by two contradictory ways of doing things. By now, readers will be quick to raise their hands and squirm in their seats when we ask, "What are they?" Of course, they are the familiar win-win or win-lose.

But here, we look at them through a wider lens. We see that they are not merely ways of gaining wealth or doing business deals. Instead, they are two opposing impulses – both of them etched deeply onto human glass. One suited mankind and his predecessors for millions of years. The other is perhaps better adapted to modern civilization. Even the most common, everyday things are illustrations of one or other of these approaches.

Do you want more sex, Dear Reader? Well, you have your choice. You can either ask for it politely, perhaps making your request in the alluring, seductive tones of a real paramour. Or you can rape someone. Sometimes, the frontier between rape and request, like the march areas between all win-win and win-lose transactions, can be unclear. They shift, too, with time and cultural trends. What was considered acceptable to the Baby Boomers, for example, may be considered quasi-rape by Millennials. Just ask Al Franken.

There is always some gray area between violence and persuasion. But that is for others to figure out. For our purposes, it hardly matters. We are just looking at the black and white parts and telling you what we see. Finer intellects with better eyesight can draw the boundaries. This theme, by the way, is one we took up because we thought it offered a simpler, and better, way to understand public life. It surprised us when we saw that it helped understand much of the rest of life, too.

We have seen already that...

...win-win promotes long-term relationships; win-lose is strictly short-term.

...win-win provides constant feedback and correction; win-lose cuts the feedback loop, allowing mistakes to continue.

...win-win is the place for entrepreneurs, businessmen, and long-term investors with "skin in the game"; win-lose is for MBAs, credential-seekers, and résumé-builders.

...win-win is universal; win-lose is tribal.

...win-win deals are best governed by common law; win-lose favors edicts and diktats.

...win-win is what they do on Main Street and in markets; win-lose finds a cozy home in Washington.

...win-win creates voluntary collectives; win-lose forces people into artificial categories and us-versus-them groups.

...win-win requires voluntary action by free people; win-lose deals need slaves.

...win-win deals increase useful knowledge; win-lose deals slow the learning process.

...win-win deals are based on fairness and reciprocity; win-lose deals are based on power and violence.

...win-win deals add to human satisfaction; win-lose deals subtract from it.

...win-win deals are civilized transactions; win-lose deals are barbaric.

We could go on. But you get the idea. So, let us now lay a bit more of the groundwork. The subject is civilization. Is it a delicate flower? Or a robust weed? Is it something that needs to be cultivated by gardeners on the public payroll, like lemon trees north of the frost line? Or something that develops on its own, no matter what we do or what we think? In this chapter, we're spraying a little Roundup around the plant so we can have a better look at it. Racing ahead, we will see that civilization – like language – is what happens when you don't prevent it from happening. Like manners, it makes relations between humans more agreeable. Like money, it facilitates commerce and makes people materially better off. And like the common law, it establishes helpful rules... sets standards and expectations... and resolves inevitable conflicts without resorting to violence.

Clive Bell, an English art critic and member of the Bloomsbury group, offered a different perspective. For him, civilization is what you get when you think and feel deeply about truth, beauty, life, justice, and other heavy themes. That is what the ancient Greeks did, he says, especially during a glorious 60-year period in the fifth century B.C. And that is why they are usually held up as paragons of civilization itself.

Bell begins on solid ground. "Civilization is artificial," he writes. He might have also written that it is "natural." As we will see, it is both. There are two sides to it. You must do some natural things. And not do other natural things. In this book, we focus on the omission side – the important things you must not do if you want to be civilized. It is on the other side... commissions... that Mr. Bell concentrates his attention.

The art critic wrote in the inter-war period of the early 20th century. He saw the destruction wrought by World War I. He anticipated, correctly, more to come. But he did not draw any broad conclusions from the extreme violence of the era or about how it might connect to the idea of civilization. Instead, he narrowed his focus onto his own, rather unique, situation. That is, rather than worry about how war fits into civilized life, the art critic chose to look at the civilized life he knew and describe it to us.

What he discovered is that civilized communities have the time to "think and feel" rather than just work. They concern themselves with art, wit, charm, style, poetry, theatre, music, philosophy, and learning – and not just with getting and spending money. In fact, Bell thought getting and spending – which is what most people do with their daylight hours – got in the way of a civilized life. This led him to conclude that if a society wants to attain a higher level of civilization, it must excuse some people – the elite – from the need to support themselves. Athens, he notes approvingly, was supported by a slave population. This allowed the best of the free men to apply themselves to higher pursuits.

One of the groups often held up as civilized and widely admired in American literature is the English landed aristocracy of the 18th and 19th centuries. Their wealth lay in the rents they were able to extract from their estates. Behind almost all of these fortunes was a crime – one that could be traced to the bloodthirsty conquest of 1066. Most of England's pre-Norman landholdings changed hands in the years following the Battle of Hastings. Land-based wealth is always subject to confiscation. But it requires the investment of time and money to make land productive. And confiscating land undermines the trust in the future needed for long-term capital investment. Thus redistributed by 1076 or so, England rediscovered property rights and became one of the leading bastions of win-win deals; its landed gentry became paragons of civilized conduct and ended up in Downton Abbey.

We have no doubt that this model found widespread support among the non-slave population of ancient Greece, just as it does among the non-slave population of modern America and the upper classes of

Britain, too. Today, we have no people we call "slaves" or "serfs" bound to the land. We have only "taxpayers." But in this context, the idea is similar. The ones support the others. We also have "wage slaves," but this term seems almost oxymoronic. If you work for wages – rather than for someone with a whip in his hand – you are always free to work for someone else… or not work at all. Real galley slaves cannot pick their masters or decide to take a holiday.

You may say, "Yeah… But we have to eat, so we have to work. We have no choice. We're effectively slaves." But if this were so, we are all slaves – to the need for food… and for shelter. And the only way we can be liberated is by enslaving someone else – forcing them to work to provide us with the things we need.

And yet, that is just what is now widely proposed – a new form of slavery, in which some are forced to support others. Today, it is called a "guaranteed universal income." The idea was championed, for a while, by Milton Friedman and other "conservative" economists, who thought it would be more efficient and less destructive than current welfare programs. Lately, it has been given energy by social engineers who think robots will displace millions of workers, who will then need some form of maintenance. Even high-profile entrepreneur Richard Branson has spoken out in favor of it.

It also dovetails fiendishly with a new, technologically advanced form of win-lose bullying. Proponents hope to combine Big Data with a guaranteed income in order to modify behavior. You would be given a "citizen score" based on whatever the insiders think would be useful. Did you vote? Do you buy "green" products? Did you get a parking ticket… or visit a "bad" website? In the Chinese version, you can also lose points for making an "insincere apology." The eye in the sky – powered by Facebook and Google Analytics – will know everything and adjust your income based on your citizen score.

But that Valhalla is still in the future.

What is unique-ish to Bell is that he believed that civilization depended on those who did not work. Instead, they undertake arts and activities that market economies might never support; they add – like Plato, Aeschylus, Aristophanes, Socrates, Praxiteles, Aesop, Hesiod, Euripides, Sophocles, etc. – to the cultural richness of the world.

If modern, politically correct readers are not shocked by Bell's attitude to slavery, they will surely be shocked by his ideas about women. The distaff half of the population usually figures only in a supporting role, as secondary characters in the drama of civilization. Greek female poets or philosophers were few and far between. Yes, there was Sappho and Aspasia. But most of the people we know from the ancient world were men.

On the other hand, the power of women is clearly on display in Greek drama. They are the mothers, daughters, heroines, and tragic figures who come upon the stage, often with blood on their gowns.

Bell believed that modern society (the 1920s) allowed only two roles for women – either housewife… or spinster. Neither would contribute much to civilized life, he said. If he were still alive, he would surely notice that women had found a whole new role – in which they are said to be, or supposed to be, equal to their male counterparts – in the work world. He would disapprove of this trend. Civilization requires detachment from… and liberation from… the need to take part in the economy, he believed.

The "hetairae" of the ancient world were mistresses, concubines, and prostitutes. Much like the geisha of Japan, they could be very well educated, and were sought out by cultivated men to contribute to their conversations. They had no work to do – other than to please their companion. And apart from physical satisfaction, the customers wanted lively, witty, engaging conversation. Bell thinks the *hetairae* added much to Greek civilization.

We have no class of women like that today. Nor do we have a class of men like those who dominated Athens before the death of Alexander. Nor even a class of men like Bell and his circle in the 1920s.

"We were very lucky," we recall our old partner, Lord Rees-Mogg explaining a few years before his death. "In Britain [in the early 20th century], there was a whole group of people who had inherited wealth and status. They went to Oxford and Cambridge. They were well educated. They had nothing to prove. They already had money and status. They were already in the aristocracy or semi-nobility, with fortunes that often rested on the innovations of the Industrial Revolution. They felt like an elite, and indeed they were. And with this feeling came a sense of public responsibility. They did not need to work, but it would have been very bad form to waste your life in idleness. So most of them set out to learn... to study... to build something... to travel... to invent... or otherwise to do something useful, or interesting, even if it had no immediate or obvious market value. And many of them succeeded quite well."

Mr. Bell, perhaps overly enthralled by the socialist tendencies of his time, reached back to the Classical period. He called upon the government to use its slave (taxpayer) labor to support an idle class. Mr. Bell would get his wish. But had he lived longer, we doubt he would have been happy with the results. Since the 1920s, governments have supported millions of people in idleness. In the U.S. today, there are 250 million adults. But there are only about 140 million with jobs. In the past, many of the jobless people would have been housewives, busy taking care of the domestic front while the male breadwinner was at the coalface. But with today's modern conveniences, small family sizes, and the shift towards women in the workplace, there must be some 100 million people who are neither breadwinners nor homemakers.

They live on welfare, food stamps, savings, pensions, and with the support of relatives. They are more or less idle. And as far as we know, not one of them has carved anything like the Danaïde, written anything approaching *Lysistrata*, or made a contribution to math and science that comes close to those of Euclid and Archimedes 2,200 years ago.

What fun it would be to have Clive Bell come to visit us in

Baltimore. He could see for himself the results of keeping three generations in idleness.

Of course, Mr. Bell is not really proposing idleness. But idleness is what shows up at the back door when the need to work goes out the front. Even in the Classical period, idleness was seen as a dangerous visitor. Here's twentieth-century English philosopher R. G. Collingwood on the subject:

> *From Plato onwards, Greco-Roman society's life was a rearguard action against emotional bankruptcy. The critical moment was reached when Rome created an urban proletariat whose only function was to eat free bread and watch free shows. This meant the segregation of an entire class which had no work to do whatever; no positive function in society, whether economic or military or administrative or intellectual or religious; only the business of being supported and being amused. When that had been done, it was only a question of time until Plato's nightmare of a consumer's society came true: the drones set up their own king, and the story of the hive came to an end.*

Idleness does not appear to lead to higher levels of civilized life. But what does? Art? Culture? Politics? The Greeks considered the tribal people who lived north of Macedonia to be roughly as low and brutish as Trump voters. But at least a thousand years earlier, the ancient Sumerians were already talking smack about them. In *The Curse of Akkad*, a story from around 2000 B.C., the semi-civilized Sumerians described the Barbarians invading their territory:

> *…they don't have grains, they don't have houses nor cities… they are not farmers, they eat raw meat, have never lived in a house in their entire lives… the Martu [what they called these Amorite invaders] are a raider people with the instincts of wild beasts.*

But is there really any important difference between the Barbarians and the people who called themselves "civilized?" If so, what is it? Rushing to judgment, we maintain that it is one thing and one thing only: a relative absence of violence.

It is common to define a "civilized" people in terms of their commissions – their cultural and political achievements. Bell added to this prejudice. The old historians focused on four paragons of civilization to make their point. Those were Athens, from the Battle of Marathon in 490 B.C. to the death of Alexander the Great in 323 B.C.... Rome, from Caesar's crossing of the Rubicon in 49 B.C. at least to the reign of Trajan in the second century... the Italian city states of the 15th and 16th centuries... and finally, France, before the Revolution in the 18th century.

But it is one thing to talk about civilization abstractly and quite another to put the label on any specific place at any specific time. And it is a challenge and a trap to base a definition of civilization purely on aesthetic or cultural markers. The trouble with basing a theory of civilization on cultural achievements is that it's very hard to get a purchase on it. As soon as you say that post-Marathon Athens was a paragon of civilization, someone will point out that the Athenians were already champions of the art world long before the Persian invasion. Then, you might be tempted to narrow your focus to the Golden Age of Pericles... until you realize that Pericles was an idiot warmonger who got Athens smashed by the Spartans and used embezzled funds to build the now-famous Parthenon.

And while we are mentioning the Spartans, they depended on slave labor, called "helots," even more than the Athenians. Today, you will have a hard time arguing that any place that relied on whips and chains for its daily bread deserves to be called "civilized" at all, let alone one of the best of the breed. And yet, wasn't Athens circa the fourth century B.C. – even with all its slave labor – still more civilized than say, Baltimore circa 2019? Imagine the students gathered at Aristotle's feet. Weren't they more civilized than the average student body of any public high school in modern Baltimore?

But wait. Our old friend, writer Richard Russell, used to say that you could judge a civilization by how it treated its women. But where does that take you? Are women in Iran or Saudi Arabia treated worse than those in Baltimore? Who knows? According to Professor Edward Westermarck, from whom Bell draws inspiration as well as information, some "civilized" communities treated their women like livestock. Some savages, on the other hand, treated them pretty well. The Andaman Islanders might have boiled up missionaries for dinner, but they were monogamous. And the Car Nicobar heathens, says Bell, were far more chaste than most U.S. presidents. Plato, meanwhile, advocated communal wife-sharing. Who's to say which is more civilized?

But it is in matters of politics and patriotism that the students of civilization tend to flunk out. The general tendency is to connect civilized periods in history with strong, resolute government. Many people – notably Steven Pinker – believe, for example, that the rise of powerful states was partly responsible for the decline in homicide rates. As we develop our theme, we'll see that the connection between government and civilization is much more complex. Or perhaps a strong government is simply a lagging indicator. When societies are cohesive and wealth producing, government tends to be strong; it can draw upon the resources of a rich economy. But since we will examine it much more closely later, we'll drop the strong government hypothesis here.

We note only that love of country is not necessarily good or bad. Bell remarks that Fiji Islanders were so attached to their homeland that they died from homesickness when they were removed from it. Other groups – especially successful merchants and traders from India, China, and Lebanon, diaspora Jews and Armenians, MBAs, and people named Patel – seem to land on their feet wherever they stumble. They don't seem to care which passport they carry, as long as it allows them to travel, learn, and do business.

Military success, too, is often confused with, or suspected of enabling, civilization. Many people believe that it was Caesar's conquest of Rome that made possible the great flourishing of civilization under Augustus. And it wasn't until Japan whupped Russia in 1905 that Japan was considered civilized by westerners. But it clearly takes more than a military victory to bring about civilized development.

In the Second World War, "protecting civilization" was again a popular justification. And it had less of a hollow, tinny ring to it than it did in World War I. But not because Germans had suddenly begun beating their wives, or forgotten how to write long, almost impossible-to-follow sentences making some obscure philosophical point... or because they were unable to string their violins. *Au contraire*, it was because they – or more precisely, their rulers – had lost the one thing that civilization requires: the willingness to leave your neighbors in peace. The Germans had gone over to the dark side – the side of violence.

THE GREATEST KILLERS OF ALL TIME

In today's world, between private citizens at least, violence is rare. There are bar fights, cases of domestic abuse, and murders – but they are relatively few. And becoming fewer. The murder rate, for example, has come down dramatically over the last few centuries.

With a generous dose of doubt and guesswork, here are the figures for the U.S. The private murder rate for the 1700s was roughly 30 per 100,000 people per year. In the 1800s, the rate fell to 20 per 100,000. Then, in the 20th century, the rate declined to 10 and below. Today, the murder rate in the U.S. is under 6 per 100,000.

That said, there are local particularities. In Baltimore, Maryland, for example, the murder rate in 2018 was even higher than it was for the U.S. in the 18th century, with 50 murders per 100,000.

And occasionally, there are spectacular murders that make the news and distort popular impressions. One week, 17 youngsters were killed at a public high school in Florida. Another week, five adults were shot dead at a small-town newspaper in Maryland. These stories make huge headlines. But they don't significantly change the downward drift of violence.

But while private murder rates have declined, the last century saw a big boom in killing as a matter of public policy. Late in the 20th century, a whole cottage industry of scholars developed around the question: Who killed more – Hitler, Stalin, or Mao? It was not an easy question. Murderous regimes do not necessarily keep, or publish, careful records about those they have massacred.

Hitler is generally credited with 17 million military deaths and another 28 million civilian deaths. Stalin killed some 20 million in his purges and mass starvations. Another 25 million or so died in World War II – many because of political and tactical directives that were criminally negligent or intentionally lethal. In this company, Pol Pot hardly deserves a footnote. Still, he murdered (or caused the deaths of) some two million people. His claim to fame is his market share. As a percentage of the population – 25% – he killed more than any of them. This figure nearly surpasses the murder rates recorded in the bloodiest ancient bone pits ever discovered.

Mao, Stalin, Hitler, Pol Pot – these four men alone were responsible for an estimated 137 million deaths, the biggest killing spree in history. Of course, you can quibble with these numbers. There is the question about collateral damage, for example. When you expel people from their homes in the dead of winter without shelter or food, you have to expect that some of them will die, especially if you load them in unheated boxcars and ship them to Siberia. So, too, if you confiscate the food peasants have stored for winter. Famine is predictable, though it may not be possible to say exactly how many will starve to death.

But on raw numbers alone, Mao seems to be in the winning position. His Great Leap Forward may have killed 45 million people. Farms were collectivized. Unrealistic production targets were set – under the fabulous reasoning that the new socialist man was more productive.

Then, Mao's goons went out into the countryside and confiscated food. They took even the seed corn, condemning the peasantry to starvation. Farmers suspected of hiding grain were tortured and killed. Even the Communist Party admitted that Mao made "mistakes." Officially, the party says that 70% of what Mao did was good; the other 30% was not.

Among the 30%, Mao told farmers to boost harvests by planting seeds closer together. Over many generations, farmers had learned how close they could plant the seeds. But Mao – well fed in Beijing or one of his many hidden palaces – had no skin in the game. He could say what he wanted. In the worst famine in human history, Chairman Mao didn't lose a pound.

DISARM GOVERNMENTS

"Thou Shalt Not Kill" is now almost universally accepted. The only exceptions – apart from the big one... killings "to the sound of trumpets" – are typically nutty. Private sector killers rarely make a rational calculation; instead, they are moved by passion, ideology, or delusion. They are mad. They are upset. They are seeking justice. Fortunately, they are rare.

Private homicide tends to go on, at low levels, more or less all the time. But homicide rates, in general, have declined everywhere, as far as we're able to tell. Public sector killing, on the other hand, is episodic. And focused in specific areas. In the just-rehearsed history of the 20th century, for example, we see public policy killings outstripping those of the private sector 10-to-1. Political scientist R. J. Rummel puts the "death by government" – what he called "democide" – tally for the 20th century at 272 million – a staggering number. If the dead measured an average of five feet tall, and were laid head to toe, they would circle the globe more than 10 times, he says.

Yet despite this evidence of clear and present danger from malign public policy, the do-gooders, the world-improvers, the media, as well as academic and political activists (both Republican and Democrat) can think of nothing more original than… more public policy! And more guns!

Another important nuance of the "who killed most" question is this: neither Mao nor Stalin nor Hitler actually did the killing. Others did it. Had they been asked, most of the killers might very well have preferred to stay at home tending their own farms and families. But the deal was asymmetrical. A very small group was able to get control of a huge society, including, most importantly, its military. This control they used to terrible effect, whether the people were enthusiastic or not.

How this happens remains to be fully explained. Part of it, of course, may be attributed to basic psychology. People – neither always good nor always bad, but always subject to influence – tend to go along with their leaders. This is especially true when they feel the group is menaced by outsiders. When a society is peaceful and expanding, people may be more civilized in their comportment. That is, they are likely to favor win-win deals.

But under stress, older, deeper instincts reveal themselves. "The veneer of civilization is very thin," said former British Prime Minister Margaret Thatcher. And it flakes off readily. All it takes is a war scare… or war fever. Or maybe just a financial setback.

Then, the old "us versus them" reaction kicks in. "Bad Guy Theory" returns. Violence, if it can be visited on others, becomes popular again. Tribalism, too. Primitive, pre-civilized responses are part of our environmental adaptation. Giraffes evolved to have long necks. And we evolved to stick together in times of attack… submit to our leaders… fight or fly… and shun, or punish, those who don't cooperate.

CAN'T MAKE CIVILIZATION

We blame Claude Henri de Rouvroy, among many others. Rouvroy, the count of Saint-Simon, was born in 1760 into an aristocratic family in France. He was a smart guy. This did not necessarily make him good at everything… or anything. In fact, he proved remarkably untalented at suicide. He shot himself in the head six times and lived!

Yet, with French philosopher Auguste Comte, Saint-Simon developed an idea that, like a malevolent weed, flourished. More on that in a minute…

It is better to be bad at some things than good. Suicide, for example. And if Napoléon Bonaparte had been less effective as a military leader, he might not have undertaken the Russian campaign of 1812. If Adolf Hitler had been less gifted as an orator, he might have lived happily, or otherwise, as a housepainter. If Charles Manson has been less persuasive, he might have died in an old folks' home, not in a prison.

What "smart" people are good at is taking in information, myths, and lies and putting them to work. That ability is very useful in the civilized world. But it must have been much less useful in the pre-civilized world from which humans are adapted. In that world, being intellectually gifted (in the modern, common sense) might have been more of a handicap than a benefit. It required a brain capacity that was only occasionally appropriate. Otherwise, there would be more smart people. Instead, as with other human traits, it was probably a good idea for a tribe to include some smart people, but not too many.

The proto-Archimedes – thinking intently about levers and arcs – might miss his shot and come home empty-handed. The proto-Leonardo – his head in the clouds, wondering about the potential of human flight – might be more likely to step on a poisonous snake. Studies have found, for example, that truck drivers are less likely to have accidents if they are not too bright. And people with advanced degrees are more likely to have traffic accidents than those with only a high school education.

The brains of our remote ancestors were pitifully small. *Australopithecus afarensis* had a brain of only 450 grams, roughly one-third the size of a modern human brain. There must have been mutant animals with larger brains, but apparently, the extra cost – in calories – of supporting a larger brain was not worth it.

Then, three million years later, *Homo sapiens* appeared with a brain three times as large. Why had smarts become so much more valuable? Well, we can guess. On the open savannah, working as a group had proved to be a winning strategy. Communicating and coordinating took more brain power. But it helped the group survive, first against the attacks of wild animals, and later against the attacks of other smartened-up groups.

And now, just as beauty will take a woman only so far and being able to bench press 200 pounds has limited market value for a man, so, too, do brains come with trade-offs. Smart people may be able to contribute to civilization, for example, but though they are tempted to try, they cannot design, create, reform, or improve civilization itself. A single brain is no match for a million years of trial and error.

We turn to the newspapers for further illustration…

AN INVITATION TO CLAPTRAP

The New York Times is probably no worse than any other newspaper. But it is the only one we had on a long trip from Berlin to Bermuda in October 2018.

What gives over at the *Times*? Most of the "think pieces" showed no signs of thinking at all. Here were some of the most thoughtful people on the planet, and all they could think of was what they wanted. David Brooks wanted more community do-goodism. Jo Piazza wanted men to be more like women. Reshma Saujani wanted women to run the world. And Nicholas Kristof wanted to do something about global warming.

At least David Brooks was right about one thing. Writing on education reform in South Carolina in the Friday, October 12, 2018 international edition, the columnist noticed:

> *Our actual lives are influenced by millions of events that interact in mysterious ways.*

That observation should have made the rest of the gang at the Gray Lady pause. For every snake we see in the grass, there are dozens more in the bush, waiting to bite us on the *derrière*.

And it should open the door to a genuinely interesting discussion. If human society is shaped by things we don't understand, can we really improve it by conscious (usually armed) intervention?

TRAIN YOUR HUSBAND

We'll come back to Mr. Brooks in a minute...

Instead, let's move on to Jo Piazza. "How I Trained My Husband to Be a Dad," was the headline. That alone calls forth a nest of viperous questions. Was this a joke? How would she know (better than he) how to be a dad? She is, after all, a mom. And what is wrong with her husband? Wasn't his role shaped by millions of years of evolutionary experience? Isn't that training now embedded in his genes, instincts, and traditions? Would the *Times* run a follow-up from him: "How I Beat My Wife Into Being a Decent Mother"?

Ms. Piazza insisted that they share the burden of baby care equally. Is that a good idea? In our experience, babies want their mommas, perhaps for purely anatomical reasons. But what do we know? Ms. Piazza doesn't know, either... and has no interest in finding out. Instead, she left her three-month-old with her husband so she could work on her novel! And her tone of self-satisfied triumphalism suggested that she believed she had just crawled out of the muck and learned to walk on two legs.

But what kind of progress was this? The earliest and most basic form of the division of labor is the cooperation between men and women. One hunts. The other gathers. One is a mother. The other is a father. One remembers the children's birthdays. The other remembers Boog Powell's batting average from 1962. By specializing, rather than by both doing the same thing, nature made it possible for them not only to have children but to build a civilization.

At one site in India, for example, there is evidence of the division of labor in making arrowheads some 1.2 million years ago. Scientists believe that men provided the brute force to break the flakes of stone loose, and women (or perhaps children or old people) fashioned them into the shapes they wanted. And today, cooperation – between specialist metallurgists, financiers, salesmen, engineers, assemblers, machinists, chemists, and so forth – produces top-of-the-line Mercedes autos, for example... which wouldn't be possible in a less-differentiated, hunter-gatherer society. Maybe nature knows something Mr. and Ms. Piazza don't... like the theory of competitive advantage!

When a man turns his attention to gathering up dirty diapers, he has less time to hunt for deals in the outside world. It's not that he can't still earn a living, but he will be at a competitive disadvantage to guys whose wives take care of the baby, leaving them to work 12 hours a day in the outside world. He will be less specialized... and less productive. The world will be less rich, too; with fewer resources to work with, people will have fewer choices.

Is that good or bad? It's none of our business how couples organize themselves. And there are surely lots of different ways to do it. But if *The New York Times* is going to put it in the public record, you'd think it would at least mention the trade-offs. Also worthy of mention was research that suggests that couples that share household chores equally – rather than specializing – are more likely to get divorced. Why? We don't know. That's why we have question marks.

Meanwhile, over on page 10 of the *Times* was another exercise in antediluvian trivia, in which Reshma Saujani suggested that "Maybe Girls Will Save Us.""From what?" was our first question. But she didn't bother with that. All over the country, she says, girls are getting turned on to politics.

The author is, of course, an activist herself. She is trying to get more girls to "code" – that is, to enter the world of computer technology. Why is it such a good idea for girls to code? We never had any interest in coding. It seems like dreary work; why try to get girls to do it?

Ms. Saujani says girls have "eclipsed boys in political participation and shown incredible moral clarity." And, oh yes, they have an "instinct for inclusiveness." Oh yeah? How does she know? And what does it mean?

Over on page 12, the smart drivel went on. There, Nicholas Kristof told us that "denying climate change doesn't stop its devastating effects." Of course, he's right. Nature doesn't care what we think. Kristof prompts a couple of climatologists to tell us that there might be a link between you driving to work in the morning and the hurricane that just washed over the Bible Belt.

Yes, there might be. Or there might not be. And maybe someday, scientists will have a better understanding of it. But today, we don't know what's going on with the world's weather. Most important, we don't know whether it's good or bad. We don't know if we could do something to change it. And we don't know if the costs would be greater than the rewards.

But Kristof can't wait. He wants "us" to do something now. As soon as you hear someone say, "We need to do something…," you can stop listening. What follows is invariably idiotic, because it always ignores those millions of inscrutable influences… and the millions of years it took to get where we are without doing it. The activist is always a scalawag. And the activist with moral clarity is dangerous.

And now, let's go back to David Brooks. Having set forth an observation worthy of Shakespeare – that there's more going on to influence our lives than we find in our philosophy – Brooks proceeds to treat it like a smelly groundling, doing his best to stay up on stage, out of reach.

He tells us that he went to Spartanburg, South Carolina and saw the do-gooders working together to improve the world. But do they do any real good? Does the investment pay off? What happens to the things that can't be done because of the time and money that have gone into these worthy projects? No one knows.

"Building working relationships across a community is an intrinsically good thing," he writes.

Is it? We don't know that, either.

But here's another question: Has a community ever actually been improved by busybodies who say they're working for the good of others?

Or, as Adam Smith suggested, are communities really improved as a byproduct of people minding their own business, looking out for themselves... making millions and millions of win-win deals, compromises, gifts, and bargains... trading, working, marrying one another, exchanging small talk and smiles in the course of business... giving and getting with no intention of forcing their moral clarity on others?

Human life is far too subtle and complicated for smart people to shape or control. It is subject to far too many baroque, mysterious influences. It can't be straightened out on an anvil by simple-minded jackasses with ball-peen hammers.

Someone should have mentioned this to Claude Henri de Rouvroy, the aforementioned count of Saint-Simon. Along with Auguste Comte, another philosopher of the 19th century, he developed an idea that soon became very popular with smart people: "positivism." By then, it was obvious that smart people could obtain "positive knowledge" about the natural world through the scientific method. Smart people could use this knowledge to build machines and organize methods of production and distribution, and thereby improve their lives. The Industrial Age was just beginning. Progress was undeniable. Smart people would lead the world forward.

"Positive knowledge" – applied to technical know-how – could make us richer, healthier, and more comfortable. Why not apply this idea to the whole society – the cultural, religious, political, and economic connections between people? Wouldn't that make things better, too?

But the relationships between people are not as simple as the relationship between a nail and a hammer. You can beat on people, too.

But it's hard to drive them straight where you want them to go. And in the 200 years that have elapsed since "positivism" made its appearance – in which the concept was exhaustively explored and employed by governments, activists, and world-improvers – no persuasive evidence of any real improvement has emerged. Smart people can make relationships between people different. They can, within limits, make them into what they want. But they can't make them better. (We will explore this subject more fully in our chapter on government. We will see that smart people, empowered by government, cannot make the world better because they don't know what better is… And they lack any of the tools that would be needed to do so anyway.)

Society evolves as people develop new ideas, products, myths, inventions, and ways of working, mostly voluntarily, with one another. One buys his bread from the corner shop because he likes the salesgirl's pretty, red hair. Another orders his cement from across town because they give him more time to pay. A third fancies a new watch that's powered by his own body heat.

Then, along come the positivists with their own ideas, imposing their own rules and policies, preventing the give and take of a free economy, setting prices, requiring licenses, blocking competition… robbing Peters to pay their crony Pauls – all in the name of making the world a better place, of course.

In their most ambitious forms, they launch sweeping programs to reorder social and economic relationships according to the fads and fashions of the time. We will all now wear Mao jackets… The intellectuals will plant cabbages… A pound of beef and a pound of steel shall bear the same price… We will speak Esperanto, tie our shoelaces together and hop to work, and wear our underwear on the outside so the authorities can verify that it is clean! As far as we know, every effort to consciously remake society – to make it more civilized by imposing win-lose deals – has been a disastrous failure. At best, they have had outcomes that can't be measured or proven out, one way or another.

In the 1930s, the positivist doctrine was given a boost. Thinkers assembled in Vienna, Austria made an impression on an English visitor named A. J. Ayer. The 24-year-old hurried back to London, wrote about it, and became the *enfant terrible* of English philosophy – promoting "logical positivism" however he could.

This school of thought, which attempted to reduce all human behavior to logical and scientific foundations, became so popular, it filled the universities, sloshing over department walls like an overflowing septic tank, and poisoning many other disciplines – notably economics. And today, there is scarcely a politician in any party who doesn't think he can pass a law to make a better society. And there is hardly an economist alive who doesn't believe that smart people can assemble "data," develop hypotheses, and manipulate rates, rules, prices, and policies to stimulate an economy or calm it down... and thereby make people richer.

German sociologist Norbert Elias believed there was a "civilizing process" that, in fits and starts, caused people to become less animal-like and more civilized over time. He attributed it to two things. First, the rise of governments – which claimed a monopoly on the use of force – concentrated the win-lose deals in the public sector. Second, win-win deals themselves – or "gentle commerce," as it was called in the Enlightenment – encouraged empathy. If you wanted to satisfy a customer, you had to think about the customer's wants and desires. The next thing you knew, you were wearing deodorant. Elias noted that this process continued "without coordination or conscious control" by any planners, governments, or smart people of any sort.

This was an inconvenient thought, of course, to a smart person. And it was widely ignored. Nature gave him a hammer. He believes he can gain money, power, and status without ever satisfying a customer; he can merely whack something. And now, almost a century after the creed of "positivism" became widely accepted, economists, political scientists, and central planners have been hammering away for nearly three generations, earning their livings and reputations by consciously applying logic and reason to make human relationships more satisfying. They no longer question it; it is as though it came from the mouth of God Himself.

But it wasn't God who pushed positivism; it was the aforementioned A. J. Ayer, who taught at Bard College in New York and distinguished himself in an encounter with American prizefighter Mike Tyson. According to press reports, Tyson was imposing himself on supermodel Naomi Campbell at a fashionable party both attended. Ayer tried to intervene.

"Do you know who the f**k I am? I'm the heavyweight champion of the world," said Tyson.

"And I am the former Wykeham Professor of Logic," Ayer replied. "We are both preeminent in our field. I suggest that we talk about this like rational men."

In the conversation that followed, Ms. Campbell is said to have slipped away. The effects of the discussion on Mr. Tyson and Mr. Ayer went unrecorded.

But Ayer is best remembered for his judgment on his life's work. Late in life, he was asked about positivism's shortcomings.

"I suppose the greatest defect," he replied, "...is that nearly all of it was false."

Fortunately, civilization does not depend on smart people. Nor does it depend on vases or sculpture... on literature or architecture... on democracy... on conquest or culture... on equality... on the rights of man... or on armies, trains, or courts. Instead, it is what you get when you remove violence and permit civilized, win-win deals to happen.

Civilization does not necessarily make you wealthy. Or happy. It is completely indifferent to you. It doesn't care what you think of it. And it doesn't feel any inclination to be what you think it should be.

&— **CHAPTER 4** —&

What Kind of Game Are We Playing?

Mr. Boche ain't a bad fellow.
You leave him alone. He'll leave you alone.
– Unknown sergeant to unknown soldier arriving
in the trenches, World War I

╍╎╍╎╍╎╍╎

A FEW YEARS AGO, we took a vague and amateurish interest in game theory; it seemed to confirm our prejudices about the way the world worked. To make a long story short, in the 1950s, the Rand Corporation (a think tank financed by the American government) began working on games in which simple decision rules were tested against each another. Assuming the players were rational (which humans may or may not be)... and assuming that complex decision rules can be reduced to simple formulae (if A does X, B should do Y)... the game might tell us something about real-life human behavior.

These tests, as simple as they were, had vast implications. Ethics, religion, politics, human relations, business, mathematics, war — everything was involved... or seemed to be. Should you do unto your neighbor as you would have him do unto you? Or should you whack him first, before he has a chance to do you any harm?

A couple of decades later, Robert Axelrod, a professor at the

University of Michigan, ran a series of computer games. He invited participants to submit computer programs, in which they would act and react with other players, earning points depending on how it went. The fourteen entries submitted came from five disciplines: psychology, economics, political science, mathematics, and sociology.

Societies work because people cooperate with one another, even if they are unaware of it, and even though they may have no particular interest in those they are cooperating with. This is what Adam Smith describes as an "invisible hand" guiding people to do things that will benefit themselves, and thereby, unintentionally, others. But how do they cooperate? When? Why? Those were the questions Professor Axelrod set out to answer.

His game was set up on a foundation of the Prisoner's Dilemma. Imagine two men are arrested on suspicion of burglary. Taken to different rooms for questioning, each faces a choice. Say nothing… and take the consequences. Or rat out the other suspect in exchange for a lighter sentence for himself. If both keep their mouths shut (cooperation), the cops may not be able to make a good case. The two may get off. But neither knows what the other will do. If either one goes along with the police (defection), bargaining for leniency in return for turning "state's evidence," the other is left holding the bag.

The computer programs submitted for the game tried various combinations of cooperation and defection, earning points more or less in line with the real rewards and punishments the prisoners described above might face. Some programs favored defection. Some favored cooperation. But the one that won the game – that is, the one that got the most favorable outcome most of the time – was one sent in by Anatol Rapoport of the University of Toronto. It was called "Tit for Tat." It was a very simple program, beginning with a cooperative move… and remaining cooperative until the other player defected. Then it defected, too. Tit for tat.

Cooperation earned players three points. An uncooperative,

defecting player, on the other hand, got five points. But defection set in motion the "Tat" response, in which each player only got one point. A defection then caused further defections – distrust begets more distrust – with further point losses.

The players learned quickly that it did not pay to defect first. The winners were "nice"; they cooperated, unless and until their opponent defected.

The competition was run again after all the participants had a chance to study the results and the winning strategies. This time, there were 62 entries from all over the world, reflecting a number of different academic disciplines. Submissions came from computer hobbyists, gamers, theorists, and so forth. Included among them was one 10-year-old boy, evidently a computer prodigy.

Once again, the winner was Anatol Rapoport, who merely dusted off his original Tit for Tat program and resubmitted it. This time, the results were signaled all over the world… and people thought they felt the earth move beneath their feet. Axelrod published the findings in the 1981 paper, *The Evolution of Cooperation*. He brought out a book of the same name in 1984.

Here was computer-simulated, mathematical proof of the Golden Rule, commonly understood as "do unto others as you would have them do unto you." Almost.

In a revised edition of his book, published in 2006, Axelrod himself disputed this finding. "In the context of the Prisoner's Dilemma," he wrote, "the Golden Rule would seem to imply that you should always cooperate, since cooperation is what you want from the other player. This interpretation suggests that the best strategy from the point of view of morality is the strategy of unconditional cooperation rather than Tit for Tat. The problem with this view is that turning the other cheek provides an incentive for the other player to exploit you. Unconditional cooperation can not only hurt you, but it can hurt other innocent bystanders with whom the successful exploiters will interact later."

Letting people get away with something spoils them, he went on to say. Jesus didn't worry about it. His instruction was to love not just friends, but enemies, too. Matthew 5:43-45:

> *⁴³ You have heard that it was said, "Love your neighbor and hate your enemy."*
> *⁴⁴ But I tell you, love your enemies and pray for those who persecute you,*
> *⁴⁵ that you may be sons of your Father in heaven. He causes His sun to rise on the evil and the good, and sends rain on the righteous and the unrighteous…*

As for those who smite you, you are supposed to turn the other cheek. Luke 6:29:

> *²⁹ And unto him that smiteth thee on the one cheek offer also the other; and him that taketh away thy cloak forbid not to take thy coat also.*

Not once, not twice, but 490 times. Matthew 18:22:

> *²² Jesus saith unto him, I say not unto thee, Until seven times: but, Until seventy times seven.*

But Axelrod insists that if you are always nice to people – even after they betray you – you'll be taken for a chump. Our personal experience contradicts this. We have met people who were always nice. As near as we could tell, they lived as well as… and were as successful as… anyone else. And they were happy.

Of course, there are several major differences between Axelrod's games and real life. First, in real life, you don't have to continue playing with every Tom, Dick, and Harry who comes along. So, even though you always forgive… and always turn the other cheek, you don't necessarily continue playing the game with the jerk.

Second, the Golden Rule is not a guide to winning Axelrod's game. It is more than a strategy. It's a moral instruction. Like the rule against murder, it is not meant to give you a leg up on the competition. It is meant, perhaps, to get you into Heaven, where God keeps score. Or perhaps it has survived and flourished simply because it provided the group – not the individual – with an advantage.

Third, Mr. Axelrod has simply goofed. The Golden Rule tells you to "do unto others as you would have them do unto you." It does not say you should always let yourself be exploited. If it were correct that "unconditional cooperation can not only hurt you, but it can hurt other innocent bystanders," what moron would want that?

"Friends don't let friends drive drunk," goes the saying. There may be an equivalent in game theory. "Friends don't let themselves be exploited by other players." Instead, they follow the Tit for Tat rule… with forgiveness. They want to be treated fairly, not obsequiously or sycophantically. But they also want their friends to cut them some slack and give them a break from time to time.

An even bigger mistake made by Mr. Axelrod is that he failed to understand what cooperation really is. We cringe and recall those immortal words of former U.S. Supreme Court Justice Oliver Wendell Holmes Jr.: "Taxes are the price we pay for a civilized society." Robert Axelrod seems to agree. And he goes further… suggesting that taxes – as well as other impositions by government – can help drive people toward civilized, cooperative behavior.

The role of government, he says, "is to make sure that when individuals do not have private incentives to cooperate, they will be required to do the socially useful thing anyway."

The "socially useful thing." What is that? How do you know? All we know about the socially useful thing is that it is what you get when people cooperate rather than defect. That is, it is a consequence of cooperation. And it is an unknown consequence. We don't know what things are worth doing until we see people voluntarily doing them. But can you get the same result if you force people to cooperate?

Let's see. How does that work? Cooperation presumes, and requires, voluntarism. If people cooperate, they must do so on their own terms. Otherwise, it's not cooperation. It's no good telling someone, "Now you cooperate, or else." Or, like a *mafioso* shaking down a small merchant: "If you cooperate, you won't get hurt." A person who goes along in this circumstance is not cooperating but obeying. Axelrod seems not to notice the difference.

The Mafia has ways of getting its own type of "cooperation." Its rules, like those of the government, raise the cost of defection. They are effective, apparently. But they are not increasing the level of real cooperation; they are changing the nature of the game.

Tit for Tat players earn points. And the only thing we know from the Tit for Tat results is that, in the context of the game at least, people who generally cooperate end up with more points. But cooperate at what? Later on, we will approach the same problem from a more traditional economic point of view, and we will look at the role of government in a larger context. But for now, we simply point out that there is no way to know what is "socially useful" outside of what the players themselves choose to do.

Axelrod goes on to argue that government can change the "payoffs" simply by taxing, prohibiting, or subsidizing certain outcomes... thus increasing the incentives to cooperate:

> *Laws are passed to cause people to pay their taxes, not to steal, and to honor contracts with strangers. Each of these activities could be regarded as a giant Prisoner's Dilemma game with many players. No one wants to pay taxes because the benefits are so diffuse and the costs are so direct. Everyone may be better off if each person has to pay so that each can share the benefits of schools, roads, and other collective goods.*

Or not... When government enters the game, it comes armed. And it changes both the outcome and the nature of the game. "No one wants to pay taxes," says Axelrod. But why? Is it possible that it is because the results really aren't "socially useful" at all? No one really wants to work in a coal mine either. But people do. Willingly. Approximately half of all discretionary U.S. government spending goes to the Department of Defense and its crony contractors. This money pays for spooks, bombs, guns, and soldiers. It pays to keep U.S. forces in the field on a variety of missions – many of which involve killing people.

Isn't it possible that the benefits are not merely "diffuse," but non-existent? Or not benefits at all, but just malign and often lethal interference in other people's win-win deals? We don't know. But neither does anyone else. Because no one gets a say. The taxpayer is never asked. And if he were asked: "If you give us $7,000 (the average theoretical contribution per household towards the military budget), here's what we'll do for you..." spelling out exactly what his money would be used for... the answer would probably be "No thanks." Yet if you asked Boeing, General Dynamics, or Raytheon if they considered the military budget "socially useful," they would surely agree that it was.

You only really discover what is socially useful by letting people play the game, in which they get to freely express their wants and desires without the feds breathing down their necks and forcing them to do things they don't want to do. That's how we know that mining coal is socially useful. Baking bread is, too. And driving taxis. As for droning people in the Middle East, we have our doubts.

Axelrod set up a game that is meant to show how people of roughly equal power (equal ability and opportunity to defect) decide to cooperate. When government enters the picture, changing the "payoffs," it sets in motion entirely different dynamics. First, you can't play a game of cooperation with someone who can decide in advance who wins and who loses. Second, you can't force cooperation any more than you can force people to love their neighbors or chocolate ice cream.

Some plants can't survive at high altitudes. Few animals can survive extreme cold. And some human activities do not improve when you add threats and violence. That's why philosopher Jean-Jacques Rousseau's quip that government is there so the citizen "will be forced to be free" is so majestically idiotic. You can let people volunteer to be slaves, but you cannot force them to be free. You can only force them to be slaves. Likewise, you can't force people to cooperate. You can only force them to do as they are told.

The key to civilization, therefore, is not commission, but omission. It was not the use of force – as in, forcing people to be free – that made them free. It was not using force upon them at all – as in not killing their men... not stealing their property... not turning them into slaves... not raping their women... and not roasting their animals. That – the absence of violence – was the thing that separated civilized people from Barbarians.

Axelrod goes on to reach a number of other dubious conclusions. Looking back, they look rather typical of the era... that is, the positive-thinking 1980s, when it still looked as though American economists and central planners knew what they were doing. He suggests, for example, that cooperation might be enhanced if we would "teach people to care about each other." However unlikely this is to work in practice, the theory is just silly. The whole idea of the Prisoner's Dilemma game is based on the rational self-interest of the player. He doesn't need to care about the other player. He only has to care about himself... and respond to the natural dynamics of the situation.

The strategies that benefit individual players later become generalized rules that have a "moral" or ethical quality to them. First, a player tries to win by cooperating. Later, players think they should cooperate because "it is the right thing to do." Cooperation – not killing each other, not stealing, not bearing false witness... that is, not defecting – became more than a strategy. It became morality, an echo of past performance.

"Morality is just a fiction used by the herd of inferior human beings to hold back the few superior men," wrote Friedrich Nietzsche. Of course, morality is a fiction. It is a myth. But it is only incidentally the kind of myth Nietzsche imagined. It is not so much the inferior holding back the superior (though restraint, being generalized, does prevent the stronger man from killing the weaker, as well as vice versa). More importantly, it restrains the great mass of inferior people from overwhelming and exploiting the few "superior men."

In any society, there are some who are cleverer, who work harder, and who are luckier. Those few are those who invent new things, build new businesses, discover new things, compose new poems, and write new novels. They are the ones who give the most to others. Civilization's restraints – against murder and theft, primarily – help make sure they get what they deserve for their efforts.

In pre-civilized life, the physically strong may push the weak out of their homes… their fields… and their hunting territories. Only the strong may reproduce. The weak may not. We don't know; it was probably more nuanced than we realize. But in civilized communities, we don't need to know. Because civilized societies depend on much more than brute force for their success. The intellectual, the innovator, or the insecure nerd may turn out to be the next Jeff Bezos or Mark Zuckerberg. Though they may be weak physically, civilized communities have rules that allow these innovators to flourish. Civilized communities have universal rules that benefit people generally, not tribal rules that benefit particular individuals or groups.

"Love thy neighbor" applies to everyone. Language is used by the eloquent as well as the babblers and time wasters. Money serves the rich as well as the poor. Property rights make it worthwhile for owners to invest in improving their land and their harvests, thereby benefiting those who have no land at all. And nobody ever knows to whom these civilized innovations will prove most useful; we do not know the future.

Civilized rules reward and protect people who may not have

survived in barbaric tribes. They may be artful with words… or with money. They may accumulate property that they, personally, have never seen and have no way to defend. And they may come and go all over the world with little fear of being murdered.

Ah… that is the evolved beauty of civilization. It elaborates myths (rules, ideas, taboos) that serve everyone, in general, and no one in particular. The mute man, though unable to speak, is still able to live in a house with central heating, built by workers who were able to pass along instructions to one another verbally. The poor man, without a dime to his name, still has the possibility of gaining a job, where in less than an hour, he could earn enough to pay for his daily bread.

If the superior man is the one who creates wealth, "morality" is a great help to him. If the superior man is the one who is indifferent to wealth, "morality" helps make his poverty more comfortable.

For the first 200,000 years, being a good computer programmer or an excellent rapper wouldn't have marked a man as "superior." Instead, being stronger, faster, a better hunter, and perhaps a more forceful personality would have made the difference. These "big men" or "aggrandizers," say the anthropologists, probably got a disproportionate share of life's good things – which were then limited to food, sex, status, and not much more. As human life evolved and became more socially and technologically differentiated, other qualities found their rewards. Being clever, cunning, deceitful, careful, friendly, persuasive, or productive gradually triumphed over brute force. The world changed. Cooperation arose… much like it did in the iterated Prisoner's Dilemma game. Then arose a culture of cooperation and trust – not because the Big Man wanted it, but because the communities that allowed it were able to build walls, guns, and cannons… and destroy the Big Man and his whole tribe.

Government is the blunt instrument with which smart people force others to do their bidding. Many other organizations share the same stated goals – the welfare of the people, healing the sick, tending the poor, avoiding war, protecting your property. These other groups can only work out cooperative arrangements with their customers, clients, and donors. That is the single thing that separates government from truly cooperative organizations, such as the Kiwanis, the Coca-Cola corporation, or the Church of Latter-Day Saints. The feds use force, holding the threat of it over every transaction. Don't want to pay your taxes? You go to jail. Don't want to comply with every crony regulation? They close your business.

Nor is government particularly interested in helping to facilitate cooperative deals between the people it governs. Professor Axelrod assumes it would want to promote cooperation because cooperation improves output and outcomes. But why do the feds care? And if they care at all, it is more likely that they would want to prevent innovation than foster it. Innovation – or any win-win deal, for that matter – threatens the existing structure of wealth, power, and status. "And if there is one opinion common to ruling classes everywhere," writes journalist Robert Wright, "it is that power is not in urgent need of redistributing."

The feds are playing a different game. They are fundamentally defectors, not cooperators.

TIT FOR TAT IN THE TRENCHES

One of the examples of spontaneous cooperation presented in Axelrod's book, *The Evolution of Cooperation*, took place in World War I.

The war had begun as a great, fast-moving, wheeling movement by the Germans. Following the Schlieffen Plan, they chased the retreating French down the Marne Valley to within a few miles of Paris. The plan called for taking Paris forthwith, but the commanding German general, Alexander von Kluck, believed the French army was broken. He thought he could continue the chase and wipe it out for good.

But the French weren't broken. Von Kluck's staff pointed out that there were few prisoners and few abandoned weapons. It did not look like an army that was demoralized or fleeing in panic. In fact, the

French were retreating in good order. And when the commander of the French garrison in Paris – the old warhorse General Gallieni – saw what was happening, his eyes lit up. "Gentlemen," he said to his staff, "they offer us their flank."

The French counterattacked from Paris, using taxi cabs to deliver soldiers to the front lines. The move caught the Germans by surprise and forced them back. Soon after, each side settled into its defensive position and stayed there. That is what gave rise to the cooperation; warfare became an iterated game. The static lines of trench warfare left groups of soldiers facing each other over long periods of time. None of them wanted to die. So, to the dismay of their officers, they devised cooperative strategies to avoid killing each other.

One officer visiting the front lines wrote that "these people evidently did not know there was a war going on." He resolved to do something about it: "I privately made up my mind to do away with that sort of thing."

There you see the relationship between the government (the officer) and the soldiers. The latter come up with ways to cooperate. The former figures out how to stop it.

British captain Bruce Bairnsfather recalls the famous Christmas Truce of 1914:

> I wouldn't have missed that unique and weird Christmas Day for anything... I spotted a German officer, some sort of lieutenant I should think, and being a bit of a collector, I intimated to him that I had taken a fancy to some of his buttons... I brought out my wire clippers and, with a few deft snips, removed a couple of his buttons and put them in my pocket. I then gave him two of mine in exchange... The last I saw was one of my machine gunners, who was a bit of an amateur hairdresser in civil life, cutting the unnaturally long hair of a docile Boche, who was patiently kneeling on the ground whilst the automatic clippers crept up the back of his neck.

Future nature writer Henry Williamson, then a nineteen-year-old private in the London Rifle Brigade, wrote to his mother on Boxing Day:

Dear Mother, I am writing from the trenches. It is 11 o'clock in the morning. Beside me is a coke fire, opposite me a "dug-out" (wet) with straw in it. The ground is sloppy in the actual trench, but frozen elsewhere. In my mouth is a pipe presented by the Princess Mary. In the pipe is tobacco. Of course, you say. But wait. In the pipe is German tobacco. Haha, you say, from a prisoner or found in a captured trench. Oh dear, no! From a German soldier. Yes a live German soldier from his own trench. Yesterday the British and Germans met and shook hands in the ground between the trenches, and exchanged souvenirs. Yes, all day Xmas day, and as I write. Marvellous, isn't it?

And Captain Robert Patrick Miles, King's Shropshire Light Infantry, wrote:

We are having the most extraordinary Christmas Day imaginable. A sort of unarranged and quite unauthorized but perfectly understood and scrupulously observed truce exists between us and our friends in front. The funny thing is it only seems to exist in this part of the battle line – on our right and left we can all hear them firing away as cheerfully as ever. The thing started last night – a bitter cold night, with white frost – soon after dusk when the Germans started shouting "Merry Christmas, Englishmen" to us. Of course, our fellows shouted back and presently large numbers of both sides had left their trenches, unarmed, and met in the debatable, shot-riddled, no man's land between the lines. Here the agreement – all on their own – came to be made that we should not fire at each other until after midnight tonight. The men were all fraternizing in the middle (we naturally did not allow them too close to our line) and swapped cigarettes and lies in the utmost good fellowship. Not a shot was fired all night.

[The Germans] are distinctly bored with the war... In fact, one of them wanted to know what on earth we were doing here fighting them... The beggars simply disregard all our warnings to get down from off their parapet, so things are at a deadlock. We can't shoot them in cold blood... I cannot see how we can get them to return to business.

Left to their own devices, even with enemy guns in their faces and the threat of court martial hanging over their heads, people generally choose to cooperate. That is the meaning of Tit for Tat.

Tony Ashworth, a British sociologist, gathered the recollections of the men who fought in the trenches. A soldier explained:

The real reason for the quietness of some sections of the line was that neither side had any intention of advancing in that particular district... If the British shelled the Germans, the Germans replied, and the damage was equal [tit for tat]... If the Germans bombed an advanced piece of trench and killed five Englishmen, an answering fusillade killed five Germans.

One of the key features of the iterated Prisoner's Dilemma game was that it was "iterated." It went on... indefinitely. This forced players to look ahead as well as behind. They could see what their fellow player did in the past. They had to guess what he would do in the future. In this manner, the future cast a shadow upon the present. If players expected continued cooperation, they cooperated. If they expected an end to cooperation – either by defection or an end to the game – they saw no benefit to further cooperation.

Likewise, a mobile war – instead of the standstill of trench warfare – offers few opportunities for cooperation. It is kill or be killed, by an opponent who faces the same challenge and the same calculation. After all, war – or any sort of aggression, for that matter – is a zero-sum game. You only win by making the other guy lose. Like chess. Or Russian roulette. Or playing cards. Or hunting.

Zero-sum games offer no upside for cooperation. You will kill the deer, or you will go hungry. There is no middle ground that allows both parties to come out ahead. You get the girl, or someone else gets her… no cooperation possible (unless, of course, you all get together sequentially or in a *ménage à trois*).

But the trenches were different. Facing an enemy who was in the same situation as he was, the typical soldier preferred to come to a mutually beneficial agreement. Live and let live. If he tried to kill his opposite number, he might succeed. Then, one would be dead. Win-lose. Or he might fail, and his enemy might kill him. Lose-win. There were also occasional instances of soldiers firing simultaneously. Lose-lose. Only by desisting from killing could both come out ahead – win-win.

No formal declaration or treaty was necessary. Nothing was ever written down or signed. No government intervened to declare or approve. The cooperation was spontaneous. A soldier recalled:

> *In one section, the hour of 8 to 9 am was regarded as consecrated to "private business," and certain places indicated by a flag were regarded as out of bounds by the snipers on both sides.*

New recruits coming into the English trenches were told by the old timers: "Mr. Boche [a term for the Germans] ain't a bad fellow. You leave him alone. He'll leave you alone."

Soldiers on both sides realized that they would face soldiers on the other side for weeks, months, or years. They came to terms in a number of ways, signaling that they meant no harm.

Artillery units, for example, would shell the enemy regularly, as commanded by their superior officers. But they would do so in a regular manner – always aiming for the same place… and always at exactly the same time. The "enemy" took the demonstration in the spirit in which it was intended: we won't hurt you if you don't hurt us.

Likewise, soldiers would fire their rifles from time to time, just to show that they did not intend to hit anyone. They would, for example, take aim at a post... or a sign... leaving a pattern that proved that they were capable of bringing down an enemy soldier, but had no intention of doing so – unless provoked.

Over time, the strategies used by individual soldiers and small groups developed into a sort of trench etiquette. It was bad form to shoot during certain hours. Shooting to kill or shooting first was regarded as unfair or unsportsmanlike. If a British soldier were killed by a sniper, for example, British snipers would retaliate by killing two Germans. Quickly, the moral code of Moses evolved: it was "wrong" to kill at all.

This ethical development is signaled in the following recollection by a British officer. By this time, the two sides had come to see right and wrong through their own battlefield lens, and were eager to protect the trust that had built up:

> *I was having tea with A Company when we heard a lot of shouting and went out to investigate. We found our men and the Germans standing on their respective parapets. Suddenly a salvo arrived but did no damage. Naturally both sides got down and our men started swearing at the Germans, when all at once a brave German got on his parapet and shouted out "We are very sorry about that; we hope no one was hurt. It is not our fault. It is that damned Prussian artillery."*

The high command aimed to put a stop to this "fraternization." They did so by shifting units around (so they couldn't cooperate; they had no expectation of seeing each other again) and by setting out raiding parties... That is, they turned the war into a mobile war again.

Did government encourage cooperation by punishing non-cooperation? Not at all. It punished cooperation and encouraged defection. Why would it do such a thing... encouraging people to kill one another? When it makes war, of course, it is not engaged in a cooperative activity. It is doing something which is the opposite of cooperation: it is using violence.

Such efforts must have been successful. It is estimated that 8.5 million solders had died by the time the fighting was finally done.

TAX PETER... PAY PAUL

While it is clear that a win-lose deal should have one winner and one loser, it is also clear that A's win will be less than B's loss. A net negative, in other words. Because transactions come with transaction costs. Friction. Wear and tear. Disincentives. Blowback. And negative feedback loops. That's why, in the real world, almost all win-lose deals are negative-sum. They are rarely zero-sum.

In the simplest example, the feds may tax Peter and give the money to Paul. But if they tax Peter $100, it is sure that Paul will get less than $100. There are costs involved. Tax forms. Tax lawyers. Tax collection. Tax enforcement. There are accountants... agents... investigators.

And those are just the obvious and direct costs. Less obvious and less direct are the costs incurred when Peter tries to dodge the tax, changes his behavior to avoid it, or simply ceases the activity which gave rise to it. If it is a tax on income, he may choose to earn less. If it is a tax on output, he may choose to work less. If it is a tax on consumption, he may consume less.

Slavery is a sort of tax. It is levied on output and collected by ruthless means. A person is put to work, and refused all choice, so that his whole production – less the cost of his maintenance – is available on the "win" side of the equation. On the "lose" side, obviously, the slave gives up his freedom and does what he is told.

All win-lose deals – into which one party enters against his will – are master-slave relationships. There is nothing "inhuman" about it. Just the contrary; it is fully human, with roots as deep and dark as our DNA. Still, that doesn't mean it is appropriate to our era.

The friction cost is apparent. Surveillance. Restriction. Policing. Punishing. Deluding. Even where whips and chains aren't needed to force compliance (say, in the U.S. tax system), there is still the need for a whole bureaucracy to explain and administer the system. Slavery costs time and money, reducing the net "win" from the deal.

In nineteenth-century America, as technology developed, it became harder and harder to maintain the level of ignorance and submission needed for slave labor. Then, as slavery disappeared in marginal areas, it became more expensive to keep slaves in the remaining slaveholding areas. Slaves ran away, increasing the cost of keeping the remaining slaves in servitude and lowering the capital value of slaves. In antebellum Maryland, for example, Frederick Douglas escaped slavery simply by leaving his farm and taking a train to Delaware. And by the time the war began, half of all slaves in the state had already escaped, bought themselves out of slavery, or had otherwise been freed. Many were freed simply because the output of a free worker had become cheaper than the output of a slave. Motivated by the promise of wages, responsible for his own maintenance, and able to increase his income by becoming more skilled, the free worker was more productive. He required no owner-supplied housing, food, and clothing. And no owner-provided slave driver or gun-toting goon to keep him in his place.

In other words, win-win triumphed naturally over win-lose. No "civil" war was necessary. The triumph was largely a consequence of the costs, both hidden and apparent, of win-lose deals. That is probably why slavery disappeared throughout the entire civilized world in the space of a few decades. Free labor was more efficient.

Try to imagine today's world run by slave labor. Imagine the marketing department of Lionsgate Films, the kitchen of the Four Seasons, or the sales department at Ralph Lauren staffed by slaves. Try to picture the engineers in Houston… the metallurgists in Duluth… or the admen in Manhattan – as slaves. The thought is almost ludicrous. All the fine judgments, skills, and incentives needed to run a modern business would disappear. A hundred or more years of progress would vanish as you tried to force someone to come up with an algorithm or a cool design... or make a sale.

Modern, complex, sophisticated, and open commerce cannot function on primitive, forced labor. It is too competitive. Too highly skilled. And too subject to sabotage. It is one thing to force slave labor to put dynamite into bombs under the watchful eye of a Nazi supervisor. It is quite another to get slaves to fend off computer viruses... program a fighter jet's software... or even wire an aircraft carrier's alarm systems. Try to fight the next war with slave labor, and you are dead before you even begin.

The Soviets gave it a try anyway. With their Sharashka program, they imprisoned Russian scientists in Siberian gulags and forced them to work on everything from increasing crop yields to building rockets. We know how that ended. The Ruskies never made it to the moon. And the Soviet Union collapsed under the weight of its win-lose deals.

ANCIENT WIN-LOSE

Even in antiquity, win-lose deals took a fearful toll. They were often extremely negative-sum... compounding so deep into negative territory that there was soon nothing left. If there were only two people in the world, and one killed the other, the "winner" would then have gained half the world. The loss, however, would have been far greater. Likewise, every murder may be said to be a "win" for the killer (otherwise, he wouldn't have done it), but it subtracts one person from the world's population – perhaps the one who might have discovered a cure for cancer.

And always, there are transaction costs. Walls are built. Guards are hired. Weapons are constructed. Young men, who might otherwise be planting wheat or building houses, put on uniforms and learn to kill.

In primitive societies, where the margin of survival was already narrow, killing could be, shall we say, fatal. That is, both killer and killee could end up dead. The effects of such "on-going, ever-present stress," writes Lawrence H. Keeley in an ethnographic, ethnohistoric study of the Illinois region from 900 to 1400 A.D., included in his landmark book, *War Before Civilization*, were catastrophic.

The bone evidence showed an abundance of crushed skulls, arrow points embedded in human bones, decapitated bodies, and scalped heads. In one location, Norris Farms 36 in Illinois, a cemetery revealed a violent death rate of 16%. Clearly there were a lot of losers, whose scalps hung on the murderers' belts. But what effect did this widespread win-lose killing have on the winners?

As the level of violence increased, tribes had to spend more of their time and resources either protecting themselves or preparing and executing revenge attacks. The result was less "wealth" for everyone. In the Central Illinois River Valley, for example, tribes had to forgo hunting and gathering to make time to build defenses. The most impressive were those built at Cahokia. There, towards the end of the 12th century, the locals put up walls around a site of some 250 acres. This wall, 3 kilometers long, required at least 20,000 logs to complete. And it appears to have been built and rebuilt at least four times within the span of just two or three generations.

War was not good for the Cahokian economy. The labor used to cut, dress, and implant logs to make a 3 kilometer wall must have deprived the community of vital resources for more important activities – such as getting enough to eat. People ended up poorer, weaker (with less to eat), and more vulnerable to attack. That seemed to be just what happened at the Crow Creek site in South Dakota (mentioned in Chapter 1). The fortified village, of perhaps 1,000 people, was attacked in the 14th century. Thomas E. Emerson describes what happened:

> *This truly was a massacre rather than a battle; most villagers appear*
> *to have been clubbed to death while fleeing. There is not an embedded*

arrow point in any of the bodies. Men, women, and children were indiscriminately killed. Their noses, hands, and feet were sometimes cut off, teeth smashed, and head and limbs cut from the body. The victims, from babies to elders, were universally scalped and mutilated. The scale of the deaths suggests that most of the inhabitants were killed.

The conclusion – if it could be backed by enough data – would surprise no one. Even today, as societies spend more of their output on their military, they have less available for other things. They become weak and vulnerable. We pointed out in our last book, *Hormegeddon*, that even Germany's famous war economy of the 1930s was a fraud. If Hitler "made the trains run on time," which is doubtful, the trains carried soldiers and war materiel. Consumer goods – including food – grew scarce, resulting in such a serious decline in calorie intake that doctors worried that young German women would be unable to conceive. Far from a model centrally planned economy suitable to supply the master race, Germany's economy failed in its essential role – to get people what they wanted.

Indeed, Hitler's pact with Stalin was made partly out of desperation; Germany had no money with which to buy resources from the West. It relied on the Soviet Union to provide them. Then, when the war began, the predations on the civilian economy increased. France, Belgium, Holland, Poland, and large parts of the Soviet Union were looted to keep the "war machine" running. But the average German had gotten poorer each year the Reich survived and was on the edge of starvation by 1945.

IS DEFECTING WRONG?

In the first chapter, we saw from the book of Joshua that there was no general proscription against killing in the Old World. Nor was widespread killing limited to the Jews. Polybius described the Romans' way of conducting warfare at the time of the wars against Carthage:

…their orders were to exterminate every form of life they encountered, sparing none… This practice is adopted to inspire terror, and so when cities are taken by the Romans you may often see not only the corpses of human beings but dogs cut in half and the dismembered limbs of other animals…

Later, as we get onto the well-worn steps of more recent history, we find killing almost everywhere – even among the highest-ranking "Big Men" of the time. In the history of Rome, almost every emperor in the third century was assassinated. This was known as the "Crisis of the Third Century." After years of win-lose military campaigns, the empire had run short on funds. So, to ensure that the triumphs continued, the emperors did a very simple thing: they began devaluing the currency.

As we will see later, when the money goes, everything else goes too. And for nearly 100 years in Rome, violence and murder were the preferred means of political ascension:

- Geta (co-emperor): Assassinated on the orders of his brother Caracalla in 211

- Caracalla (emperor): Assassinated on the orders of Macrinus in 217

- Macrinus (co-emperor): Executed on the orders of Elagabalus in 218

- Diadumenianus (co-emperor): Executed on the orders of Elagabalus in 218

- Elagabalus (emperor): Assassinated by the Praetorian Guard in 222

- Alexander Severus (emperor): Assassinated by his own troops in 235

- Maximinus Thrax (emperor): Assassinated by the Praetorian Guard in 238

- Pupienus (co-emperor): Assassinated by the Praetorian Guard in 238

- Balbinus (co-emperor): Assassinated by the Praetorian Guard in 238

- Gordian III (emperor): Possibly assassinated in 244

- Trebonianus Gallus (co-emperor): Assassinated by his troops in 253

- Aemilian (emperor): Assassinated by his troops in 253

- Gallienus (emperor): Assassinated by his generals in 268

- Aurelian (emperor): Assassinated by the Praetorian Guard in 275

- Tacitus (emperor): Probably assassinated in 276

- Florian (emperor): Assassinated by his troops in 276

- Probus (emperor): Assassinated by his own troops in 282

- Carus (co-emperor): Probably assassinated by the Praetorian Prefect Aper in 283

- Numerian (co-emperor): Perhaps assassinated in 284

In the history of Florence and other Italian city states, we see similar runs of homicide. Almost constant feuding left a trail of bodies over many generations. The most famous example is likely the feud between the Medicis and the Pazzis. In 1478, at High Mass, Bernardo di Bandini Baroncelli and Francesco de' Pazzi attacked brothers Giuliano and Lorenzo de' Medici. One of the de' Medici brothers died. The other escaped.

And the Hundred Years' War saw marauding bands of pseudo-armies, brigands, and mercenaries romping across Europe... killing, stealing, and raping. You will notice that all of these murders (not to mention the especially bloody 20th century) occurred after the rule against murder had been announced and widely accepted as a moral law.

"Thou Shalt Not Kill" was prominent on the list when Moses handed down the Ten Commandments. That interdiction didn't stop murder. Killing continued. Civilization is not immediate. Or automatic. Or guaranteed. Cooperation comes gradually. Little by little, the game changes. And the residual killers go on the government payroll.

FORCE IS NOT PERSUASION

Whether by direct force, the threat of violence, bullying, or fraud, when the feds enter the game, it ceases to be cooperative. It becomes a game of another sort... a game dominated by force rather than persuasion and cooperation. Generally, the more government you have, the more force you have in use... and the less cooperation is possible.

The best example of this is the familiar one – the Soviet Union, which came to a sad end in 1991. After the Russian Revolution of 1917, the insiders who took control of the machinery of violence – the army, police, bureaucracy, etc. – were especially ambitious. They replaced the normal, cooperative, "bourgeois" arrangements with state-dictated orders. Who should work for whom... How much they would be paid... What hours they would work and under what conditions... What money they would have available to them... What resources they could draw upon... What prices would be charged... What products would be on the shelves... Who could get an automobile, a radio, or a train ticket. Win-win deals – big and small – were abolished; apparatchiks, nomenklatura, and party members were the new deciders. And if the common man refused to go along, he faced a disagreeable stay in the gulag.

This was defection on a massive scale. The government itself was not going along with the Tit for Tat program. Doing away with the cooperation that normally takes place in a group, the Soviets also did away with civil society entirely. Everything – or almost everything – was determined in a win-lose deal. From employment to everyday shopping, every transaction was carried out on unequal terms: the consumer/citizen/employee was treated like an army recruit. Journalist Debra Kocher reports:

> *Buying anything in the store was always an adventure. First was the line to tell the salesgirl what you wanted to buy. She would sneer out at you, in her uniform and kerchief on her head, then grudgingly give you a chit of paper. You took that for payment in a new line.*
>
> *At the head of that line, you would get the once over as the shop girl pondered why an obvious foreigner was buying Russian goods at a government store if they didn't have to. Then it was back into the original line with receipt in hand, to pick up your stuff, more often than not wrapped in old newspaper. All this while being jostled by angry, hefty, frazzled Russian women in a hurry.*

It didn't matter how inconvenient, disappointing, or humiliating the shopping experience was; the consumer had no choice. He could not take his custom elsewhere. He could not "vote with his roubles." He could not express his preferences or instruct the economy with his decisions. The whole system had gone deaf, dumb, and blind.

Naturally, a huge black market developed, much of it furnished with goods "taken from work," that is, stolen. Often, this black market was the only part of the economy with its eyes open; the only place to get quality goods... or goods of any kind.

Even in the gulag, people found ways to cooperate. Prisoners traded information, clothes, and food between themselves and with the guards. Codes of behavior developed, just as they had in the trenches. But they did so under the constant threat of violent defection. *Gulag Voices*, edited by Pulitzer Prize-winning journalist Anne Applebaum, includes an account by Kazimierz Zarod, a young Polish civil servant and army reservist who, with many others, fled east from Poland's capital Warsaw when the Nazis attacked on September 1, 1939. But when the Soviets invaded Poland on September 17, he was arrested.

After interrogation, he was sent to a Siberian forestry camp, which he knew only as Labour Corrective Camp No. 21:

> *If a prisoner stole clothes or tobacco and was discovered, he could expect a good beating from his fellow inmates. But the unwritten law of this camp was that anyone caught stealing another man's bread earned a death sentence. An "accident" was not difficult to arrange in the forest.*

The Soviet system was based on defection, not cooperation. Defection strategies lowered scores for individual players. And for the whole group. Defection set off more defections. It was rude, unproductive, and wasteful, with falling real aggregate income for everyone. Just as game theory would predict.

There is nothing particularly new about this. It's just a new way of looking at it. Game theory put the invisible hand right out in broad daylight… suggesting that looking out for Number 1 really does benefit the other guy, too. Tit for Tat seemed to prove that win-win won. It also showed that Jesus was not just a religious figure, but an economic genius. It showed that being "nice" was not a strategy for weak losers, but a winning strategy for everyone. And the Soviets' 70-year experiment with win-lose social and economic planning seemed to confirm it: win-lose was for losers.

Tit for Tat seemed to show, too, that Darwinian evolution applied not just to the physical plant and animal kingdoms, but to humans, too. And not just to their bodies and mental hardware, but to their software… their morals and myths… and their spontaneous organization as well. One strategy was tried. It survived, or it didn't. Gradually, the unsuccessful mutants were eliminated. Left were the strategies that worked, which established not just individual decision rules but also the "customs," "habits," and social rules that came to dominate the "society." As the winning rules crowded out the losing ones, players came to expect that other players would follow the same strategies they did. They expected other players to be "nice" – first, because it worked, and later, because it was expected of them. They expected other players to cooperate – first, because the cooperative strategies beat the uncooperative ones, and later, because cooperation became the only socially acceptable approach.

In the real world, however, things never stay the same for very long. And success inevitably leads to failure. The success of potato farming in Ireland, for example, contributed to the largest famine in the country's history. The success of the Roman Empire led to its decline and fall – the biggest setback for civilization and progress of all time. The success of stock market trading and the economic boom in the 1920s – led by skyscrapers, electric motors, automobiles, and assembly lines – was followed by the crash of 1929 and the Great Depression.

So, it shouldn't be a surprise that the trust created by a winning cooperative strategy leads to something else. Naturally, it gives way to distrust. You can see how this might happen. When liquor stores become so trusting that they leave their doors unlocked at night, sooner or later, some dipsomaniac is bound to help himself. And when investors lose their natural skepticism, they become easier to fleece. As trust increases, the payoff for defecting also increases. Trust builds wealth. Then, it becomes easier and more profitable for the Steppe Barbarians to take it away. As the return on cheating rises, you have to expect the number of cheaters to increase, too.

An illustration frequently used is that of vaccinations. When the chance of contracting, say, tuberculosis, is high, the vaccination may involve some risk, but the payoff from cooperating, and getting a vaccination against the disease along with everyone else, is also high. But after everyone is vaccinated, and the odds of getting the disease are low, there is a strong temptation to defect. Let others run the risk of inoculation.

In a small society, trust can be maintained by laws, myths,

proximity, and social pressures. In such a society, people know what is true and what is false, and who can be trusted and who can't. They have well-developed BS detectors, and the facts are near and obvious. A few common myths and rules can hold the group together, reinforce trust, and avoid costly errors.

But as the group grows larger, new myths evolve. "Cultural innovations – new memes – can be introduced purposely," writes Robert Wright. And new gaps open between what is... and what might be. Instead of reflecting the distilled, hard-won lessons from generations past, there is more room for fantasy, hocus-pocus, and the self-interests of the most powerful groups. And the information needed to separate a useful myth from a predatory myth is so degraded by time and space, the public can't tell the difference.

Tit for Tat still works in the private space. And, in most of the world, it still governs most of our transactions. If we want a smile, we give a smile. We shake hands. We go along and get along. But the public space is different. There is tit, but no tat. Instead, transactions come under the spell of win-lose deals operated for the benefit of the elite.

This is not always a bad thing. But the elite has power. And power is always an invitation to corruption and parasitism. Then, the system becomes extractive rather than productive. And civilization walks backward.

CHAPTER 5

Win-Win... Or Lose

The message of Genesis is that in the most vital areas of human life there can be no progress, only an unending struggle with our own nature.
– Philosopher John Gray

WE ARE GOING TO BACK UP to the very beginning, *ab ovo*, just to make sure we're all in the same coop. There are only two ways to get what you want: win-win deals or win-lose deals. There is no other way. You either cooperate or you defect. You either give to get... or try to get without giving anything in return. It's either reciprocal or it's not. It's either voluntary or it's forced.

Of course, there are gray areas. The two parties to a transaction can have very different opinions about what actually went down. Juries are often asked to decide when a woman has succumbed to seduction... or when she has been raped. Likewise, sometimes salesmen are so persuasive that customers later feel like they've been robbed. Over hundreds of years, people learned how best to manage these frontier areas. They developed the "common law" as a way of settling disputes and establishing a legal principle to help judges and juries make their decisions. *Stare decisis* means "to follow precedent." It is a conservative legal principle, allowing each new generation to build on the decisions of the past.

But while it is "conservative," it is not trying to stop progress. Instead, common law is cumulative. One decision helps bring forth another one. Judges and juries don't have to figure it out from scratch. They just have to plug the facts into similar fact patterns. Then, they are expected to follow the precedent decision while continually taking old principles and applying them to new situations, helping people figure out – even in entirely new circumstances – what is acceptable behavior... and what is not.

The frontier between the two is never fixed or permanently settled. One set of facts falls in the "good salesmanship" category. Another is considered "fraud." One man is shamed as an "aggressive cad." Another is convicted of "rape." Following precedent removes some of the uncertainty, clarifies the acceptable limits of win-win deals, and maps out the borderlands between civilization and barbarism. Like market prices, right and wrong are discovered, not decreed, in real time... as the future happens.

Jesus simplified. He described how to do cooperative deals – in business, in personal matters, and in all other aspects of life:

Do unto others as you would have them do unto you.

Why does the rule work so well? Why is it so important? Win-win deals are voluntary. They do not need to be enforced or policed. Theft, by contrast, is a win-lose proposition. Even if it weren't illegal, the civilized vernacular has turned against theft (more on that shortly). Proscribed by the *polizei* and spurned by his fellow man, the thief must operate in the dark. He must hide his ill-gotten gains; he must protect them, too, from other thieves, who operate on the same uncivilized code as his own. All of these things increase his costs (including lifestyle, psychological, and status costs).

A win-win transaction can be as simple as exchanging currency for a boat; it can be done in a few minutes. No muss, no fuss. The buyer can immediately enjoy his new yacht. But the thief gets no rest. He has to overcome police, alarms, locks, and other barriers... And not just at the moment of stealing the boat – further downstream (so to speak), he has to avoid detection, reclamation, and punishment. He will find it hard to enjoy his tub at all!

In a modern economy, crime doesn't pay very well – again, unless it is approved by the feds. Wealth is relatively easier to create than to steal. The risk-return ratio in banking, fishing, baking, or almost any other profession, is probably better than it is for larceny.

THE IMPORTANCE OF THE VERNACULAR

An important term to understand in this chapter is "vernacular." As defined by the dictionary, it means a dialect or language native to a culture or region. Why do Northerners wonder "how everybody is keeping," for example, but Southerners inquire "how y'all are doing"? Vernacular.

If you hear someone speaking a foreign language, you can go to the grammar books and dictionaries to try to find out what he is saying. There, you'll find out not what he is actually saying, but what he's supposed to be saying. In English, for example, a proper response to the statement, "I'm looking for Mr. Jones," could be: "I am the person of whom you speak."

But people don't say that. They say: "That's me." That response is welcome if you are serving a summons. But it causes grammarians to squirm.

The vernacular evolves... often in response to the formal rules. Many people today are afraid of the word "me." They recall vaguely that the grammarians disapprove of it. So, they go with "myself," even though it doesn't make much sense.

"Who was playing the guitar?" "Joe and myself."

They are also afraid of being politically incorrect. So, instead of saying, "Everyone thinks he should speak correctly," they say, "Everyone thinks they should speak correctly," which is both incorrect and idiotic. Still, it seems to have become the new, officially approved grammar.

Winston Churchill once mocked people who tried to speak "correctly," saying: "This is the sort of bloody nonsense up with which I will not put."

But let's not get sidetracked... We're stalking bigger game here. There are formal structures – ordained by law, legislation, and official proclamation. And there are other things that better describe how we really speak, do business, and get along with each other. This we know as the vernacular.

There is a difference between what is and what is supposed to be in other things, too. Over thousands of years, vernacular, architecture, manners, rules, transportation, law... and even money... have evolved into what we know as civilized life. It is a life in which people can go along and get along, because civilization imposes standards that make the actions of others predictable. Usually, strangers won't kill you. They won't rob you. They won't rape you. Instead, normally, they will say "please" and "thank you," and will get along tolerably well.

No government declared gold to be money, for example. Instead, it arose naturally as people found it useful. Later, governments declared other things to be "money." These monies work more or less well than gold, but in a crisis, people tend to go back to the vernacular.

No law requires people to say "please" and "thank you" either. But they generally do... And they generally find it makes casual exchanges more agreeable. Occasionally, as in the fervor of a revolution, these "bourgeois affectations" are dropped in favor of some ideologically correct claptrap. "Vive la Révolution!" was popular for a while. "Heil Hitler," had a run, too. Both were soon dropped in favor of the vernacular.

As far as we know, no government has tried to stop people from smiling. That, too, is a vernacular way of signaling that you have no harmful intentions towards others. However, in the Soviet Union, an example to which we will return often, the delicate fabric of civilized life was so rumpled and stretched during the 70 years from the Russian Revolution to the fall of the Berlin Wall in 1989 that, even today, people in Russia are reluctant to smile.

Likewise, there is the formal government... and there are the informal rules, customs, and standards that people use to govern themselves. Many of the colonies that gained independence after World War II, for example, took France, Britain, or the U.S. as their templates. Some created systems which, on paper, were almost exact copies of the U.S. or European dioramas. They had bicameral legislatures, independent judiciaries, checks and balances – the whole kit and caboodle. But the new democracies in Africa and Asia didn't always function like their Western role models.

A French joke illustrates the power of the vernacular: The mayor of an African town in one of France's former colonies came to pay a visit to the mayor of a French town of more or less the same size. He was astonished at the mayor's office. It was full of fine furniture, expensive paintings, and rich decorations.

"How can you afford these things on a mayor's salary?" he asked. The French mayor beckoned him over to the window. "See that bridge? 10%." It took a moment for the African mayor to get the message. But his eyes lit up when he did.

Years later, the French mayor visited the African town. In the mayor's office, he was shocked to find even more luxury than in his own – including Aubusson carpets, delicate Chinese vases, and Old Master paintings.

"Now, I have to ask you the same question you asked me," he began. "How can you afford all these things?"

The African mayor pointed out the window. "See that bridge?" he asked the French mayor. "Well... no... I don't see any bridge," replied the French mayor. "Right. 100%."

Now, in the U.S., the Constitution still sits in its glass case. The Supreme Court still sits on its bench. Members of Congress still sit in camera. And bureaucrats and nomenklatura still plop their fat *derrières* down in their seats of authority.

Officially, nothing has changed.

But in the vernacular, nothing is the same. Anyone with any brains knows his congressman is a scoundrel… Everyone knows his Constitution – except the Second Amendment! – is ancient history. Everyone knows his vote is mostly symbolic. And everyone knows that as long as the Dow is going up and unemployment is going down – even just on paper – he doesn't give a damn.

How did this happen? The answer, we believe, is in the word vernacular.

The classic win-win deal is not the law of the land anywhere; it is the vernacular. It was never invented by anyone… No one got the Nobel Prize for coming up with it… And some of the smartest people on the planet don't believe in it. Still, most people generally follow the rule on an everyday basis. If they want a burger, they give some money to the burger store. If they want money, they offer their time to an employer. If Ford wants to sell its pickup trucks, it does its best to make people want them.

That is the commonly accepted way to get what you want and need in life. If you want a wife, you have to offer her something that makes it worth her while. If you want a loaf of bread, you have to give something of equal value to the baker. Whether it is love, respect, a fortune, or a bag of Frito-Lay corn chips you are after, the best way to get it is to make a win-win deal.

Note also that this vernacular – this set of rules, manners, customs, money, language, and myths that make modern civilization possible – is a collective achievement. An individual can't be "civilized" on his own. It is as meaningless as a phone system with only one phone. Civilization must be shared. It must be a system of interaction. When you smile, you must smile at someone. And it must be voluntary.

Only crooks, cads, and governments operate on the uncivilized model. They do unto others, and they hope to God others can't do likewise unto them. Attila was widely esteemed for robbing and murdering hundreds of thousands of strangers. He was probably one of the world's richest people at the time. He probably would have been named *TIME*'s "Person of the Year" for 450 A.D. had the magazine existed at the time.

But morals evolved with productivity. Today, the world's richest people generally make their money by producing wealth rather than stealing it. Presumably, Attila would be unwelcome in today's prosperous, polite society. At the very least, he would be exceptional. The vernacular has changed.

A LEARNING SYSTEM

Everything is made from the same atoms. We all have the same basic matter at hand; it all depends on how we put it together. A skyscraper is nothing more than various basic elements assembled in a certain way. Poor tribesmen in the Amazon don't know how to do it; rich people in New York, Tokyo, or Paris do.

The difference is knowledge. It tells us how to build a nuclear power plant... or make ice cream. Information and knowledge are also critical to an entire economy. How many ice cream parlors do we need? How much steel should we produce? How do you make a hit TV show?

But there are two forms of learning: technical and social. They are both essential to civilization and our advanced living standards. And they are very different.

When we think of "progress" or "wealth," however, we think of stuff – cars, monorails, iPhones, and air conditioning. It's hard to imagine any other kind of progress. But there is social progress, too – innovations in the way people get along with one another, do business, and cooperate. These, too, build up as a form of social capital.

Some of the most basic forms of human social innovations predate the evolution of our species. Things such as smiling at one another to signal peaceful intentions, or the division of labor between the sexes. Then, there are things such as getting to work on time... saving money... "early to bed, early to rise"... property ownership... and simply working hard (an innovation that developed after the agricultural revolution).

Psychology professor William von Hippel names the habit of forming a line as one of the most important social innovations because it makes it possible to process transactions (and information) in an orderly, predictable way. These social innovations are what make technical innovations possible. There would be no use in discovering the formula for open-hearth steelmaking if you couldn't accumulate capital, hire able, willing workers, protect your property, and so forth, all of which require a common understanding of how to act.

Elsewhere in this book, we characterize innovations as a kind of software. Just look at the way dogs and cats act to see it at work. Cats curl around your ankles, expressing what appears to be affection. Or they catch mice... and lay them at your doorstep. Dogs, too, try to make themselves loveable and useful. They wag their tails. They lick your hand. They fetch the birds and rabbits you shoot. They help round up your cattle and herd your sheep.

Why do they do these things? Our guess is that those that didn't were the ones eaten first and whose software was not carried to the next generation.

Perhaps the best way to understand the difference between this kind of software and the more recent, less instinctual social innovations can be found by simply looking more closely at computer software. There is major software – such as the disk operating system – and there are minor apps, such as software that allows you to do mathematical computations on your cellphone.

One of the most important social innovations by humans was an operating system that allowed us to live and work together in communities. On the African savannahs, man's ancestors had to learn to cooperate, to hunt and fight together, or they would have been dead meat.

A much later app extended the principle of reciprocity beyond the tribe to the whole human race. This app is the key to civilization and both social and material progress because it allows us to learn from people we've never met – through writing, money, and markets. This app – do unto others as you would have them do unto you – permits the exchange of information, as well as stuff, without being afraid of getting ripped off or murdered.

Progress requires learning and accumulated information. Can you make a profit selling ice cream cones to Eskimos? What is the real price of capital? What will happen if I ask the girl on a date?

Life gives you the answers. But it must be allowed to speak the truth. Bring out a pistol and the room goes silent. Win-lose deals – made at the barrel of a gun – tell you little. Societies, or more modestly, groups of people, learn from their experiences and follow up, applying the lessons to do better in the future. But that involves a process that the economist Joseph Schumpeter described as "creative destruction."

Win-win deals create. But they also destroy, regularly ditching mistakes. Otherwise, bad chefs stay in business... bad drivers stay on the road... and bad money stays in circulation.

Of course, no one wants to admit failure or see his business go belly up. He will ask the authorities for a handout, a subsidy, or a protective tariff to help him stay in the game. But then, learning... innovation... and experimentation slow down. Old businesses are kept alive; geriatric governments are propped up by propaganda and armed guards; new choices are squeezed out by gun-backed monopolies.

When a company goes bankrupt, it should be taken out and given a proper burial. This would liberate time, money, and resources for other projects. Keeping it on life support, on the other hand, by providing below-market financing... and rewarding its managers with million-dollar bonuses... sends the wrong signal. Imposing a winner, too, distorts the picture and stops the learning process. It is like the "intelligence" tortured out of a prisoner; rely on it at your peril.

As we will see more clearly later, "reality" consists of conventions, ideas, protocols, fabrications, myths, and lies – things that aren't real at all. Prominent among them are the taboos and codes – the software – that have arisen over thousands of years. They developed freely, without anyone's say-so. But the authorities find they are easy to manipulate, too. Recognizing that this reality is not a physical, objective thing, but merely the furnishings of a civilized mind, elites are always tempted to redecorate… and always with appalling consequences. Thus does reality bend in their direction… until it snaps back suddenly.

Humans want silks, frescoes, lamb with mint sauce, and slaves to do their bidding. They want these things because they give them status, theoretically improving their mating opportunities. But how could anyone know what these things are worth or to whom they should belong? The idea of status is to impress others. Should they buy a polyester leisure suit or a house in the Bronx? How could they keep track of the currents of fashion and technology?

Win-win deals – made possible by the "do unto others" app – were the only way, letting markets tell their tales. Voluntary buying and selling discovered prices. Not only did these prices inform the whole system, as noted above, they also directed output towards the things people actually wanted. People got more of what they wanted because they bid for them on the open market. Knowledge comes from conducting trial and error experiments – millions of win-win deals… social, commercial, and technical… over many centuries. The results, gathered over centuries of win-win deals, congeal into a vernacular culture of relationships, language, technical know-how, architecture, rules, manners, customs, old wives' tales, and moral lessons.

People don't have to know how an internal combustion engine works; they can just turn the key. And they don't need to figure out why they don't kill each other or why they get up early, comb their hair, and get to work. They just do. And doing so, apparently, gives the group an advantage over those who don't.

World-improvers, do-gooders, and pathological maniacs may have their own ideas. But the only way to increase human satisfaction is to back off and let people seek it, in their own way. Freely, in win-win deals. That is the elegant justice meted out by the "invisible hand." Everyone does his best to get what he wants. But to get what he wants, he has to give his counterparty what *he* wants. The result is more satisfaction for all. And civilization. As people compete with one another for status, they find new and better ways to express it. Art, manners, dress, output – all are trappings of the civilizing process. More important, as they try to satisfy each other's needs and wants, they develop keen sensitivities to others. Pretty soon, they've forgotten they ever wanted to kill them.

In an earlier book, *Hormegeddon*, we explained civilization, at least to our own satisfaction:

> *I propose a simple way to conceive of civilization. Readers will recognize that it is not necessarily what any particular civilization is at any particular moment, but rather what it ought to be all the time.*
>
> *Forget the ancient Greeks... Forget Aristotle... Forget also the religious interpretations... And put aside prejudices based on culture, race, aesthetics, technology, politics, or other bugaboos.*
>
> *Instead let us simply divide the human experience into two big periods. The first was "mean, brutish, and short," to use the pithy phrasing of Thomas Hobbes. The second, in which we are living today, is basically a civilized world with frequent relapses into barbarity. What's the difference? Just one, and only one, thing makes sense of it: the role of violence.*

Now, we go back and embellish. Our landmark insight was largely ignored by the world's thinkers, who probably felt insulted by it. The idea is that the decline of violence was an evolutionary adaptation, not the product of the thinkers' thoughts, planning, or good intentions.

Several of these thinkers even dare to add a whole new phase of human social development to our two.

They believe we can think our way to a higher form of civilization by consciously and deliberately insisting on new and better social norms. The language can be transformed, for example, to eliminate "masculine takes precedence" pronouns. So, too, can separating your trash become a moral rule. But as we will see more clearly, we regard this third and more flattering phase as a dangerous conceit.

Typically, trust expands during a period of peace, often with the help of a government, which provides a uniform and reliable system of weights, measures, and rules, and a way to resolve disputes without bloodshed. The Romans were a win-lose, hard-fighting group. But once conquered, people were free to do win-win deals under the protection of the empire. During the Roman Era, there was a great expansion of trade, technology, and wealth. Evidence can be found as far from Rome as Gloucestershire in Britain, where a third-century villa shows all the trappings of civilized life of the time, including running water, central heating, and floor mosaics, as well as wine and olives from the Mediterranean, silver from the mines of Spain, and carpets from the East.

This was only made possible by the Roman's vast road networks and the trade routes that traveled it. Government protection of property rights removed some uncertainty. Government also helped make sure contracts were enforced and violence was limited. If anyone were to be robbed or killed, it would be the feds who did it!

Another great expansion took place under the British Empire in the late 19th century. Economist John Maynard Keynes wrote about what a remarkable thing it was:

> *The inhabitant of London could order by telephone, sipping his morning tea in bed, the various products of the whole Earth, in such quantity as he might see fit, and reasonably expect their early*

delivery upon his doorstep; he could at the same moment and by the same means adventure his wealth in the natural resources and new enterprises of any quarter of the world, and share, without exertion or even trouble, in their prospective fruits and advantages.

A third great period of "globalization" occurred under the watchful eye of the post-Cold War Pax Americana. From the fall of the Berlin Wall in 1989 to 2007, trade boomed. The world had never seen such an increase in wealth. Author Matt Ridley explains:

In [the last 50 years] we have gone from 75 per cent of the world living in extreme poverty, to just 9 per cent. We have increased human productivity by some 3,000 per cent.

Nobody seems to know this. The late Hans Rosling conducted a poll in which he asked people if the proportion of the world living in extreme poverty had doubled, halved or stayed the same in the past 20 years. Just 5 per cent of people thought it had halved, which was the right answer.

Why does globalization work so well? For the same reason the Soviet Union worked so badly. Win-win deals expand prosperity. Win-lose deals reduce it. Adam Smith announced the principle of "absolute advantage," referring to trade between nations:

If a foreign country can supply us with a commodity cheaper than we ourselves can make it, better buy it of them with some part of the produce of our own industry, employed in a way in which we have some advantage. The general industry of the country, being always in proportion to the capital which employs it, will not thereby be diminished... but only left to find out the way in which it can be employed with the greatest advantage.

More trade means more transactions, more competition, more choices, more learning, and more specialization. That's how an economy moves ahead. It's also part of the explanation for why some groups are rich and others are poor. A rich economy is open to trade. A poor economy is closed off – either by physical barriers, culture, or politics. As the trade zone shrinks, so does its wealth. Generally, the smaller the isolated group, the less it is able to specialize and the less rich it is. We see it up at our ranch in the mountains of Argentina. All the locals know the same things – how to plant corn, how to cure hides, how to protect the sheep from the puma, and how to build a mud roof.

In a rich society, people know very different things. One knows how to program a computer. Another knows how to fix the toilet. Still another knows how to bake bread. In the modern economy, the rich guy is rarely a jack-of-all-trades; he's the one who figures out one *métier* better than others. Then this dispersed, specialized knowledge is brought together through trade and markets.

Early-nineteenth-century English economist David Ricardo explained the principle of "comparative advantage" further, still addressing the issue of international trade. He asks us to imagine that England is more efficient at producing cloth and that Portugal is more efficient at producing wine. Portugal could spend its time stitching cloth and England could try its hand at growing vines. But this is not the most efficient use of resources. By each country focusing on producing what it is most efficient at producing, and trading with countries for goods it is not efficient at producing itself, the whole world grows richer.

There is no qualitative difference between trade across borders and trade across the street. As long as you are free to trade with whomever you want, on whatever terms you want, you will always try to expand your trading circle to get the best deal you can.

And the win-win trade is not a zero-sum deal. It is a positive-sum deal. Political economist Robert Torrens showed how to compute the gain:

[I]f I wish to know the extent of the advantage, which arises to England, from her giving France a hundred pounds of broad cloth, in exchange for a hundred pounds of lace, I take the quantity of lace which she has acquired by this transaction, and compare it with the quantity which she might, at the same expense of labour and capital, have acquired by manufacturing it at home. The lace that remains, beyond what the labour and capital employed on the cloth, might have fabricated at home, is the amount of the advantage which England derives from the exchange.

A win-lose exchange would have had England getting lace worth (to her) less than the broad cloth she had given up. An even exchange would have meant that each side got exactly the same value in return for what it had offered. But the win-win transaction goes beyond an even exchange.

France is better at making lace (she can make more lace of higher quality while using fewer resources). England is better at making broad cloth. By trading, both come out ahead. Though on the surface, the exchange is registered as "fair" and "even," England ends up with more than she had before. So does France. Win-win makes the world a richer place.

The same thing happens when you trade with the people in your village. The pigherd, Albert, raises hogs more efficiently than you do. The butcher, Louis, is better at cutting them up. And Jack down the street has a refrigerated truck to deliver the meat. Specializing, and trading output, leaves everyone happier. And richer. Civilization – including property rights, money, and "morality" (no killing, stealing, or lying) – makes it possible.

Mutual trust, a common language, a common coin of the realm, and the common law that allows you to go about your business in relative safety – these things... these restrictions and the win-win deals they permit, including markets and manners... are how the common good is discovered and developed.

There is, alas, nothing that guarantees eternal progress, prosperity, or civilization. Win-win deals proliferate, and then – here come the parasites!

NO SATISFACTION

And here, we give the devil his due. We have seen why win-win deals are so important to civilization. They allow for material and social progress. They make it possible for people to learn and to share. They permit people to divide tasks among themselves, thus specializing and becoming more productive. Then, they aggregate the increased output and information through consensual markets. They permit people to get along and go along, peacefully. Why, then, are win-lose deals still so popular?

To answer the question, let us begin by backtracking, perhaps a million years. There, perhaps on the banks of the Jordan River, pre-man, a form of *Homo erectus*, was throwing a party. When a new couple arrived, the males at the party eyed the new fellow… They may have looked for a smile… or perhaps the relaxed posture of someone who posed no threat.

Then, they turned to the female and looked her up and down, too, with longer, more careful leers. She was the one that really interested them. The other females scarcely bothered with the male at all. They looked at the female too, gauging the competition.

The same phenomenon was evident at our office party before Christmas. Men looked mostly at women. Women looked mostly at women, too. And women, in their colorful fabrics, sparkling jewelry, and painted nails, seemed to want to be looked at.

What to make of it?

Man is a social animal. With no one to stand beside us, we might as well not stand at all. Only in groups are people able to get their bearings. They compare everything – their looks, health, clothes, houses, autos, manners, education… you name it. That is how they know who they are, where they fit in, and what they want.

Pre-man faced stronger, faster predators. He could only survive by developing his social skills, which is probably what turned him into man. He needed others to watch his back. And he learned that the best way to get others to look out for him was to look out for them. Together, they could use sticks and stones to keep the lions and jackals at bay. Man learned, too, to share... and to participate. Just as it took a group to protect each other, so did it take a group to bring down the big game... or even the little game. And so did it take a group effort to protect the tribe from other tribes eager to take away its women or drive it away from its hunting ground.

Working together to hunt, to defend themselves, and to divide up the work so they could be more productive – mankind flourished... and eventually dominated the whole planet.

EAT AND PRODUCE

All of us alive today are the descendants of people who figured that out... and also wanted to mate and reproduce. That desire is, in addition to survival itself, the *sine qua non* of existence. If you don't want to eat or procreate, your genes will not be passed along. Obviously, we are the products of those whose appetites were satisfied... at least for a while. That is why most of us have appetites, too. We inherited them.

Both procreation and eating involve competition. The world's natural food resources are not infinite. In any given area, there are only so many ripe fruits and slow animals. In the millions of years in which human evolution made us what we are today, there must have been many proto-humans who were too slow, too dumb, or too unlucky to get enough to eat.

Whole tribes – perhaps whole subsets of primates – disappeared, as did our other human competitors. *Homo neanderthalensis*, for example, survived for hundreds of thousands of years. Then, *Homo sapiens* (we) arrived on the scene. Within a few thousand years, Neanderthals were history, leaving only a trace of their DNA – in us. They may have starved to death. They may have been killed. Either way, competition took its toll.

There is also competition to mate. Women can only have a few children each. At the margin, the women whose children survived were probably those who were most selective about their mates. They chose (when they could) men who were strong, fast, smart, and successful. This increased the odds that their children would get those traits too.

Even today, at parties, men and women still look at each other. Unconsciously perhaps, or instinctively, they have one eye out for suitable mates... and the other on the competition. Who's strongest? Who's fastest? Who's smartest? Who's most attractive? That's why we put on nice clothes and makeup, even if we have no current intention of mating; "flaunting it" is embedded in our genes as an instinct.

Since the agricultural revolution some 5,000 years ago, survival has been man's number one concern, but only occasionally. Famines came from time to time. Mating, meanwhile... finding, attracting, forcing, or seducing... was always on his mind. He wanted to make himself better so he would have more mating opportunities. But it was a relative "better" he wanted, not an absolute "better."

He only had to be stronger, richer, smarter, and more able than his rivals. And there were two ways to do it. He could improve himself – working harder to make himself more attractive. Or he could try to take the competition down a peg. So, in addition to becoming a cooperative, win-win dealmaker, he also became fiercely jealous, competitive, deceitful, power-mad, ruthless, murderous, and vengeful.

In the purest, simplest, crudest form of competition, he could simply kill his rival. *Voilà* – he was then the best available mate. He got the girl. And we got his genes, his instincts, his strengths... and his weaknesses.

As we've seen, taking your competitors down a peg was practically the only way to win before the Neolithic Age. And even today, it is often an attractive alternative. It can be quicker and much more effective than improving yourself. And as we will see, it is the only way to harness the power of government to your cause. Government cannot make people richer. But it can easily make them poorer. So, if you and your crony friends can get control of a government and use it to impoverish most of the population (even if you do not gain a penny), you have won. Yes, all flesh is heir to that win-lose temptation as well as the inclination to win-win.

TRUST

Civilization and its win-win deals both require trust. And they help bring it about. You need to trust that your barber won't cut your throat and that your money will still be worth something tomorrow. Then, the more often you get shaved without having your throat cut, the more you trust that your barber won't slash your throat – ever.

Trust is probably deeply etched in our social programming. Out on the savannah, a pre-human had to trust that his companions wouldn't run away when they faced down a pack of hyenas. Survival required those in small groups to trust one another... to use all available eyes to watch out for trouble and all available hands to fight off danger. And even today, cowardice in the face of the enemy – being untrustworthy in battle – is the worst sin a soldier can commit.

Generally, "high-trust" societies are more prosperous than low-trust societies. Switzerland, for example, has a much higher per capita income than Haiti or the Congo. Trusting societies are richer because trust increases the efficiency of investment and economic activity of all sorts. If you trust that your investment firm won't rip you off, you can save on the amount of research and due diligence you might otherwise have to do. If you trust that your investments will always go up, there will be no need to hold unproductive cash as "insurance" or "hedge" positions. With less need for investigation and protection, you can simply take someone "at his word." You can do more win-win deals. Knowledge and wealth grow faster.

And if trust is widespread, so is credit generally available on easy terms. When creditors are assured of getting paid back, in money that has not lost its value, they offer better terms. One of the strange things that happened in the last few years was that creditors made money available to selected borrowers (large institutional borrowers and governments) at negative rates. In theory, borrowers were paid to take money off lenders' hands.

This was so bizarre (suggesting that lenders had more than 100% confidence that nothing would go wrong) that we will explore it further in a later chapter. Our point here is that the safer the currency, the market, and the firms in it appear, the richer the society... and the more tempting it is to defect. Typically, markets go in cycles, roughly corresponding to the ebb and flow of trust. As trust recedes, so do asset prices. Bond prices, for example, fall and yields rise as people lose faith in the future.

But remember, there are two ways of doing things, and two ways of getting what you want. And they're not permanently fixed. As a society does more win-win deals, it becomes richer and more trusting. Then, win-lose deals and defection become relatively more rewarding. There are fewer armed guards, fewer locks, and fewer skeptical widows. Generally, as people become more trusting, it is easier to rip them off.

So, too, "pacifist" nations become easy targets for warlike people. Steven Pinker explains:

> *If a nation decides not to learn war any more, but its neighbor continues to do so, its pruning hooks will be no match for the neighbor's spears, and it may find itself at the wrong end of an invading army.*

In a broader sense, trust and the progress of civilization itself are cyclical, too.

THE GREAT LEVELER

A billboard in the Baltimore area simplifies the message of a local firm specializing in tort cases. "Get More!" it says.

Chasing ambulances is a competitive business. It is not enough for a lawyer to promise a courtroom victory. After all, it's not the principle of the thing. It's the money. So, one billboard advertises "More Aggressive" lawyers. Another suggests that "You may be entitled to a big settlement." Still another, from Johnnie Cochran's outfit (Cochran is the attorney who helped O. J. Simpson beat the murder rap), says, "Turned down for disability? Let us help you get the money you deserve."

This "Get More" message is not aimed at the rich. Instead, it is aimed at the poor and middle classes, where the target market seems to know exactly what it means. It is an effective message, too; it appeals to basic desires: greed, envy, and sometimes, larceny. If you get in a traffic accident, slip on ice, or end up with a limp after hip surgery, you may have a chance to "get more" in a settlement. All you need is a mad-dog law firm fighting for you.

The ad, however, sounds a little crass, crude, or vulgar to most people. And in matters of public policy, they prefer to talk of "alleviating injustice" by "palliating inequality." The name "Piketty" is frequently invoked.

In 2013, Barack Obama described the "defining challenge" of our time. The problem, he said, was a "dangerous and growing inequality." He never explained why it was such a problem. In fact, we've never seen any real explanation. Some say it "causes instability." Some, including Mr. Obama, say it's "unfair." Others think it "inhibits growth." Most just don't like the idea that some people are getting more than they are.

Getting more than the other guy is the theme of a book by Walter Scheidel. In *The Great Leveler*, the Stanford professor worries about the inequality of income and wealth. He wonders – but not too hard – what causes it… and observes the awful circumstances in which the playing field is commonly leveled.

The phenomenon is well documented. The rich get richer. And richer. And richer. Why do the rich get so rich? Partly because they are smart, disciplined, and hard-working (the traditional Republican view). Partly because they are greedy capitalists, who use their money to gain more capital (they "make money when they sleep," as French President François Mitterrand put it). And largely because the government colludes to rig the system on their behalf (our focus here).

Most people have nothing against the "deserving rich." If they have done more win-win deals than others, they should enjoy more of the fruits. Nor does it bother us that people save their money rather than spend it, and that by putting it out to hire, they make more money for themselves. Nor does wealth "inequality" itself seem sinister or unjust. It doesn't stick in our craw that we are much richer than the typical Pakistani peasant or much poorer than Donald Trump and his crony friends. The evidence suggests, at least to us, that it is not really wealth inequality that makes people mad; it is the win-lose deals that cause it.

Clever, ambitious people always want to get ahead. When they exercise their ambitions honestly, few complain. Periods of stability give them a chance to multiply their wealth by doing more win-win deals. Each win-win deal advances, in some small or large measure, the "wealth" of society and the satisfaction of the people in it. These win-win deals create surpluses, from which we get savings – capital – which can be applied to even more wealth-building. In the aggregate, everyone is better off.

The trouble is, there is always a temptation to cheat… to defect… to gain wealth, power, and status in the fastest, surest way: by taking it from someone else. That is how the win-losers benefit from periods of stability, too, burrowing into the rotten wood of government and building their nests in its nooks and crannies.

Over time, the number of chiselers and malingerers increases; the number of people contributing to growth and prosperity goes down. Insiders gain more power. The swamp gets deeper. This is why, too, after a war, it is frequently the losers who end up the winners. In the winning camp, the insiders get more and more of a hold on old industries and corrupt, geriatric government. In the losing camp, the old government has been dismantled… cronies and zombies have been chased away or killed; people are free to build new wealth on the rubble.

After World War II, for example, which were the world's most dynamic economies? Germany and Japan. Within a single generation, the two bombed-out economies were back on top of the world, the second- and third-largest economies (after the U.S.) – until China took the lead in the 21st century.

The U.S. was king of the hill after World War II. Its industries were intact. Its ships ruled the seas. Its salesmen roamed the land, offering quality, American-made goods to a grateful world. But the Republic was already 170 years old. The beasts were already slouching towards the District of Columbia, bringing win-lose deals by the thousands. They were soon embedded in the 178,000 pages of the Code of Federal Regulations... and 75,000 pages of the U.S. "tax code." The Obamacare regulations alone are eight times longer than the Bible.

HISTORY OF INEQUALITY

Rolling down the tracks on Mr. Scheidel's train is slow, tedious, and predictable. But if you want to take a trip through the history of financial inequality, you might enjoy the ride. You will see, in suspiciously precise detail, how the Gini coefficients of Greek, Roman, and other ancient civilizations evolved over time. The illustrations continue, measuring income inequality and wealth disparities everywhere from ancient Assyria to the Tang Dynasty in China to Europe through the war years of the 20th century.

What the long trip reveals is what we expected. In fact, it is pretty much what Italian economist Vilfredo Pareto described a century ago. Whenever a society is stable, ambitious people figure out how to "Get More" by gaming the system, just like Baltimore's ambulance-chasers do today.

Wealth itself is created by win-win deals that require hard work, sacrifice, luck, innovation, time, and all the other things that are difficult to predict or control. But once created, wealth is exposed to predators

– like a sheep that has been fattened by a careful shepherd. Wealth cannot be created by win-lose deals, but it can be taken away by theft, confiscation, and redistribution. Like many of his contemporaries, Mr. Scheidel approves of these win-lose deals if they are done for a good reason, such as leveling out wealth. Inequality, he believes, is always a bad thing, no matter what the real source.

That's where the feds come in. It is too bad they don't get more attention from Scheidel on this trip. They pop up in nearly every scene. But he acts as if they had only supporting roles. Clearly, they should get top billing. In most work on the subject, the feds – with their earnest, conscious efforts to right the world's wrongs – are presumed to be the antidote to wealth inequality.

Benign and well meaning, they often intervene to "do something" to correct the imbalance. But, as the author notes, they almost never seem to solve the problem (at least, not without making the overall situation worse). Could it be that when it comes to wealth inequality, Ronald Reagan was right: Government is not the solution; it is the cause? Once you make a lot of money, you have the means to bribe your way into the heart of the political process. Then, you may use the feds' muscle to "Get More."

In a free economy, wealth moves around. So, if you are on top of the world today, knowing that tomorrow brings risks, your instinct will be to try to stop tomorrow from coming. That is, you will want to prevent not only the win-lose deals by which your wealth could be taken away, but the win-win deals, too. Markets… competition… upstart entrepreneurs… new technology – all threaten to diminish your wealth relative to that of others.

As we will see in a later chapter, government is always a deeply reactionary institution, used by the few to exploit the many, and always looking ahead to try to keep the future from happening. That is, it is always trying to turn a positive-sum, win-win economy into a negative-sum, win-lose economy. When the rich are in cahoots with the government, controlling a stable, perhaps stagnant, economy, the share of wealth in the hands of the elite increases, as you would expect, and as confirmed by Mr. Scheidel's figures. The obvious conclusion: The insiders use the government to take wealth (including wealth that has not yet been earned – government debt) from everybody else.

STABILITY LEADS TO INSTABILITY

Take a drive around the Washington, D.C. beltway; you'll see dozens of sparkling new buildings. More and more corporate headquarters are moving from the industrial heartland, where the work is done, to the nation's capital, where the favors are passed out. In 1980, Washington, D.C. enjoyed per capita income that was 29% above the national average. By 2012, it had risen to 75% above average.

In the win-win world of wealth creation, the feedback loops are fast and accurate. A customer says "no." A deal falls apart. A company goes broke. The incompetent chef has an empty restaurant. But the win-lose world distorts the information flow and retards progress. Customers are given no choice. Deals are imposed, not negotiated. Interest rates and prices are fixed, not discovered in open markets. Companies are granted monopolies. And the rich are protected from their own extravagance, laziness, and bad judgement by forced extractions from the general population. The win-losers, leeches, and schemers gain more and more. As the aforementioned French economist Thomas Piketty put it so succinctly (and incorrectly):

$$r > g$$

The returns from investment (r) outpace the general growth of the economy (g). The rich get richer, in other words.

FOUR HORSEMEN OF LEVELING

But you can't keep this jig up forever. Eventually, as American economist Hyman Minsky reminds us, stability leads to instability. You rescue the stock market... prices go higher... weak businesses are protected… bad investments go uncorrected… the rich get richer… the rest get restless… and the system becomes more vulnerable.

Then, something always happens that the insiders can't control. Scheidel lists four possibilities, which he refers to as the "four horsemen of leveling": warfare (with mass mobilization), revolution, government collapse, and lethal pandemics.

It doesn't take too much imagination to see why these things would have a leveling effect. They destroy the cozy relationship between the rich and the rulers. That is, they reduce the ability of government to rig the system with win-lose deals. In desperate circumstances, in which their own privileges are threatened, rulers will not shirk from despoiling the rich to protect themselves. And when governments fall – either in revolution, war, or extreme financial distress – the rich who depended on them are often wiped out financially… or killed.

Pandemics, too, shake things up for everyone. In the Great Plague, for example, in some places, half the labor pool died. Workers found themselves in a much better bargaining position. Also, much productive land was abandoned. It was relatively easy for the poor and middle classes to gain wealth.

Again, it's a shame the feds don't get the attention they deserve. They are at the center of the whole inequality story. They allow their rich cronies to get richer (through taxes, licensing, privileges, redistribution… and preventing the free expression of inconstant fortune). But then, when they are overwhelmed by some calamity, they lose power and the slaves slip their chains.

And here, we add a corollary to Scheidel's observations: The bigger and more ambitious government is, the more win-lose deals it insists upon, and the greater the inequality – even when it claims to be leveling. The case of the Russian Revolution is worth exploring in more detail. It shows what can happen when a government consciously undertakes to do something about inequality.

In 1917, most of the wealth in Russia was in the form of land ownership. This is where Lenin attacked first, with his "Land Decree" of November 8th:

> *The landowners' right of property in land is herewith abolished without compensation... The right of private property in land is to be abolished for all time. The land shall not be bought, sold, leased or otherwise alienated... The right to use the land shall be given to all citizens, regardless of sex, of the Russian state who desire to work it by their own hands... Hired labor is not permissible... The lands shall be distributed among those who use them on the principle of equalization...*

The "war to the death against the rich" had begun. Farmers who owned their land resisted. But Lenin knew how to deal with them. In August 1918, he wrote to a provincial commissar:

> *Comrade! Hang (and I mean hang so that the people can see) not less than 100 known kulaks, rich men, bloodsuckers... Do this so that for hundreds of miles around, the people can see, tremble, know, and cry: they are killing and will go on killing the bloodsucking kulaks.*

The program worked. Income differences were leveled. Scheidel reports:

> *...between 1912 and 1922, the proportion of rural peasant households having no horses or only one horse rose from 64 percent to 86 percent, whereas that of households having three or more fell from 14 percent to 3 percent. Villagers were now poorer overall — but more equally so. Rampant inflation contributed: by 1921, prices were almost 17,000 times as high as they had been in 1914. Barter increasingly replaced money, and the black market boomed.*

Government cannot level up. It can only level down. Often, way down. Inequality lives by the sword; it dies by the sword, too. But even as the feds use epic levels of violence to level, the elite – relatively – still rise. While Lenin and his friends enjoyed the power, status, warm fires, and red meat of a Moscow winter, 7 million kulaks died, most from starvation. Later, as the nomenklatura and apparatchiks solidified their positions, their standard of living far surpassed that of the average Soviet citizen. They had nice houses, chauffeured cars, heat!, airplanes – and a *dacha* in the country. The typical citizen had almost nothing.

In terms of living standards, in 1989, when the Berlin Wall came down, the difference between the Soviet elites and the common people was actually greater than that between the American 1% and the rest of the population. The American rich had much larger bank accounts and lived in better zip codes, but they drove similar cars, ate similar food, used similar appliances, and watched the same stupid shows on TV from the comfort of their airconditioned rec rooms as poorer Americans.

Win-lose, even when well-intentioned (if it ever really is)… and even when done in the name of some great cause… is always a loser.

ADDING IT UP

Win-lose deals are net losses. The more of them you have, the more you lose. Here's a simple formula:

$$TS = rv \ (w\text{-}w - w\text{-}l)$$

That is, Total Satisfaction (TS) is equal to the real value (rv) of win-win (w-w) exchanges minus the loss from win-lose (w-l) exchanges. Yes, it's as simple as that. Like a whittler working on a piece of wood, we've shaved so much off, there is nothing left of it… except the essential heartwood. And here, we aim – modestly – to overthrow all modern economics and provide a deeper insight into what real people actually want… how economies really work… and what "wealth" really is.

Here's a question for you: Which would you prefer? You grow up with an inferiority complex. You hate your mother. She hates you. You compensate by starting a successful business, hiring thousands of people, and making millions of dollars. You work night and day. Your wife hates you, too (because, subconsciously, you despise all women... thank you, Mommie dearest). And nobody much cares when you drop dead at 40, filthy rich, after battling a terrible, disfiguring disease for years.

Or...

You come from a good family. You always feel loved. You work as a rural mail carrier. You marry the woman of your dreams. The two of you have a small family and live on a small farm. You never make much money. In fact, you eat mostly from your own garden. But you are in good health and live happily into your nineties.

Which would you choose?

The problem with economics – especially the voodoo variety, as practiced by the witch doctors in universities and at the Federal Reserve – is that it cannot tell the difference. It can't measure quality. It can only measure quantity. It has numbers. And nothing more. Fives. Sixes. Sevens. There are only 9 basic numbers, which economists slice and dice... and add zeros, decimal points, and a few Greek symbols to. Using these numbers, they focus on the quantity of output, jobs, new roads, trade, and dollars earned and spent.

Everyone assumes more is better. More jobs. More factories. More malls. More credit. More spending. More autos. More houses. More of everything they can count. The fellow who creates and spends a fortune is the hero; he has more stuff.

Economists then promote policies that encourage larger numbers. They aim to stimulate growth, employment, productivity... and so on. Trillions of dollars have been spent as a result.

We'll have more on this in a subsequent chapter. Here, we just point out that the whole concept is warped and confused. More is not necessarily better. Economists can't measure "better" or "satisfaction." Our formula avoids the problem. It is so breathtakingly simple... so bewitchingly useful... and so shockingly revolutionary, we can hardly believe we didn't steal it from someone else. And perhaps we did. We just can't remember from whom.

Here's how it works. You have a cow. Your neighbor has a chicken. You give him milk. He gives you eggs. Note that it isn't an even-steven trade. Your wealth is created and enhanced when the cost of producing the milk is lower than the value of the eggs received in exchange. The difference can be called "profit"; it is the measure of new wealth created, as described by Robert Torrens in the French lace and English broad cloth trade above. Markets, prices, equities, bonds, yields, derivatives, swaps – all are merely elaborations of the basic win-win deal.

And all government policies – Quantitative Easing (QE), Dodd-Frank, trade tariffs, tax rates… everything – should be judged by how they affect these win-win exchanges. Is a proposed law or rule change good or bad? Does it make these win-win exchanges safer and easier… or slower and harder?

The other way to get what you want is to take it without giving anything in return. You shoot your neighbor's cow and roast it for dinner. The neighbor complains; you shoot him, too. That is a win-lose deal. You win. He loses. Win-lose deals do not create wealth; they merely transfer it. The math is easy…

A win is a plus. A lose is a minus. A plus added to a minus equals zero ($-1 + 1 = 0$). The world's wealth doesn't increase. It can't. Because the gain came at someone else's expense.

Of course, there are transaction costs and perverse incentives involved. The neighbor, fearing you may kill his cow, doesn't bother to raise it. Or he may erect a high wall to keep you away from his livestock. Or he may butcher his cow, just to avoid having it stolen from him. Or he may kill you. All of these things destroy satisfaction because people get less of what they really want.

When we first put our formula forward, in our daily e-letter, *Bill Bonner's Diary*, we got feedback. Some good. Some bad… And some that left us scratching our head. Some readers wondered what they could do with it... or how the government could capture this insight and put it to work.

Some were disappointed that it wasn't more politically charged, like Thomas Piketty's silly "r > g" formula. Piketty had become the lion of economic literature with his 2013 book, *Capital in the Twenty-First Century*, in which he argued that returns on capital (r) grow faster than the economy (g). This led the elite classes to imagine that they could solve the problem of inequality with various win-lose programs designed to diminish the return on capital. Taxes, for example.

Our $TS = rv$ *(w-w – w-l)* formula, on the other hand, will delight no activists. No ambitious politician will find it useful for speeches. No think tank will raise money from rich donors by promising to turn it into a new federal program.

Ours is not a formula for action. It is a call to inaction, a call to the feds to back off and let people do their best. It is just a description of how a civilized economy actually works. And it leads to a shocking and treasonous question: If win-lose is always negative... and if government only traffics in win-lose deals, why do we allow it? (We will address that question more fully in a later chapter, too.)

But setting aside that question, we merely note that win-win produces more human satisfaction – in a modern economy – than win-lose. It has become the vernacular of everyday transactions, the default morality for the private sector in the 21st century. We assume, we expect, and we insist that others – all over the world, in different countries with different cultures, different languages, and different gods – follow it.

ℏ— CHAPTER 6 —ℏ

Fake News

So you think you can tell Heaven from Hell, blue skies from pain
– "Wish You Were Here" by Pink Floyd

✞·✞·✞·✞

IF YOU WISH to visit us in Argentina, you can fly to Buenos Aires, and then to Salta, a city of about 600,000 people in the northwest of the country. From there, you will get in a 4-wheel-drive vehicle and travel for another five or six hours, depending on which route you take. In either case, the pavement will run out after an hour or two.

You will drive along on dirt roads through a vast, empty wilderness. Depending on which route you take, you can drive for hours without seeing another car... or scarcely a house or another living soul. If you are unlucky, you will get stuck behind a truck on a long, winding road and be unable to pass. The dust will block your view and force you to roll up the windows.

Imagine, then, arriving in a tiny village of mud- and concrete-houses with mud- or tin-roofs. There are few visible signs of commercial or cultural life – save an occasional little sign offering *empanadas* or to repair your flat tires. But you notice something remarkable – street lights.

For nearly a mile leading into town, the road is graced with modern lights mounted on tall, metal poles, curving over the road and giving off a yellow glow over the dusty main drag. There are no cars on the road... no houses near the road... no sidewalks next to the road... and no pedestrians walking on them. Welcome to Angastaco. Population: 823.

We tried to imagine the town council meeting. Almost the entire voting population of the town might have crowded into the hangar where Luis changes tires… or the little restaurant where Marta serves homemade *empanadas*.

"We have before us a proposal to put in street lights," begins the mayor. "It will cost about $20,000 to put them in… which is about our entire annual budget. And it will cost about $2,000 a year to maintain and power them. All in favor raise their hands."

No hands go up.

"Wait," says the mayor. "It will be paid for by Buenos Aires."

All hands go up.

Porteños, as people from Buenos Aires are called, probably have a hard time imagining little Angastaco. Sixteen hours away by car, Buenos Aires has European-style buildings, skyscrapers, chic restaurants, paved streets, and thousands of cafes, bars, shops, and factories. Almost all the streets and highways are lit. And almost all the important decisions requiring an enlightened government are made there.

It must have taken some effort to get the government in Buenos Aires to see the need for street lights in Angastaco. Lobbyists for the power company, the engineers, and the installers all probably had to talk it up, and perhaps reward the right people at the right time. And, of course, compromises were probably made. Instead of putting in one lightpost every 100 feet, perhaps there is only one every 200 feet. And maybe the power company had to cut back on its initial estimate of the cost.

We don't know how the deal went down, but there they are… bright, shiny street lights on a deserted road in the middle of nowhere, serving no good purpose whatsoever… eerily lighting up nothing, for nobody's sake. And using energy that comes from distant power plants at who-knows-what real cost.

The citizens of Angastaco know perfectly well that the street lights are a waste of money. But scale, space, and time corrupt information. To the government in faraway Buenos Aires, with so much else on its mind, the cost seems almost trivial. And the apparent knowledge – that safe, well-lit streets are a good thing – seems almost self-evident.

In Angastaco, the facts about its street lighting are direct, immediate, firsthand, and close. In Buenos Aires, they are distant and mostly theoretical. Or mythical. "Good lighting" is something people believe in… but without any real evidence as to why.

And here, we undertake our most important contribution to the whole genre of civilization studies. That is, we attempt to understand how private information and public information differ.

FACTS AND MYTHS

The reader will say: Well, of course they are different. Public life is bigger; there's more information in it. Yes, it is bigger. And yes, there is more information available. But the quality of the information changes as the quantity increases. In Angastaco, street lighting is a fact. In Buenos Aires, it is a myth.

Myths are not true or untrue. They are simply unprovable, more like an opinion than a scientific hypothesis. Do street lights reduce accidents? Crime? What about in a town that has neither accidents nor crime? How do you figure it? You say, "It is a myth that throwing a virgin into a volcano will appease the volcano gods." And yes, it is certainly a myth. But that doesn't mean it isn't true. It is a different thing altogether, not subject to proof. Like street lighting. Is it better to light the streets leading into a small, remote town? Who knows?

Meanwhile, in a little village in France, we frequently pass a soccer field, now being used to grow hay. Slowing down for the new traffic-easing roundabout and speed bumps, we see a sign warning us to watch out for children. Only there are no children. There's no traffic, no one on the streets, and no one to play soccer.

This is just another of the thousands of geriatric towns in France.

It has almost no young people and little public life of any sort. But the national government in Paris thought that it should have street lights, a soccer field, a roundabout, and a sign warning the rare driver to keep his eyes open for the even-rarer child.

But let's stick with the more sensational example. Everything we know about volcanoes suggests that tossing in a virgin will make no difference to the volcano's behavior. But we don't know everything. And there is no way to know whether what we don't know includes some important detail concerning the use of virgins. You could conduct all the experiments you wanted. You could toss one virgin in… then two… then three. You could toss them in dressed in white… then black. You could throw in a few matrons, too.

Then, you could watch. Did the volcano erupt? No? Why not? Perhaps the virgins really did the trick. But even if the volcano erupted, you still wouldn't know anything. Perhaps it didn't like that particular virgin. Or maybe she wasn't really as chaste as she claimed.

PRIVATE MYTHS

And you, Dear Reader, what myths do you live by? We write the stories of our lives; we're the heroes. We create dragons… and then we slay them. We are "the able and loyal worker," for example, triumphing over want, idleness, and irrelevance. We are the "good husband," walking the line… providing for our families… preparing the way for our children. We're the "good citizen." We read the papers. We vote. We join. We participate. Or we're "a rich guy." We have a big house, a big boat, and a big stock market portfolio. We are enlightened… and progressive. Or we are a good conservative… maybe even a Conservative Christian.

These descriptions may be "true"… until they are upended by events. The good employee gets fired. The good husband meets a fetching cocktail waitress. The rich guy gets wiped out in a market crash… and has to fly economy. And the Conservative Christian votes for Donald J. Trump!

Yes, Dear Reader... we are all human. Not always good, and not always bad... but always subject to shifting influence. We need myths to make sense of who we are and what we do.

Once our heroic story is undone, we must tell a new story. The good employee becomes the victim of a rapacious employer. The good husband buys a convertible and becomes a *bon vivant*. The rich guy becomes a Marxist. And the Conservative Christian thinks it is time for a change.

When things go wrong, you blame someone else. Or simply deny the obvious contradictions. Did we run off with the cocktail waitress? Or did our wife lose interest and drive us away? Did we really fail to do our job properly, as charged? Or was our employer merely trying to reduce his payroll by getting rid of his most senior – and most competent – workers?

Should we have known that it was a bubble? Or are bubbles as unpredictable as Alan Greenspan says they are? As for The Donald, there is nothing Christian or conservative about him. But who knows? God works in mysterious ways!

Myths are wily, elusive things. Like fake news.

"Fake news" became a household term when Donald Trump used it to describe any media report that was critical of him. Some news, of course, is just purely made up for the purpose of entertainment or influence.

In January 2016, a satirical website reported that a "meth-addled couple" had eaten a homeless man in New York City's Central Park. Later, another such site, *Now8News*, reported that a can of cookie dough had "exploded in a woman's vagina"; the woman was alleged to have been shoplifting. One of our favorite fake news stories appeared years ago in the *Weekly World News*. It showed a dim photo of a B-24 bomber on what appeared to be a desert landscape, with this headline: "World War II Bomber Found on the Moon."

What fun it must have been to work at the *Weekly World News*, making up loony stories to amuse yourself and your friends. It must have been a laugh a minute in the "news" room. The newspaper made no pretense of truthfulness. But what did it matter if a World War II bomber had been found on the moon or not? It was fun to think about it... imagining the crew wondering if they had flown off course... thinking about how far it must have gone... wondering how the navigator could have made such a big mistake... and what the crew must have thought as the moon loomed before them. Was it simply a case of "pilot error"?

Yes, it was a fantasy. But it was the kind of falsehood that actually strengthened our grip on reality. We had to think about gravity, distance, air pressure, and all the other things that make it impossible for a World War II vintage airplane to fly to the moon.

Most of the news, however, is not so clearly preposterous. As such, the truth of it – not being plainly made up – is less apparent. It is less "truthful" in the sense that the real meaning is more obscure. It falls in a shadow area, between the light of day and the darkness of night, between what is true and what is false. Or more precisely, it is obscured from the whole truth and nothing but the truth by such a fog of myth, illusion, and wishful thinking that its information content can be very hard to judge.

When we first began writing this book, we believed that fake news was something new. Until the age of mass media, there was little news of any sort and little opportunity to mislead oneself or others with "fake" news content. What people knew was immediate, close, and clearly established – much like what Angastaco knew about its street lighting. Perhaps more importantly, falsehood was readily identified and discarded.

"We have plenty of food for the winter," a tribal chief might say. Then, as the tribe starved to death, the "fake news" and its purveyors would be eliminated. "The neighboring tribe is no threat to us," could also be disproven. So could, "Yes, that mushroom is harmless." And these last words, "Nice kitty," spoken to a saber-toothed tiger, put an end to that illusion.

In the private world, feedback loops tend to be quick, accurate, and unforgiving. You think you are a genius. Your wife, children, neighbors, co-workers, and friends all set you right. You think deficits don't matter... until they repossess your car. You drive on the wrong side of the road... drink too much vodka... tell your mother-in-law what you really think of her – all of these things generally result in immediate correction.

But there are persistent myths in private life, too; we could scarcely live without them. It is largely a matter of scale, space, and time that separates them from the grand delusions in the public sphere. If you see a grizzly bear running towards you, growling and snarling, the information content of that observation is likely to be very high. He is right there in front of you. You see him with your own eyes. It is happening now, not 1,000 years ago. And the consequences could be very important to you.

If it were 1,000 years ago, and you were in what is today Austria, and someone you knew ran into your village yelling, "The Huns are coming! Run for the hills!" – that, too, probably would have had a very high information content. Perhaps not quite as high as the previous example, but still substantial.

Life is always lived in the dark, as Lucretius might have said if he'd thought of it. But in the very old days, at least the ground was mostly free of banana peels and booby traps laid out by grand-scale mythmakers and the fake news media.

Let us go to 2003. Colin Powell, then U.S. Secretary of State, is addressing the United Nations. He says Iraq has "weapons of mass destruction" and something must be done about it.

Information content? You've never met Colin Powell. Is he an honorable, stand-up kind of guy? Or is he a bounder? You've never been to Iraq either. You have a vague feeling that it is next to Israel. You wonder what the difference is between a weapon of mass destruction and any other modern weapon. You don't know Mr. Powell's motives. You don't know who he is working for. (Yes, he works for the U.S. government... but what is that? Who controls it? What is it trying to do?) You don't know where he got the information, from whom, nor what their motives were. How accurate is this information? You have no way of knowing. And even if it were accurate, you don't know whether or not the alleged weapons pose a danger to you. And even if they do, you don't know what could be done about it. Or at what cost. Most important, you don't know the answer to the most essential question: So what?

The information value turned out to be negative. After you heard the speech, you had less real knowledge than you had before. Worse, you were likely to go away with false notions that would get you into a lot of trouble. Because not only was the information false, the myth on which it rested, like a prehensile tail, was better suited to an earlier stage of evolution.

Mr. Powell's news was the fakiest kind of fake news. It was untrue. The information was phonied-up in order to justify a war with Iraq. And even if it were true, it had very little valuable content. Almost all nations have "weapons of mass destruction." Iraq had them too? What was new?

And here we offer a simple rule: Like radiant heat, the information content of any news declines by the square of the elapsed time and distance from the source. Call it the Angastaco Effect.

In the beginning was the word. But a word is not the same as a thing. No two objects or events are exactly the same. Two tables may look alike. But close inspection will show slight differences. They are not made from the same piece of wood, for example. (Even if they are made from the same tree, they are – necessarily – made from different parts of the tree.) There may be a slight difference in color. They may have scratches, perhaps imperceptible to the eye. And so on.

Except for electrons, every object is unique and could be identified in a number of ways – a four-legged thing, a wooden thing, a thing for eating at, a carbon-based thing, a brown thing...

The "table" tag is just an identifier. It is not specific to the thing. So, when we say, "It is a table," what we really mean is that it could be placed in a category which we choose to call "table." Or not.

And as our thoughts fill with words, so do they fill with compound identifiers that become more and more remote from the actual truth. A "table" may be simple enough and close enough to the real thing to be fairly safe, serviceable, and reliable. But when we get to really abstract and aggregated words – such as "The Reformation" – we are lost in a fantasy world.

Likewise, at some level, all information is fake. We think in words. And every word is at best, a metaphor, and at worst, a lie. This was comically illustrated when Bill Clinton, defending himself against impeachment, challenged the meaning of "is." If the most common verb in the English language is subject to interpretation, so is every other word. Each one bends the light in one direction or another. Put words together and it is easier to lie than to tell the truth.

We only have five basic senses: sight, sound, touch, taste, and smell. From these senses come data that our brain interprets according to various mythical formulae. As Plato pointed out, we have in our minds an idea – a myth or "form" – about what a chair is. That chair does not exist. It is idealized and given general characteristics so that any real object may be compared to it. So, when you say, "This is a chair," you are not stating a fact. You are just jumping to a conclusion.

Some things are not fake, of course. If you are fair-skinned and go out into the sunlight for too long, you'll get a sunburn. It doesn't matter whether you think the sun is a burning ball of gas… or a god. Likewise, if you stand in front of a speeding locomotive, you will get run over and die. Again, it doesn't matter what you think is going on. The locomotive is real, even though it wouldn't exist without the myths that guide human action.

The amount of data coming to us from our senses is practically infinite. We could look at a tree and see an almost unlimited amount of detail... which we could examine for an almost unlimited amount of time. Instead, we compare the incoming data to some preprogrammed model, as quickly as possible, and come to an almost immediate judgment: this is a tree.

This is what German philosopher Immanuel Kant called the "categories of understanding." If we weren't able to categorize the incoming data, we would be paralyzed by our senses, receiving "information," but literally unable to know what to make of it.

For millions of years (even long before we were human), our brains developed ways of using fake news – myths – that were useful to us. Abstract thinking evolved and adapted along with our hand tools. Myths that helped us kill the game, beat back an attack by another tribe, or find the good mushroom were, presumably, kept. The others were either discarded... or the people who believed them were weeded out of the gene pool.

Myths do not have to be "true" or verifiable to be useful. Socrates, as quoted by Plato in Book III of *The Republic*, mentions "noble lies." He recognized that the Greek myths were fake news and the Greek gods were phonies. But he believed they were useful for teaching moral lessons: forbearance, courage, greatness of the soul, etc.

This is true today, too. Stalin's 1941 appeal to comrades to rise up in defense of Mother Russia, rather than the Soviet Union, was a form of noble (or ignoble, depending on how you look at it) lie. Mother Russia was a myth. His appeal to protect her had little more reliable information content than Colin Powell's address to the United Nations.

If we think of "myths" as a kind of software for the brain, we can also see that some software is helpful. Some is not. Some, like malware, is destructive.

LARGE-SCALE MYTHS

Myths survive, or die, like ethologist Richard Dawkins' viruses... along with the brains they infect. A myth that forbade the use of weapons, for example, was likely to doom a tribe to failure. A myth that eating meat was "wrong" was probably fatal, too. Even in recent history, various beliefs have sidelined, or caused the extinction of, whole groups of people. Stuck with eighteenth-century technology, the Amish have become a tourist attraction. Shakers, an eighteenth-century Christian sect, believed that sex was the root cause of sin. At their peak in the mid-nineteenth century, there were roughly 6,000 believers. Unable to procreate, the movement died out.

We don't know what myths caused the extinction of ancient groups; they died and took the evidence with them. But nature suffers fools more gladly now than in the past. They used to be punished with death. Now, they are elected to public office. Readers will think we are joking. We are not. On a small scale, foolish myths are quickly corrected. But on a large scale, they are often rewarded... for a while. Politicians traffic in them.

We turn briefly to the German elections of 1932. The voters spoke and gave Adolf Hitler's NSDAP, the Nazis, control of the legislature. A few months later, the Reichstag, now in Nazi hands, passed the Enabling Act, giving Hitler almost unlimited power. Thirteen years later, the country was bankrupt, bombed out, defeated, with 8 million people dead. And it would be occupied by foreign troops for decades to come.

There were some 40 million adults in Germany in 1932. Out of so many, how could voters choose the one – and possibly the only – person who could destroy the country so thoroughly? Chosen at random, Herr Schultz or Herr Baumann probably would have muddled along. He (the randomly selected leader) probably would have drawn on his instincts, training, and the experts available to advise him, and tried to make peace with the communists and the trade unions. Maybe he would have been overwhelmed by the Bolsheviki. Maybe there would have been widespread disorder, strikes, street brawls, etc.

But who knows? Other European countries seemed to keep their wits about them, and muddled through, more or less. Except Italy, which had the extremely bad judgment to team up with Hitler.

Picked at random, the German leader most likely would have stuck to the bourgeois script. He would have negotiated with France and Britain, rather than confronting them head-on. He would have ignored the gays, Jews, and gypsies, rather than trying to exterminate them. He would have been so busy just trying to maintain basic law and order that he wouldn't have had the time, energy, or money – let alone the desire – to attack Poland, the Soviet Union, Belgium, France, and Britain.

Almost anyone, no matter how incompetent or how irresolute, no matter how crooked or corruptible, no matter how delusional or insane, would have been better than Herr Hitler. No Hitler, no World War II, they say. No World War II, no holocaust.

Why, then, did the Germans pick him? What kind of trick were the gods playing? What kind of perverse fate brought Herr Hitler to lead 66 million civilized men, women, and children into one of the most uncivilized disasters in history? That is the power of what advertising genius David Ogilvy called the "Big Idea," and what we are describing as a "Large-Scale Myth."

Many of the leading myths of today are so big, we scarcely realize they are myths at all. Neither necessarily bad nor necessarily good (we'll get to that later), we take them for granted… as though "that's just the way it is."

Global climate change (we have no way of knowing for sure what is going on)… Majority rule (why is that better?)… Murder is bad (who says?)… Genocide is even worse (why is that?)… Hitler was a bad dude (not what his mother said!)… Racism (does it really exist?)… Gender differences come from socialization (do these people have children?)… Child labor, torture, inequality, slavery – all are bad.

MAKE AMERICA GREAT AGAIN

There is the myth of the nation state, for example. It suggests that there is something inevitable, natural, and end-of-history-ish about a political organization in which a nation of people and a government are one. Closely connected is the myth of democracy: that it matters what people think, and that a nation should be governed according to the wishes of the majority. They express their desires and opinions through the ballot box; their ideas are transformed into the law of the land. Myth makes reality.

And here's another Grand Myth: the myth of "progress." We tend to think that things get better all the time, and that the world we know today is better than it has ever been. There is a contradictory myth, too, that things were better in the "good old days."

And yes, of course, technological and material knowledge accumulate. But we don't have any way of knowing whether they make life better. We don't know what "better" is; we only know what we like and what we want.

The hydrogen bomb was a big improvement over old-fashioned dynamite. But being able to kill more people faster is not necessarily better. Is an eight-lane highway better than a two-lane blacktop? Is a McDonald's Happy Meal better than home-cooked grub?

Do these innovations make us happier? Do they make the world better? Who knows?

Most people believe "progress" happens, that it is a good thing, and that governments that promote progress are better than those that impede it. But there is no reason to think that our political and social institutions are better today than they were in the past. We don't even know how to measure real progress, or how to describe it. Suppose some pharmaceutical breakthrough made us all happy all the time – would that be better? Would that be progress?

We pause to backtrack. Myths are ancient. Older than human beings. That is, even before other human-like species evolved into *Homo sapiens*, myths already made it possible to think, to make decisions, to act, and to live with other, similar animals.

One myth that almost surely predates humans is the "us versus them" concept. In the long struggle for life pre-history, "us" was the group that carried common genes and helped each other survive. Starvation was an almost ever-present threat. Animal numbers tend to grow to fill the feeding niche available to them, so any setback – drought, disease, storms... or population growth – could be an existential threat. There was also the ever-present threat from "them," who were competing not only for the same food resources, but also for the same procreation opportunities. For the male of the species, or the tribe, "them" was lethal competition.

Steven Pinker adds another evolutionary angle. People may have been wary of other tribes, other races, other cultures, and so forth because they posed a biological threat. Groups were separated for many thousands of years by rivers, mountains, and deserts... as well as by mutual animosity. Germs developed along with the separate groups. Before the days of antibiotics, contact with another group might have been fatal, as it was for the Aztecs when the Spanish reached them. So, the myth – fear or dislike of other groups – may have a hidden prophylactic *raison d'être*.

Of course, it was still a myth. You never knew who carried which germs, or whether the "us" were friendly and the "them" were enemies. Nevertheless, the "us versus them" software must have been useful at some point, or we wouldn't have it today.

"Us versus them" invites "us" to participate in murder, war, fratricide, genocide, and massacres. It invites "them" to do so, too. And probably, during the millions of pre-human years... and at least 295,000 of our 300,000 years in existence as humans... the best strategy was probably to try to exterminate "them" before they did the same to you... or at least to try to maintain such a plausible balance of power that they didn't dare try.

The Jews were the "us" of the Old Testament. Everyone else was the "them." It made sense in a tribal world. But does it make sense today? Who's us? Those who speak the same language? Those who worship the same god? Those from the same city, the same state, or the same country? Does the Goldman Sachs hot-shot in New York have more in common with the hick in a Kentucky hollow than he does with his colleague in London? Does "us versus them" make any sense at all in a modern, globalized, win-win world? The myth, now embedded as instinct, or near-instinct, was developed under conditions very different from those of today.

Colin Powell's speech to the United Nations served its purpose. Millions of people felt that they should take up arms. They had never been to Iraq. They couldn't find it on a map. They didn't know its history, its culture, or its politics. They didn't know how, or if, it might represent a threat to them. (A moment of reflection would have revealed that it posed no menace at all.) Still, people were ready to carry out acts of violence against Iraq and kill its people; they were "them."

The idea that Iraq should be attacked was a form of myth. There was no proof that by going to war, the world would be a better place. The machinist in Duluth or the plainsman in Kansas certainly had no way of judging any of the claims and predictions made about the forthcoming war. Would it be easy, quick, and cheap, as the warmongers promised? Would U.S. troops be welcomed as liberators? Would the costs be covered by Iraqi oil revenues and the whole investment made profitable? Would Iraq turn into a Muslim USA, a model of liberal democracy and consumerism in the heart of the Middle East?

These were all myths – the soldiers-as-liberators, the quick-and-easy victory, the oil revenues, and the model democracy. But they weren't necessarily untrue. And from such a distance, who could tell? We know now that the information value of all these assertions was less than zero. The claims were made in bad faith, based on faulty, and/or intentionally misleading inputs, supported by incompetent reasoning, and driven by absurd, venal, and vainglorious motives. But few people realized it then. Scale and distance had stripped the information of all useful content. All that was left was a vestigial myth, which people believed to their cost.

THE TROUBLE WITH THE TRUTH

In the fifth century, Christian scholars counted 88 different heresies. Arianism. Eutychianism. Nestorianism. You name it. One argued that there was no such thing as "original sin." Another denied the trinity. Still another claimed Jesus was not divine. Which one had the truth?

Not waiting for divine revelation, people formed up into "us" groups and fought it out in the streets... in wars and mass murders. For 1,000 years, off and on, heretics were persecuted, tortured, and burned at the stake.

The truth is hard to see. And hard to tell. We say, "Time will tell." But often, even time can't get the words out. You listen carefully. All you get is a garbled message echoing from the past, full of maybes and caveats. Between cause and effect, the noise can be deafening. And as the scale grows, so does the noise level. Put out enough noise and the listener can hear anything he wants. And what does he want to hear? Lies.

Even in personal matters, lies are generally more appealing than the truth, to teller as well as listener. A lie, like smooth whiskey, goes down easy... and leaves the drinker with a little glow. Researchers have found that when people hear what they want to hear, it releases dopamine, giving them a little buzz. Of course, you have to be careful how you phrase things. "No, Dear, that dress doesn't make you look any fatter than you actually are," may not be the winning lie you expected. But generally, soothing lies are more warmly received than jagged truths.

It's hard to tell the truth, too, because it's not available to us. Often, there is none. In public, myth takes the place of truth. But the problem with myth is that it is often abominably stupid... and, as we have seen, inappropriate. Rather than the "noble lie" that Socrates had in mind, it is a scurrilous one, put forth intentionally.

As Adolf Hitler explained, big lies have:

> *...a certain force of credibility; because the broad masses of a nation are always more easily corrupted in the deeper strata of their emotional nature than consciously or voluntarily...*

In August 2018, *The Washington Post*, which had been keeping track, tallied 4,229 "false or misleading statements" made by Donald Trump since he became president. A substantial portion of the public loved every one of them.

Even though fake news and fake myths are ubiquitous, they're still fake. You may jump off a cliff hoping to float in the air. Then, you discover that gravity, like truth, still exists. As we've seen, private errors, pretentions, and delusions tend to be small and are quickly corrected or forgotten. Public errors, pernicious myths, and mass delusions can persist for many years, often on a huge scale. The poor Russians, for example, endured their Soviet system for 70 years. The poor Chinese suffered Mao's mass murders and starvation for 30 years. And pity the poor Egyptians – they slaved in the stifling heat, putting up huge monuments to their elite, for thousands of years.

We say they "slaved," but they weren't necessarily enslaved. Myth can substitute for force. Dressed up in the proper myth, a win-lose deal can become a win-win deal. Egyptians loved lies as much as anyone. Egyptologists tell us that some "slaves" might have been doing a form of community service, perhaps in lieu of taxes or military service. It would have been impossible, or nearly impossible, to mobilize that much labor over such a long period of time with brute force alone. They must have had powerful myths that kept the leaders "on message"… and the people on the job… for centuries. It is even likely that these laborers took up their work as modern volunteer soldiers pick up their rifles and veterans' benefits – with pride and satisfaction. Which merely illustrates how vapory the frontier between win-win and win-lose can be. The masses are often so captivated by the myth – even a predatory myth – that they neither resent nor resist. Instead, they take to their labors like an old workhorse to the harness, longing for the lash.

Pyramid-building may have consumed the entire economic surplus of the Nile Valley for hundreds of years. Wealth that might have been used to improve the lifestyles and living conditions of the average family was instead used for the glorification of the ultra-elite, in whose reflected glory, perhaps, the common man, too, basked with pleasure.

Was this a good idea? It is not for us to say. Some will argue that the myths made it possible for the society to do something that it would never otherwise have attempted. No man, no matter how rich, could have organized and carried out such an immense resource-consuming project on a win-win basis alone. Nor could win-win have developed the Manhattan Project, for that matter.

You may describe these as "big wins for mankind." "Yes," you may protest at all that you have read so far, "if you want a big win, you're bound to suffer some big losses, too."

And you would be right. The myth-making techniques that gave rise to the Acropolis were also what created Auschwitz. The deification of the emperor may have contributed to the glory of Rome, but that same myth of a "glorious leader" was also used to legitimize the rule of Josef Stalin.

But let's keep looking.

FAKE MYTHS

There is nothing unusual about Rhinebeck, New York. In the center of it is a monument put up to honor America's soldiers who died in World War I. A bronze statue depicts a muscular soldier with his rifle. And at the base of the statue is a plaque that reads: "They died that we might live." Over the decades, the townspeople and visitors must have read this inscription many thousands of times. Has anybody noticed that it is not true? Probably not.

In World War I, never was there any risk that the Huns were going to invade New York State and put the citizens of Rhinebeck to the sword. Then, as now, anyone would have laughed at the idea. But the plaque remains. It is part of the mythology of modern life. Soldiers are meant to believe that they are protecting the homeland. And we are supposed to believe that our boys in uniform are doing us an important service.

There are real myths. And there are fake myths. The reflex of taking up arms to attack or defend may be based on a real myth, for example. It is precious experience embedded as instinct. But fake myths are made-up myths… concocted to put something over on others, and inappropriate to the cause of civilization. Entering World War I was on the basis of a fake myth. It was a misadventure organized by the Wilson administration that had nothing to do with protecting American lives. Instead, it did the exact opposite. It endangered them. The war got 117,465 Americans killed. Had the U.S. stayed out of the war, in all probability, they would have lived. The plaque lies.

Also in Rhinebeck, in our hotel room, was a notice. We were told that if we hung up our towel, it wouldn't be laundered. It was advertised that this would "Save the Planet." Was it true? Of course not. It may or may not be true that humans have the capacity to heat up the Earth's atmosphere. They may even be able to destroy themselves. But it is certainly not true that they can destroy the planet. The planet will survive anything we can throw at it. We could set off every nuclear warhead on Earth; the planet would still be here. As the Marquis de Sade remarks in the play *Marat/Sade* by Peter Weiss, "Nature herself would watch unmoved if we destroyed the entire human race." So, there is no way on God's green Earth that humans are going to "save the planet" either. It is a phony myth.

Myths have power. People recycle their trash. They invest in "green" technologies and worry about their carbon footprints; they want to believe they can save the planet. And, if challenged, they will say, "It can't hurt to try."

But in the end, the planet is indifferent.

When virgins were thrown into volcanoes, the authorities had a theory: Volcanoes had "spirits." These spirits needed to be appeased; otherwise, they would show their displeasure by exploding. This hypothesis has not been confirmed by modern science, which sees no causal link between maidens and volcanic eruptions, or the lack thereof.

But the witchdoctor who said, "Well... it can't hurt... And who knows, it might work" would have had a point.

MUSHY FACTS

Useful myths are forms of condensed experience, heated white hot in the fires of history, and hammered hard by countless trials... and errors. Fake myths tend to be invented more recently... and are conveniently exploited. These more modern myths are often based on interpretations of history and recent events. But even the truest and most indisputable public facts on which they rest are mushy.

You say that World War II began when Germany attacked Poland on September 1, 1939. Then what about the German Abwehr attack on Jablonków on the Slovak/Polish border on August 25? What about the invasion of Albania by the Italians on April 7? What about the German occupation of Czechoslovakia in March? But wait... If you say, "Hitler invaded Poland," you are definitely wrong. He was in Berlin the whole time. So, to make it a true fact, you'd have to say: "Germany invaded Poland." But that's not correct either. Germany is a country. The mountains of Bavaria didn't exactly attack the mountains of Poland. So maybe you could say, "The Germans attacked the Poles." Of course, that wouldn't be true either. Few Germans had anything to do with it. And probably, if asked, most wanted no part of it.

You could be more precise and say that the "Wehrmacht invaded Poland," but it surely wasn't all the Wehrmacht either. Some members of it invaded. But one soldier crossing the border would not have begun the war. Then, two? Three? How many had to cross into Poland before the war officially began?

We presume the Wehrmacht, Hitler, and Germany all acted with a single mind... as a single actor. But is that true? And did they really "invade" Poland? Not according to Hitler. He was merely trying to protect "German interests." There were many ethnic Germans in Poland who didn't consider it an invasion at all, but a liberation. Danzig, for example, had a majority German population.

Besides, 17 days later, the Soviet Union invaded Poland, too. Perhaps Germany really was just trying to protect its civilians in Poland. But what was the Soviet Union doing? Maybe the war really began when the Soviet Union invaded.

You get the point. Actual history is infinitely complex… infinitely detailed… and infinitely nuanced. You can't possibly know what actually happened (you would need the mind of God). So instead, you come up with a simplified narrative that you can handle. Since this story is necessarily a simplification, an abbreviation, and a bowdlerized version of what really happened, it is also false. It is not what happened. What actually happened was far more complicated, with thousands of details, any one of which might be far more important and meaningful than those we chose to highlight.

What is true of history is true, too, of contemporary events. When People's Republic of China leader Zhou Enlai was asked by Richard Nixon what he thought was the effect of the French Revolution, the Chinese leader replied: "It is too soon to know." (There are some accounts claiming that he was referring to the communist revolution in China or the student riots in France in 1968…)

Historians believe that it is impossible to get a grip on history until at least a quarter of a century has passed. It takes that long for the dust to settle and for you to be able to see "what it meant." But as you move away from events, the confusions and contradictions are harder and harder to see. Then, you can develop a storyline that is comfortingly flattering and satisfactorily false. It is not what really happened, but a myth that makes sense of otherwise incomprehensible data.

Looking at history is a bit like trying to understand Nietzsche by looking at his skull. You will see something that was once part of the man known as Nietzsche, but it will be far from the real thing. And yet, from these dried-up and bleached-out bones, the lessons of history are drawn.

The most evil man of the 20th century, in the popular mind at least, was Adolf Hitler. And the biggest mistake of good men was that of former British Prime Minister Neville Chamberlain, who allegedly "appeased" the monster at the Bad Godesberg conference in 1938. This lesson seemed obvious and irrefutable to most Americans: There are bad people; you have to stand up to them. But it is merely a myth. And perhaps a toxic one. A broader, more universal, and more useful truth from the history of the 20th century may be that even the most civilized people in the most civilized nations are capable of slipping into barbarism. The old elites are discredited by failed wars, hyperinflation, and bankruptcy. A new elite arises that's capable of rousing the masses to mischief by appealing to atavistic sentiments. They identify the "them"… the bad guys. But the trouble is, these new "bad guys" could be you. And the "facts," always pliable, will bend themselves to suit the favored myth.

COLLUSION OF THE PRESS

If you read that a black safe dropped out of a window at 23 Larkins Lane on June 3 at 11:27 in the morning, and that it fell on the head of Walter Scheming, killing him instantly, the account is probably fairly close to the truth. That is, it is almost as good as private information. The reporter has merely passed along the same thing that an eyewitness would have seen.

But enter larger, more remote, more abstract news – with a more substantial myth component – and the "public news" that results is fantasy. The same comment applies to "history," insofar as it is distilled from public news. News is rarely what it pretends to be. It is not a bloodless recitation of indisputable facts, like a list of the temperatures recorded at the North Pole. Instead, it is informed and persuaded by a web of ideas, myths, lies, and misconceptions. Otherwise, the news would be meaningless.

Mr. Jones says something to Mr. Smith… a cold breeze blows across the public parks of Duluth… a bird flies into a window pane in

Georgia. If you really wanted to report what happened, you'd have an infinite amount of material. Obviously, you couldn't do that, even if you knew what had happened. So, you apply some artificial standards. You try to make sense of the world and its goings-on by labeling things and putting them on shelves. It is one thing for a man on the streets of Lagos, Nigeria to kill another man in the heat of passion. It is quite another for a man in Ankara, Turkey to gun down the Russian ambassador. Both involve passion. Both involve men. Both stories end with a corpse. But the former is not newsworthy. Different label. Different shelf. The media decides. It tells us that whatever Mr. Jones said to Mr. Smith, it is not worth reporting. It leaves the cold breeze story to The Weather Channel. As for the poor little bird, who gives a damn?

Mr. Smith has bought a loaf of bread from Mr. Jones for $2.30. Miss Dupree has agreed to go out on a date with Mr. Carlton. The young Billy Owens hit a baseball so hard it went through Ms. Catterton's front window. The national press will not trouble itself with all the millions of private win-win deals. Instead, it will focus on win-lose deals. A man was stabbed at the Four Corners Bar last night. Two high school teachers were arrested for stealing from the basketball fund. Russia invaded Crimea.

Violence sells newspapers. Readers think it is important to know about it; and there's hardly anything more satisfying than violence happening to someone else. Real fake news (if we may use that term) is a form of entertainment (or propaganda) that makes people feel smart, heroic, and honorable. The public wants lies, in other words, and the media provides them.

People don't want to pay for news that makes them feel uncomfortable, inadequate, or stupid. The last thing they want is any serious thought or real insight. The truth is too difficult to get ahold of and too bitter to swallow. They want news that makes them feel taller and slimmer.

Mass media also needs a mass audience. So, it cultivates mass themes, from which nuance, irony, and doubt – the particularities of local content – have been removed. It wants cartoon heroes and "us versus them" stories that leave no doubt that "us" is the side of the angels. The atavistic "us versus them" gives readers a sense that they are somehow engaged in the events and that they are part of an "us" that is under attack, being ripped off, in danger, and so forth.

The media speaks to the public about programs, wars, disasters, policies, politics, celebrities, sports... and other collective myths. The talking heads chatter about nations, teams, companies, groups, religions, political parties, red and blue, different races, conservatives and liberals... rich and poor. It is about "us."

It is no coincidence that the editorial pages hector readers with "We need to do this..." or "We should do that." Nor is it a coincidence, then, that mass newspapers came into existence at about the same time as the nation state. The newspapers provided the "us" narrative, leading people to think that they had something in common with other readers... and other members, citizens, and subjects of the nation state. It was only with the rise of these mass communications that the French, for example, came to see themselves as French... citizens of the Republic... speakers of a national language... guardians of a national culture. Previously, as late as the French Revolution, regional differences were so pronounced that people from different provinces often could not understand each other's dialects. Each province had its own weights and measures. There were 13 different appeal courts, each with its own jurisdiction. The laws themselves were different, too... with mostly customary, vernacular law in the North and a written code in the South.

What changed? Many things. Railroads and canals made moving around easier. A national system of schools and centralized authority brought a further sense of unity. A national postal service improved the flow of information. But arching over all these things was a myth. It was the myth of the French nation. They weren't just Picardians and Girondins trying to get along with each other. They weren't just

Bretons and Poitevins trying to talk with one another. Instead, they were all French. They shared a common narrative. A common history. A common destiny, that had brought them together and made them citizens of a great nation. And a common enemy: "them."

The "them" changes. Before the Revolution, France's hereditary enemy was England. But France was not yet a nation state, so the antipathy towards the English did not run very deep. The typical resident of the Massif Central or Savoy may have had no idea that the English were an enemy. During the Revolution, "them" were the aristocrats who had escaped the Revolution and were fomenting trouble abroad. This "them" worked throughout the Napoleonic Wars, as France was still surrounded by monarchies, which *les citoyens* regarded as natural and implacable enemies.

Then, after the revolutionary tumult was over, "them" became the Huns. It was the Prussian field marshal Gebhard Leberecht von Blücher, after all, who smashed Napoléon at Waterloo. French troops attacked the Prussians in 1870, but they were quickly and decisively defeated. Humiliated, France's win-lose military caste dreamed of a rematch for the next 40 years. Even then, it was hard for the periphery to keep up with the center.

Not long ago, a friend recounted the story of a recruiter in World War I, who had gone to a small, isolated village to recruit soldiers. One particularly out-of-touch new recruit saluted and replied, "Oui, mon Lieutenant, finally... we'll teach those English a lesson!"

It was fake news, in other words, that created France. And Germany. And Italy. And almost every other country in the world. Fake news created an "us"... and a "them." Fake news is always heavily weighted towards win-lose... and, specifically, towards the most dramatic win-lose deal of all – war.

The level of myth-making depends on the scale of the war. A war between two small, primitive tribes is relatively free from mythical claptrap. It really is "us" against "them," with little pretense of a larger purpose. Almost all modern wars, by contrast, are myth-based. Now, there are rights and wrongs at stake that exist only in an elaborate, highly abstract, and largely mythical space. There are bad guys. And good guys. Needless to say, ultimately, the bad-guy tag is placed on the losers. The Germans were, arguably, no more responsible for World War I than the other combatants. But as the losers, they were named the bad guys. Twenty years later, they got a chance to confirm it.

In today's world, at least for the last few centuries, almost all wars have been supported by instinct and the press but based on myth and nonsense. Taking the U.S. as an example, the revolutionaries of 1776 claimed to be acting in the name of liberty. But there is no evidence that the typical American was appreciably freer after the war than before... or freer than the still-loyal Australian, Canadian, or Englishman. Using taxes as a measure, he was surely less free after the revolution than he had been before. Taxation with representation turned out to be a lot easier to impose and collect than taxation without representation. Taxes were few and feeble before 1776. Government agents were rarely seen.

When the American Revolution concluded in 1783, colonists might have thought themselves finally free from the heavy hand of government. So, when a tax collector showed up in Western Pennsylvania trying to collect a tax on artisanal whiskey production, they rode him out of town on a rail. But soon, Alexander Hamilton was underway... just like the British Major General Edward Braddock before him... leading an army to bring the wild western counties under elite control.

The War of 1812 we will pass over with no comment; it was a war for no apparent purpose, with no apparent gain on either side. The final battle, the Miracle of New Orleans, highlighted the pointlessness of it. As the popular Johnny Cash song puts it, the redcoats "ran through the briars and they ran through the brambles; and they ran through the bushes where a rabbit couldn't go." But they might as well have not run at all. The war had already ended two weeks earlier, with the signing of the Treaty of Ghent.

The War Between the States, on the other hand, was a disaster for both sides. It could be said that it served the useful purpose of freeing the slaves. But that was not Lincoln's intention when he invaded Virginia. Southern politicians won office by proclaiming the myth of God-approved slavery. Northern politicians won office by proclaiming the myth of God-disapproved slavery. There was no way to reconcile the two sides. Still, all other civilized countries also freed their slaves at about the same time, with no need for a war.

The Spanish-American War was a shameful exercise in win-lose imperialism, ginned up by newspapermen Joseph Pulitzer and William Randolph Hearst. Writing to artist Frederic Remington, who he had dispatched to illustrate the revolution erupting in Cuba, Hearst remarked, "You furnish the pictures and I'll furnish the war." The news was largely fake. But the war was real; it sold newspapers.

America participated in World War I largely on the basis of fake news, too – fake atrocities allegedly committed by the Germans, and a fake war goal (to make the world safe for democracy – a strange goal for a country coming in on the side of Britain, which ruled over more non-voting peoples than any government ever had).

Only World War II seems like a fairly straightforward, no-claptrap, no-myth war. After all, the U.S. was attacked. But there's more to the story. The U.S. had already taken over Hawaii under the mythomaniacal banner of "manifest destiny." Perhaps the country had a destiny. But manifest, it certainly was not.

Then, the Roosevelt government put its fleet at Pearl Harbor so that it could throw its weight around in the Pacific. (Some say the real intention was to lure the Japanese to attack.) The U.S. had taken over the Philippines as part of the booty from the Spanish-American War. It then felt a desire to protect its territory. And in 1941, the U.S. cut off Japan from its oil exports, which the Japanese regarded as vital to their war machine.

The Japanese, meanwhile, had their own myth-based military policy. They believed they had a manifest destiny, too – and it involved taking over, by force, much of East Asia in order to secure raw materials for, what else, its defense! In the context of these rival myths, what happened next was almost predictable. The threat of U.S. warships interdicting its supplies of oil was too much for the Japanese to stomach. In response, they did the one, and almost the only, thing they could have done that would have brought destruction to their whole society: they bombed Pearl Harbor.

Before we move along to a more recent example, let us note that none of the "reasons" for war were ever subject to any kind of proof. In the War Between the States, the North said it was "protecting the Union." But what kind of union was it that meant you had to kill a substantial part of the population to get the other party to go along? And why was a "union" a good idea in the first place? And wasn't it completely contrary to the Declaration of Independence, which flatly proclaimed the right of a people to decide for themselves how they would be misgoverned?

Nor in World War I was there any way to prove that democracy was a better system than all the others… or that the world was unsafe for it… or that it could be made safe for it by defeating the Germans and their allies. As for "manifest destiny," the term invites ridicule, not challenge.

In World War II, American men once again rushed to put on uniforms to "protect our country." Or to "defend our liberty." But neither the country nor its liberties were ever seriously in jeopardy. Germany had a two-front war going already; it had no conceivable way to attack America, too. And Japan may have endangered the liberties of others and been capable of bombing an island Navy base, but it had no plausible way to invade the continental United States.

"WELL, IT'S ONE, TWO, THREE… WHAT ARE WE FIGHTIN' FOR?"

But now, we move along to a more recent war and a more modern example of fake news… with devastating real consequences. Beginning in 1950, the U.S. began funding France's war to hold onto Indochina. Even from the get-go, you had to buy into a number of grandiose myths to make sense of it. Why was France in Indochina? And what dog did America have in that fight?

At first gradually, little by little, and then all of a sudden, the U.S. took over the white man's burden, spending more and more money and sending more and more troops. And here we see the full power of fake news in all its sordid glory. There were specific, falsely reported or fabricated "news" stories – such as the second Gulf of Tonkin attack, which the NSA said in 2005 never happened.

That phony attack led to a huge increase in America's bombing and ground-troop campaigns. And there were ongoing, faked reports on the progress of the war – coming from generals in the field and U.S. Secretary of Defense Robert McNamara – which helped keep the American public in the dark about what was really going on.

Here we see how fake myth and fake news work together. There was, of course, the familiar "us versus them" myth. In this case, the "them" was the communists. You had to believe that communism was not just a mistake (which would be self-correcting), but evil (which is a whole 'nuther thing). You had to believe, too, that those people America was trying to kill in Vietnam were communists. (What else did "we" have against them?) You had to also believe that the communists could be stopped. You had to believe it was worth stopping them. You had to believe that, if the communists were not contained in Vietnam, other Southeast Asian nations would fall "like dominos." And of course, you had to believe that it mattered.

In his memoirs, Robert McNamara regretted that nobody ever asked "them." If they had, they might have discovered that the whole war – with as many as 2.5 million casualties – might have been avoided. But Vietnam is a long way from Washington... and from Dubuque, Albuquerque, and San José. The myths stretched out to the point where they were useless and senseless. The information value of the news on the subject – mostly telling Americans that there was light at the end of the tunnel – was negative.

The Washington Post deserves a special cameo appearance in this show. The whole press corps swinishly followed the lead of the Pentagon in providing fake news to readers. Few bothered to question the strategies or check the facts. The press – propagandist, cheerleader, and myth-monger for "us" – rarely questioned the foundational myths of the war.

We only single out *The Washington Post* because it is now hailed as a hero. A movie appeared in 2017, *The Post*, presenting it in a flattering light for its publishing of the "Pentagon Papers." But this was the same paper that was – and still is – a booster for almost every misbegotten military adventure to come along. In the run-up to the Iraq war, for example, American journalist James Bovard reports that *The Washington Post* ran 27 editorials in favor of America's attack on Iraq and 140 front-page articles in support of the Bush administration's arguments for war. Newspapers sell fake wars. Fake wars sell newspapers.

FAKE TRUTH

If mockery is an art, in 2017, Mr. Robert Mueller called out for the talents of a Leonardo. Clean as a whistle. Hard as steel. Incorruptible. Unstoppable. He just kept going… hammering away until he nailed a dangerous felon… or railroaded someone else.

In the public space, some people disseminate fake news. Others pretend to counter the fake news with the truth, which is also fake. In February 2018, after months of investigating Russian meddling in the 2016 U.S. presidential election, Mueller handed in his indictment. Now, it was serious, or so they said. After so many months of rumors, accusations, countercharges, and fake news, with the newspapers following Mr. Mueller day after day, headline after headline, we finally had a federal prosecutor who'd managed to collar a gang of real desperadoes.

Who were these hellish perps? What mayhem and murder had they committed? Had they raped and killed a whole convent of nuns?

Did they plant a charge of dynamite under the Capitol dome? Have they given the nation's nuclear codes to our mortal enemies? Thank God we had crime fighters like Robert Mueller on the job! He was assuring the safety of our citizens and the integrity of their vital institutions.

After months of following clues and spending millions of dollars, at last, he nabbed some fiendish criminals. Who? A retired St. Petersburg police officer, a 31-year-old web designer, and various others who were paid $4-$6 an hour to post messages on the internet! That's right – and here, we turn pale and recoil at the sheer horror of it – they were tweeting… posting… blogging… and generally clogging the worldwide web with messages such as: "Trump is our only hope for a better future."

And now that it was all out in the open, we saw that the whole Russia-meddling-in-U.S.-elections story was nothing but claptrap, as we suspected from the get-go. The Russian government may or may not have been involved. What did it matter? The meddlers spent a trivial amount of money putting out dumb messages, most of which were never delivered and never read. They organized protest marches to which no one showed up… and must have had zero impact on the election.

But wait, five months later, Mr. Mueller came forward with yet more indictments. These included some Russian military personnel; it was alleged that they had hacked into voting software. Here was yet more proof that the Russians had tried to undermine America's democracy.

Except that the whole story was probably fake from the very beginning. Two retired NSA and CIA analysts, William Binney and Ray McGovern, with a combined 63 years of experience, came forward days later and made the astounding charge. They said the hack – made by a program called "Guccifer" – was almost certainly an inside job, carried out by America's own intelligence professionals, who were, apparently, trying to set the Russians up. "Want to know where Guccifer came from?" asked the two intelligence experts. "Ask the FBI." But the mainstream press made Mueller the Hero of the Hour… and the Pride of the U.S. Legal System – proof that the system works!

We wondered what Mueller thought of himself in the dark of night… without his suit and tie… without the public media egging him on… when stark reality hit him like a recurring nightmare. He is not a dumb man. He had taken on a silly, woebegone project; he aided and abetted a fake news story and made a federal case out of nothing. Would future legal scholars regard him as a hopeless laughingstock?

Ronald Reagan used to tell the story of a little boy who was given a pile of manure as his birthday present. The boy dug into the pile joyfully. When asked what he was doing, he replied: "There's got to be a pony in there somewhere."

But there was no pony in the Russiagate story. Just a remarkably dense pile of B.S. myth. You had to believe that U.S. elections were otherwise pristine affairs, in which only registered voters expressed opinions. You had to believe that it mattered what the voters thought, and that it mattered which candidate won… and that the Russian choice would be the wrong one (what would be the problem if Russian interference helped the best candidate win?). You had to believe that there was a "best" candidate… and that voters could know in advance who the best candidate actually was. You had to believe that this candidate would have an effect on the lives of some people, somewhere, and that the Russians had to know this, too, so they could undermine him. On… and on… and on. You had to believe in the myth of elections – that they produce the "right" leader. And in the myth of democracy – that somehow, the will of the people, expressed through elections and public opinion polls, produced a just government with the right to boss the rest of us around.

Of course, nobody really knew any of these things. Nobody knew the future. Nobody knew which candidate would be best-equipped to deal with it. Neither U.S. voters nor Russian meddlers.

"It's the principle of the thing," says the patriot. "I don't want Russians meddling in our elections." But why not? Would the outcome be better or worse? No one knew. As for the principle, it is pure myth and subject to any amendment you care to make. Why shouldn't Russians have a say in U.S. elections? They may be affected by them.

You will say, "They don't pay taxes here." But neither do half the U.S.-based voters.

"But they don't live in the U.S." Neither do thousands of absentee voters.

"They weren't born in the U.S." Neither were millions of other naturalized citizens.

They're not American citizens, either. But why should that be a requirement for voting in U.S. elections? Why should an accident of birth – conferring automatic citizenship – give someone the right to tell others what to do?

You can put the parameters of a myth wherever you want them. Only freeborn, propertied males could vote in ancient Athens – the cradle of democracy. Now, most democracies allow almost all adults to vote. This is the general rule, even where as many as half the voters receive money from the government and, therefore, really should recuse themselves; arguably, they are unable to separate their personal interests from those of the nation.

Many, if not most, eligible voters decide not to participate in the mythic ritual (realizing that their individual votes will have no effect on the outcome). That is, they put the value of their vote at zero. Or deem it to be of so little value as to not be worth the time it takes to exercise it. Many others consider the act of voting to be not just useless, but immoral. Unless it is decisive, a vote has no more substance than an opinion poll. And in the extremely unlikely event that it tips the election, the voter imposes his own prejudices and desires on nearly half the population – who are clearly against them.

In this light, giving the vote to foreigners would not be much of a stretch, since you are giving something that is worthless. Or wicked.

But the Russiagate story was not even about voting, it was about influence – using your time and money to express your opinions in the hope that you would influence others. What myth opposes such a thing? If there is one, it doesn't seem to apply to the U.S. government itself. The aforementioned *Washington Post* reported that the feds have been intervening in foreign elections since the end of World War II. Citing the work of political scientist Dov Levin, the paper showed the U.S. and Russia intervened in a total of 117 elections around the world from 1946 to 2000, an average of two per year.

Sometimes, the interference was "soft" – intentionally spreading fake news and propaganda and financing candidates. Sometimes, U.S. meddlers backed assassinations and/or *coups d'état*. Naturally, these were done in the name of a myth – such as protecting the world from communism and putting in place a more U.S.-friendly regime.

But sometimes, it was just plain win-lose corruption. In 1954, for example, Jacobo Árbenz, democratically elected president of Guatemala, sought to reduce the influence and pare the landholdings of the United Fruit Company. Allen Dulles, then head of the CIA, rarely missed an opportunity to intervene in someone else's business.

Egged on by the United Fruit Company, he recruited, armed, and trained a small force of 480 men. He also set up a fake radio station, the Voice of Liberation, which pretended to be broadcasting from the Guatemalan jungle, but was really doing its recordings in Miami. The broadcasts told Guatemalans what awful people were currently running the government and urged them to support the invaders. As the action on the ground developed, the Guatemalan military would have little trouble defeating the inept CIA forces, but Árbenz feared giving the U.S. a pretext for a full-scale invasion. He resigned. And the CIA-backed military took over.

SOFTWARE OUTLIVES ITS USEFUL LIFE

Driving down the road in rural France one evening, we observed a rabbit in front of the car. The animal feinted to the left, and then to the right, trying to fake-out its pursuer. The tactic, passed along by the survivors of past win-lose encounters, was now embedded as instinct. Had the rabbit been chased by a dog or a fox, it probably would have given him a slight advantage. Against a Nissan Patrol, however, it was counterproductive. Embedded myths, like moral lessons, are dependent on the conditions in which they were derived. Had the animal simply jumped out of the road, it would have survived. The car paid no attention to the feint. It ran right over the rabbit.

The instinct to fight... to defend... to take up arms against an invader... was embedded in a time when the scale of information was much smaller. Back then, all the available information was private. Its quality was very high.

As civilization evolved, with larger and larger communities, information evolved, too. It got bigger and more abundant. But the quality was less sure. Myths filled in for truth. Some were more appropriate to the new circumstances. Others, nourished by the new media, stirred old instincts... and brought disaster.

In 1945, people in Hiroshima went about their business. But things were getting tough for the Japanese. The U.S. controlled the seas and the air. This cut Japan off from its supply lines, leaving it hungry... and without any real means to defend itself. People were already dying of hunger-related diseases – such as tuberculosis and beriberi. Young and old had been enrolled in the war effort, responding to air raid drills daily... with buckets of water at hand to put out fires, and practicing diving under beds to protect themselves from bombs. Every house also had a sharpened bamboo stick at the doorway to fight off American soldiers.

Any sober observer could see that the situation was hopeless. An observer with access to details of the Manhattan Project could see that the threat was existential. Bamboo spears and mattresses were no defense against an atomic bomb. But the Japanese – or some of them, at least – believed that Emperor Hirohito was divine. It might be hard going now. But when they looked ahead, the myth blocked their vision.

They couldn't see how they could lose the war, because that would mean that the Emperor had lost to mortals... and not even Japanese mortals at that.

The Japanese discovered the weakness of this myth on August 6, 1945. It was not only inappropriate, it was deadly. Within seconds, the rabbit was crushed – the center of Hiroshima was obliterated as temperatures rose higher than on the surface of the sun. Steel melted. Internal organs vaporized.

LEAPING TO ABSURDITY

The average man can't know what is in his hotdogs or how his nation's medical system works. Even its weights and measures are a mystery. He believes in ghosts; he doubts that a moon landing ever took place. He wonders how many inches to a gallon. He can't find Ukraine on a map... he believes the Declaration of Independence is a terrorist document... and as for Muslims, he is sure they are up to no good, even though he's never met one. He relies on his elites to deal with these complex matters... and counts on them to treat him fairly. When they don't, he gets a noose in his hands and looks for someone to hang, though not necessarily the fellow who has it coming.

There will always be some people who are stronger, smarter, faster, more charming, better marksmen, more productive, etc. Society always sorts itself into a hierarchical, pyramidal structure, with the elites on top and the masses at the bottom. The elites help the masses by separating good myths from bad ones... facts from lies... and foolish notions from useful ideas. They help administer justice with calm, sensible, common-law courts, rather than lynch mobs. They provide the technical expertise for indoor plumbing and computer networks. They offer spiritual guidance and make the trains run on time.

Elites have power. And power invites corruption. In a modern, large-scale empire, the elites have so much power that double-dealing is almost inevitable. Then, the elites turn the rest of the population into chumps. Instead of challenging and correcting the fake news that motivates the mob, the elites encourage even more extravagant illusions.

We have to annihilate ISIS in Syria or no man in Iowa will be safe. The Fed makes our economy stronger by faking interest rates and flooding it with "savings" (credit) that no one ever saved. The Department of Education can make us smarter... the Department of Defense can make us safer... and the Department of Gender Affairs can make us better human beings. All they need is more power and more money!

The typical citizen is expected to believe six impossible things before breakfast and another half dozen before lunch. He has no easy way of distinguishing a fake myth from the useful myths that are essential to his survival. He's too far away in every sense.

In the 21st century, he hears terrorists pose a threat... and he puts it in the same box as an imminent attack by a hostile tribe. His emotions – not his mind – are engaged. He sees his wife ravaged in front of his eyes... and his children carried off into slavery. He leaps to absurdity... taking up arms against an enemy that exists only as a mythical public artefact... and choosing as his champion the biggest, most self-confident alpha-male numbskull in the tribe.

Then it gets worse.

The "us" enterprise – whether it is a war on terror, a war on drugs, or a war on poverty – depends on keeping "us" in line. Myths need believers. And when people stop believing... Poof! The myth disappears. That's why there is so much pressure to NOT think independently, but instead, to go along with whatever cockamamie program is in the news. That's why you must be *solidaire*, as the French say, with public policy, no matter how absurd it is.

Fortunately for the myths and the people who benefit from them, most people go along. They stand behind their leaders, no matter what pathetic losers they are. And they regard anyone who doesn't as a traitor.

LOCAL HEROES

One November, when we were working in Paris, we turned to our trusty assistant, Beirne. "Beirne," we said gravely, "tell me about Thanksgiving in Mississippi."

Beirne proceeded to tell us about a Mississippi bluesman named "Son" House, who lived to be 86 by doing what bluesmen tended to do… chasing bad luck, bad liquor, and bad women.

"What has that to do with Thanksgiving?"

"Nothing," he replied… whereupon he drew on the resources generously provided by Britannica.com, formerly of Chicago, lately of cyberspace, to get the needed research.

In a country where roots meant almost nothing, where people were ready to pick up and move at the drop of a hat… Thanksgiving served to provide a unified, national myth…

Beirne hails from Mississippi. And Mississippians sit down like the rest of the nation and tuck into their turkeys with equal relish… perhaps only substituting bourbon pecan pie for the sweet potato or pumpkin pie enjoyed in Maryland. But it was not always so.

Somewhere deep in the most primitive part of his medulla oblongata, the part of the brain where race memories are stored, Beirne resists Thanksgiving. It is, after all, a Yankee holiday. In the middle of the War Between the States, both sides would proclaim days of "thanksgiving," following the progress of the war as we now follow the progress of the stock market. After each of the first and second battles of Bull Run – which sent the Yankees fleeing back to Washington – the Confederates proclaimed days of thanksgiving.

But it was Lincoln's day that stuck. Declared after the battle of Gettysburg – the last, great, boneheaded Napoleonic charge of military history – Thanksgiving was set for the last Thursday in the month of November, commemorating the Northern victory. Beirne doesn't say so… but this fact must stick in his craw. It doesn't help that the original celebration took place in Massachusetts. And that it was hosted by a dour bunch of Puritans, who probably wouldn't have been able to enjoy a good dinner if their lives depended on it. But they certainly had a lot to be thankful for.

As *The Wall Street Journal* reminds us annually, they nearly exterminated themselves in typical Yankee fashion – by wanting to boss each other around. Intending to settle in the more hospitable climate of Virginia, which had been colonized more than 10 years before, they had arrived in Massachusetts by accident and bad seamanship. Once in Massachusetts, they proceeded to set up such a miserable community that surely most of them, had they lived, would have longed to return to England.

The Soviets could have learned from their example and spared themselves 70 years of misery. Only after they abandoned their communal form of organization and allowed people to do their own win-win deals did the colony have a prayer of survival. But victors write the history books. And now, this precarious celebration by a feeble group of religious zealots has turned into the most American holiday. After the Battle of Appomattox in 1865, the South was helpless. Its natural leaders, the plantation aristocrats, were either dead, bankrupted, and/or discredited. Many of them went to northern cities like New York or Baltimore, where, American journalist H.L. Mencken tells us, they "arrived with no baggage, save good manners and empty bellies." They enriched the North.

But back home, they were sorely missed. "First the carpetbaggers ravaged the land," says Mencken, "…and then it fell into the hands of the native white trash…" The old elite had been eliminated; a new elite was in town.

Thanksgiving was declared a national holiday in 1863. Through the Depression and then World War II, Thanksgiving grew in importance. There were huge differences in what people thought and how they lived, but Thanksgiving brought them together in an idyllic scene most popularly expressed in Norman Rockwell's 1943 Thanksgiving cover for *The Saturday Evening Post*.

Roots mean more in Mississippi than they do in California. The myths are deeper, richer, with less space between them and the people who live by them. Local myths tend to be useful and subject to constant correction. National myths are often gaudy fantasies.

"No man is himself," said William Faulkner, Oxford, Mississippi's most celebrated alcoholic. "He is the sum of his past." Unlike so many other American writers of the 20th century, Faulkner stayed home.

The foreword to the *Encyclopedia of Southern Culture* has a passage from Faulkner saying, "Tell about the South. What's it like there? What do they do there? Why do they live there? Why do they live at all?"

Even in Faulkner's Mississippi, Thanksgiving is now part of everyone. Where Beirne goes, it goes, too. Even all over the world. But genuine attachments, emotional and cultural, diminish as the scale increases. In other words, the larger the "us," the less us we are.

Our own sense of "us" is extremely limited and combined with a deep skepticism. Even as to our fellow tidewater residents of the Chesapeake Bay area we have our doubts. Our family has been there for more than 300 years, so a DNA test is bound to show a connection to the old families. But how many are still there? And how many are still attached to the land and the seasons? How many still gather up oysters in the bay? And now, when we talk to our young neighbors about cutting or hanging tobacco, they have no idea what we are talking about; they think planting tobacco should be illegal!

The real dividing line between the South and the North is Pratt Street in Baltimore. South of Pratt Street, the land is flat. You can raise field crops. So, field hands – slaves – were in demand. North of Pratt Street, the land rises. It is rocky and hilly – not very good for field crops. Not surprisingly, people there had little use for slaves.

When the Massachusetts Regiment marched through Baltimore on April 19, 1861, it came down Charles Street in good order. When it reached Pratt Street, people began throwing rocks at it. The Yankees fired their guns, producing the first casualties of the War Between the States.

Culture is local. Genuine sentiments and affections are specific, direct, and personal. Love at home is indifference abroad. That's why the contrived "us" is always so disappointing. And the bigger the contrived myth that holds "us" together, the more sterile and puerile it is.

NUMBERS LIE TOO

In early 2017 came news that Maryland had slipped in Bloomberg's ranking of the states based on "gender equality." Bloomberg included a companion report that the Trump administration was hiring "three men for every woman."

Right away, we could feel the greasy water dripping from our skin; splashed by political correctness, now the "us" was meant to be everyone who cared about "equality." We all know the two sexes are different. If they weren't, we'd only have one sex... and about a million fewer jokes... half our libraries would be empty... the internet porn industry would be left as limp and flaccid as a joint session of Congress... and we wouldn't exist.

What shallow and depressing lives these equality warriors must live! Such a simpleton's universe, with no truth, no art, no irony, no genuine sentiment, and no real emotion or authentic beauty. Have they had children? Have they watched a man and a woman dance the tango? How could they believe they were equal in any way?

All they have is numbers, measuring quantity... leaving out the important parts. Imagine the poor dimwit who tells you he has fallen in love. Why? "She is 5'4" tall, weighs 112 pounds, and has an IQ of 125," he says.

A human being can recognize thousands of different faces – each with its own story of heartbreak, betrayal, love, and joy etched on it. A competent chef can whip up an infinite variety of dishes, each with its unique flavor, from hundreds of different ingredients. Look up at the stars at night; you will be awed by the infinite possibilities of an unknowable universe. But a world-improver has only 10 digits to work with, which he piles up like lumps of limburger cheese in a bigger and bigger heap, not noticing that the whole thing stinks. How many women are on corporate boards, they ask? How much does the average woman earn? How many female executives are there? How many women has Trump hired?

Why not ask: How much joy does a woman get from doing what no man can – having a child? How much poetry is in her soul? She lives, on average, six years more than a man; how much is that worth to her? The blind prophet Tiresias of Greek mythology was transformed into a woman by the goddess Hera after striking a snake. The prophet said he got more pleasure from sex as a woman than he did from sex when he was a man. True? The improvers have no idea… The concept is made even more absurd… Bloomberg went on, with no trace of self-awareness or hint of much-needed sarcasm:

> Diversity *"leads to better problem solving, better outcomes, and, in some cases, better financial performance,"* said Brande Stellings, *vice president of corporate-board services at Catalyst, a nonprofit organization that promotes women in the workplace.*

Ms. Stellings didn't fall into the trap of false knowledge. She jumped in and then wallowed in it. Is she saying that if the Wehrmacht had had more female field marshals, it might have won World War II? If there had been women priests aiding the Inquisition, would the heretics have been burned faster?

Better what? Better problem-solving? Better outcomes? Are you kidding? How would anyone know? "Better" is qualitative; it can't be measured with numbers alone. It can be felt and appreciated locally and personally, like an act of kindness, a smile, or a hand on a shoulder when it is needed. But it can't be digitized and projected onto a large screen. Again, it is not that the drive for "equality" is untruthful… it's just that there is no truth in it. It is "public information," based on compound myths and fake news.

We have a friend who has managed to mock the whole business... In Europe – perhaps in the U.S., too – the push for gender equality and transgender rights led governments to allow citizens to choose their own gender. The mischief in this fantasy went unnoticed by almost everyone, but not by our friend.

He has a business. Another of the legislative diktats designed to encourage gender equality required that corporate boards have at least one woman on them. So, he declared himself to be a woman. No operations or drugs were necessary; he was a woman simply because the law gave him the right to be one. Problem solved.

The legislature, in its wisdom, passed the law. The law now says he is a woman. So, there can be no doubt. He is a woman. Women are equal to men, said a further law. So now, he is equal to a man in every way. Even the essential ones.

Athletes have caught on, too. By 2017, "biological males" were setting new records in practically all women's sports. Men and women clearly were not equal when it came to power or speed. But the new drive for "equality" left biological women coming in second or third.

"But wait," we can hear readers reply. "This is not just about myth. Shouldn't women be treated equally in the workplace? Shouldn't they be paid equally for equal work? Isn't that what it is all about? Isn't that real?"

MYTHS IN COLLISION

The streets were crowded when we visited Barcelona in April 2018. On the main *Ramblas*, so many people were strolling about, we could barely cross the intersection. Many of the women held single red roses.

It was the Day of Roses and Books, Sant Jordi's Day, in the Catalan capital city. Women are given roses to celebrate the slaying of the dragon by Sant Jordi in the fourth century. Men are given books, coincidentally, to recall the deaths of the two giants of Western letters,

William Shakespeare and Miguel Cervantes, both of whom died on about the same day, April 23, 1616.

Myths and legends, like political slogans, federal budget projections, and declarations of eternal love, are not subject to proof. According to legend, the town of Montblanc in Catalonia had a dragon infestation. In order to keep the dragon satisfied, the town fed it one person every day. And the person selected for April 23, 303, was – improbably – the town's princess. It was on this day that Sant Jordi – Saint George – a Christian knight, showed up and quickly went to work. He drove his lance into the beast. The dragon was killed. Its blood spilled upon the ground. And from the blood-soaked ground grew a red rose.

The story is probably fake news. If historians are to be believed, the real Saint George was not in Montblanc that day in 303. Instead, he was in Nicodemia, undergoing the kind of punishment that Donald Trump proposed to give drug dealers. Saint George offered religion. Christianity, to be specific. And Emperor Diocletian had declared war on Christians. He ordered that all Christian soldiers were to be arrested. According to this account, George refused to renounce his religion. His head was cut off, making him a martyr to the cause.

As we have already seen, history is cluttered with fake news. The bare facts may be reported correctly. But the facts lack all sense and meaning unless you put them in context. In addition to the what, where, and when, you need a "why." And the "why" is almost always so distorted by time, delusion, and wishful thinking – not to mention distance and scale – that meaning is more myth than reality.

Barcelona's streets – at least in this part of town – are wide, with a center strip for pedestrians, and protected from the Mediterranean sun by sycamore trees on both sides. Buildings are handsome, nineteenth- or early-twentieth-century constructions, many with elaborate, overhanging balconies, often set distinctively on the corners, and often enclosed in stained glass.

Architecture is important; the city is often remembered as the home of Antoni Gaudí, whose works are remarkably inventive, clever, and playful. But when he began his career, it was not at all clear where he would end up. When he graduated from his architecture school, his class director said: "Today, we give this degree to either a fool or a genius. Time will tell."

We went to visit the pride of Barcelona, the Sagrada Família, an extraordinary cathedral designed by Gaudí, to make up our own mind. Gaudí was a devout Christian. He saw the cathedral as a way to express his profound, and perhaps very original, faith. It is breathtaking. And it shows what you can do when you are daring enough.

Gaudí began the building in 1882. He kept at it – off and on, sometimes living on site – for the next 44 years. Then, crossing the street, and perhaps looking back to admire his creation, he was struck by a tramway car and died. At that point, people were still not quite sure whether he was a genius or a fool, but they knew he was extraordinary. Thousands of them came to the funeral and accompanied the body into the crypt of the church he had designed.

We have done a little "experimental" building ourselves. Many years ago, we built an in-ground, solar-heated "hobbit house" out of ferro-cement. As far as we know, no one had ever before built a house like that in the entire U.S. And no one ever did after. Because departing from the traditional designs and evolved vernacular architecture is a form of arrogance, and almost always a mistake. At least we were modest enough to keep it to a small scale and paid for it with our own money. Not Gaudí. Every detail, from the doorway to the soaring towers to the windows and altar, is big, staggering, new, and bold.

Boldness in architecture is usually a dismal failure. And for good reason. It took hundreds of years for the pleasing, familiar shapes of traditional architecture to evolve. Arches were developed 2,000 years ago. Columns, maybe 3,000 years ago. These, and many of the "classical" shapes we take for granted, are physical forms of condensed wisdom, information, and style. They're like that for a reason – like language and manners – even if we don't know what the reason is. The "moral" of the story may not be obvious, but that doesn't mean there isn't one.

After World War I, architects consciously rejected the past. And when you reject the lessons of the past – whether in economics, religion, marriage, manners, morals, or aesthetics – you risk creating monsters. The Russians, for example, rejected the conventions of bourgeois capitalism, and created the catastrophe that was the Soviet Union. The Brazilians rejected organic, traditional architecture, and created their capital city – Brasília – while architects the world over, such as those of the Bauhaus school, intentionally stripped their buildings of the ornaments and refinements of the past in order to give them a new, modern look.

And in economics, to which we will return until we are sick to death of it, classical insights were rejected in favor of claptrap modern theories – especially those of John Maynard Keynes. The result? A monstrous mess, which we will take up in the next chapter.

EQUAL PAY FOR EQUAL WORK

And with that preface, we return to the question posed at the end of the last section: Shouldn't women get equal treatment in the workplace? The question was put to us by one of our female colleagues in Barcelona.

"How would we know?" we replied.

This was not the answer that would bring a smile to her lips. We fear that many readers' lips are turning down, too. But we are exploring the role of fake news and myths, and "equality" is one of the great myths of our time. Not just equality in the workplace, but equality in all manner of settings. And not just between men and women, but between people of different races, creeds, club memberships, hair colors, and just about everything else.

It's a founding principle of the United States, where "all men [including women] are created equal." They are equal before the law. They are meant to be treated equally by the police and by the government.

Laws require that businesses not discriminate against certain categories of them.

But we all know it isn't true. Maybe it is a noble lie. Or an ignoble one. People are not equal in any way. They get stopped by the police at different rates – depending on where they live. They pay different insurance premiums. They pay different tax rates. They run at different speeds. Some are fat. Some are skinny. Some are smart. Some are dumb. Each is different.

The idea of equal pay for equal work is a myth on several levels. We've been in business for 40 years. We've never seen two people do equal work. Each one works differently. Some better. Some worse. Even where the output is roughly even, one requires more handling than the other. One is more loyal. One is more fun to work with.

The only place where we have seen roughly equal pay for equal work is in the vineyards, where grape pickers are paid for each container of grapes they fill. This is as close to equal pay for equal work as you can get. Vineyard owners are completely color- and gender-blind. They don't care who picks the grapes… just so long as they get picked. But guess what? Female pickers end up with only about half to two-thirds as much money as the men. On average, they just don't pick as many grapes.

Is that fair? It is just? Is it equal?

You see the problem. Myths collide. There are four of them, that we can think of, coming together in this example.

Myth #1: People should be able to decide between themselves how much each is paid. After all, it's a free world. We allow win-win deals. Either side can walk away.

Myth #2: People should be paid the same thing for the same work (as with piece workers, commission salesmen, and profit sharers).

Myth #3: Women should be paid the same amount as men when they have the same job description and responsibilities.

Myth #4: Women and men should earn the same amount,

regardless of output.

All are myths. Unless you have the judgment of God Himself, there is no way of knowing which is "better" or "worse."

Gaudí's work is exceptional. Yes, it looks a little like it has escaped from some eccentric's back yard and been enlarged 1,000 times. But it is breathtakingly original and refreshingly *sui generis*. We have seen hundreds of churches... but none like the Sagrada Família. It turns its back on traditional architecture in favor of bold new shapes and imaginative designs. It is exhilarating, like meeting an attractive lunatic. But our guess is that it is an evolutionary dead end. Because time hides its lessons in tradition. We don't really know why chimney tops have corbelling... or why many languages have a "subjunctive mood"... or why people smile and say "good morning," even to total strangers. But they do.

Even music follows patterns which most people cannot identify, but nevertheless recognize. Listening to a song you never heard before, one note follows the next, so that the next note is not exactly predictable, but can be anticipated. If the notes are too predictable, the song is boring. If they are too unexpected, the music is unsatisfying and discordant, like the music of John Cage or Meredith Monk.

Rules are made to be broken, of course. You could just say, "Go to hell" to everyone you meet. Some people do. But they are rare... and rarely have much social or business success. Readers are invited to try it... and report back.

We don't know exactly why the traditional "rules" are what they are. And we don't know the consequences of breaking them. But there is almost always a price to pay. As Emerson tells us, "all the world is moral."

In 404 B.C., the war between Athens and Sparta ended. It was an on-again, off-again war... for over 27 years. At low points, the Athenians wanted to stop the killing. But the Greek statesman Pericles, in the famous funeral oration recalled by the historian Thucydides, bade them continue:

So died these men as becomes Athenians. You, their survivors, must determine to have as unfaltering a resolution in the field, though you may pray that it may have a happier outcome.

Bad advice. The Athenians, urged on by Pericles, went back onto the battlefield. By the end of the war, almost all of Athens' soldiers had been killed, or captured and enslaved. "Put your sword back in its place," said Jesus.

The gods are jealous; they don't like to see people contradict or ignore their "natural" laws. They have their moral rules, and woe to the poor mortal who defies them. One of the "rules," learned over thousands of years of bitter experience, was the one that Athens ignored: you shouldn't go to war unless you have to. "He who lives by the sword, dies by the sword," is an expression attributed to the Greek Aeschylus, or the Gospel of Matthew. Dying by the sword is not something most people would like to do. The reasonable inference is that you should avoid picking fights.

But that lesson is easy to forget. Especially when you get too big for your britches. Then, you can pick fights with people who pose no real threat to you. That is what the Pentagon has done since the end of World War II, using fake myths to rally support. These fake myths are intentional uses of myth-making to gain money, status, and power.

Real myths arise naturally, organically, like the other key innovations of civilization. They evolved long ago. They were developed, unconsciously, by people now dead, for reasons we can never fully understand. Fake myths engage the self-interest of living people for reasons that are all-too-obvious. Today, no sparrow can fall anywhere in the world without a push from the Pentagon and a payoff to a crony arms dealer. In other words, these are not fools behind these lethal U.S. adventures. Instead, they are knaves.

WHY WE LOVE FAT PEOPLE

Tradition – often expressed in aphorisms, rules, adages, and proverbs – distills the lessons of centuries. Individuals do not always see the benefits of following these rules; often, there are none… for them. As mentioned earlier, the "survival machine" is the group, not the individual.

We have spent many years living in Europe. And every year, in the springtime, restaurateurs and hoteliers begin making jokes about the invasion of the "fat Americans" that is about to begin. They reinforce their chairs and floors. They increase food portions and raise prices. Beds are examined; elevators are tested; doctors are put on alert.

Why does nature put up with so much obesity? The fat person is slower – making him an easy and choice target for beasts of prey. He is less able to defend himself from enemies, too. Nor is he much help in the hunt. Why, then, does he exist? The answer, of course, is obvious. An individual may or may not benefit, individually, from his culture. He may be born into a war-like, Spartan culture, for example; yet he may be soft and sensitive, with a poetic soul. Or a girl may be born into a culture that believes in female genital mutilation; half the population may be victims. Or the culture may call for the sacrifice of the first-born child – hard cheese for them!

Myths are often harmful to individuals (think of the virgins tossed into volcanoes… think of the draftees in the Great War), but they may still confer an advantage on the group. "Thou Shalt Not Kill" may not be the best rule in individual cases, for example. Imagine that you were King David and saw Bathsheba bathing on the roof; you'd be better off if you could get her husband, Uriah the Hittite, out of the way. Or suppose you had a chance to kill Adolf Hitler in the trenches in 1918; wouldn't we all be better off if you had pulled the trigger? Alas, we never know the future. For all we knew in 1918, the young Hitler might have grown up and discovered a cure for cancer.

Still, groups that don't believe in killing each other seem to have an advantage, at least in the modern world. And myths, though they might be a nuisance for individuals, could still benefit the group. The myth that Pharaoh was divine, for example, might have helped unite the people of the Nile Delta and enabled them to operate a complicated irrigation system. Even building the pyramids – though perhaps it did nothing positive for the thousands who labored on them – may have brought some benefit in terms of social cohesion or sense of purpose.

So, too, a group's survival may be enhanced when it has members who, on their own, are poorly adapted for survival. Fat people, for example. Before the Agricultural Revolution... and long before the invention of canning, curing, and refrigeration... it was difficult to store food. A tribe lived hand to mouth. If the weather turned against it... or hunts produced no meat... it could quickly be close to starvation.

The cats and dogs would be slaughtered, with the least loved doomed first. (When a dog wags his tail, it's not because he likes you; he just doesn't want to be eaten.) Then mice, rats... whatever they could find. Having someone in the tribe who naturally packed on a few extra pounds was like an insurance policy. *In extremis*, he could survive... or be consumed by the others. In either case, he might ensure the survival of the tribe. His own sluggishness might help the others survive, too. Imagine that the tribe was being chased off its land by fierce warriors from another tribe. They might kill the fat boy and take time to eat him, giving the others a chance to get away.

As recently as the early 20th century, explorers and anthropologists in the Amazon reported encountering a tribe with two relatively fat girls among an otherwise thin group. Asked for an explanation, they were told that the girls had been captured from another tribe as children... and that they were being fattened for a feast. The girls may not reproduce. But they may help others do so.

In the ancient world, fatness may have been an advantage to the individual (who was able to survive a famine) and/or to the group (which survived because of him). In today's world, it seems out of fashion, as incompatible with modern life as an Adam's apple is with shaving.

Fatness no longer appears to give an advantage to the individual or the group. It is widely frowned upon, like bad table manners. But buried deeper than myths, or even instincts, the phenomenon persists.

And why do men and women still marry each other? The union probably provided a benefit to early groups. But now, marriage rates are falling. Is it no longer needed, or inappropriate?

"We're not married," said a young friend recently. "We just live together. It's got to work for us both. And when it doesn't work, well, we don't want to be stuck in a loveless marriage."

"Well," we replied, speaking from much experience, "it doesn't work every day!"

People often chafe against the rules and restraints of tradition. And civilization. They build zany cathedrals. They kill one another. And why not? Why should they be bound by old wives' tales and silly old conventions, they wonder. Why should music follow scales and patterns? Aren't we smart enough to figure things out for ourselves? Can't we intentionally and intelligently rise above these "irrational" restrictions?

In his great novel, *Crime and Punishment*, Dostoyevsky explored the subject. The protagonist, Raskolnikov, is convinced that he is above and beyond the rules that other civilized people obey. He challenges the most widely held taboo in Christendom: Thou Shalt Not Kill.

Today, most people believe that murder is not only illegal, but immoral; you shouldn't do it, even if you're sure you could get away with it.

Dostoyevsky's lead character discovers that there is more to these prohibitions than just the law, or any other obvious result that can be tallied or measured. There is conscience, for example, a residual feeling, or a kind of hard-wired sense of right and wrong. That's the whole idea of morality… that there are consequences, often unseen and unexpected. You can tell yourself you didn't drink too much last night. But that doesn't mean the headache goes away!

And poor Florence Newton. The young woman was tried as a

witch in Youghal, Ireland in 1661. It was alleged that she kissed another woman "violently" and that the victim experienced fits, cramps, and visions. In another instance, she kissed the hand of an imprisoned man, who subsequently died. Today, we think of "witchcraft" as hocus-pocus. We deny any cause-and-effect relationship between Ms. Newton's kiss and the prisoner's death. Myth, in other words.

Today, sorcery has no more truth in it than a campaign promise. But a kiss is still a kiss. A penny saved is still a penny earned. And a fool and his money are still soon parted.

And now, we return to the critical question, the one that drove Nietzsche crazy and got Socrates killed: How do we know if what we are doing is good... or bad?

We've seen that myths collide. We've seen that even real, useful myths go out of style and get out of date. We've seen that they can be manipulated and used to mislead and harm.

We've seen, too, that the vernacular rules of civilized life are not the product of intellect. They are the consequence of trial and error. Turn your back on them and you court disaster. But courting disaster is what some people are bound to do. Just as some people are programmed to get fat and others are programmed to go to war, still others can't resist wanting to try something new. The society that stops them from doing so also stops the learning process and its own development.

To simplify, there are two kinds of innovation – technical and social. Technical innovations are brought about consciously (with some measure of luck involved) and then accumulate. One advance can lead to others, and to what we know as progress. Social innovations are much less subject to conscious thought and intentional effort; rather, they are the result of something much more elusive, like evolution, where we don't know exactly why we do what we do (we invent explanations after the fact). Real myths are those social innovations that rest on generations of experience, contribute to the survival of the species, and are compatible with modern civilization. Fake myths are those that spring from conscious or semi-conscious reasoning, often driven by self-interest. How to tell them apart?

We give you four tests:

1. Time

As we've seen, time weakens information. But it strengthens myths. How long has the myth survived? Generally, the older, the better. Myths survive when they tell us something useful... often some enduring truth that would be painful or impossible to learn on our own.

The idea of saving money, for example, is ubiquitous and as old as the hills. "If you don't save for your retirement, you could end your days in misery," say the old timers. But you only live once. You can't learn this lesson on your own. If you reach retirement age, and haven't saved, it's too late to say: "Okay... I won't do that again." You must learn it from the experience of others... by following the myths, old wives' tales, and moral lessons of the past.

Short cut: If the myth is of recent vintage, give it a few centuries; see how it holds up.

2. Simplicity

"Thou Shalt Not Kill" is only four words. Easy to remember. A "clash of civilizations" or "global climate change" take whole books to explain. They are probably 90% fake – too big, too vague, too grandiose to be useful. Real myths are easy to understand and require no complex assumptions to make sense of them. Their simplicity makes them useful for individuals, who can use them for moral guidance. Fake myths – based on counterfeit knowledge and compound presuppositions – are invitations to mischief.

Short cut: The simpler it is, the more likely it is to be useful.

3. Universality

"A bird in the hand" may or may not be worth two in the bush. But the adage tells us something important that will work on a small scale as well as on a large one: Beware of empty promises and guesswork about the future.

On the other hand, every fool knows that the "deficits don't matter" myth won't work on an individual basis. But he imagines that there might be some magic that makes it work on a large scale.

And yes, of course, the feds can get away with more foolishness for longer – and on a much bigger scale – than you can. But nature doesn't change just because you've got a gun in your hand and a printing press in the basement. Deficits might not matter to the debtor, but we can't all be debtors. Someone must lend. The bird must come from somewhere.

Short cut: If the myth can be useful to anyone and everyone, it is probably worth paying attention to.

4. Violence

The surest test is this: Is the myth backed by win-win or by win-lose? Today's useful myths benefit anyone who takes them seriously. The saver. The hard worker. The generous spirit. The caring parent. The good neighbor. And they do so without harming anyone else. The saver is better off. But so is the borrower; he has more funds available. The hard worker adds to the world's wealth, not just his own. The generous spirit helps others… and himself. The caring parent spares his children the crippling effect of too much money and too little affection. The good neighbor builds a good fence.

The convenient lie, on the other hand, is win-lose. It only benefits some people – at other's expense. "Us" versus "them." Mexicans, terrorists, Muslims, Catholics, drug dealers – you can choose any "them" you want. Someone will find a way to make it pay. Great for demagogues, witch hunters, and cronies. Everybody else loses.

No myth backed by violence is too loony, too murderous, or too counterproductive not to be cherished for centuries. Using the violence that is theirs... the feds burn witches at the stake; they hang Irishmen, Catholics, and blacks... they send Jews and Gypsies to the gas chambers... they put the guillotine to work on the necks of aristocrats in Paris and shoot the counterrevolutionaries in St. Petersburg. They tax, regulate, control, fix prices, pay off cronies, go to war... backed by large-scale violence and myths so absurd as to make gods chuckle...

Short cut to myth-testing: If the myth requires backing up by the feds, it is almost surely a convenient lie, not a useful myth.

Now that we have our tests, let's apply them: Equal pay? Or free pay? Should the feds force employers to pay equal amounts to men and women? Or should people be free to decide for themselves who works for whom at what compensation?

1. Time

Free pay wins; it's an older myth.

2. Simplicity

Equal pay is a huge idea, and almost impossible to administer. What's "equal" work? Free pay is a concept that can be used by anyone, anywhere. Employer and employee can decide for themselves... as they have for thousands of years. Free pay is simpler; it wins.

3. Universality

Free pay again... the "equal pay" rule can only be applied in favor of some people and against others.

4. Violence

Equal pay would have to be forced onto people. Resistance would have to be punished. Free pay requires no enforcement. It wins again.

And how about looking at it from the abiding premise of this book, that "win-win" deals are more appropriate to a modern, civilized society than "win-lose" deals? "Free pay" is a classic win-win; both sides come out ahead, or they wouldn't make the deal. "Equal pay" is a win for the person whose salary is raised, by force, and a lose for the person paying it. Free pay wins again.

So, free pay is the useful myth. Equal pay is a fake.

We've ranged far and wide in this chapter. But the important thing to remember is that we are a myth-making species. Primitive myths ("I'll watch your back; you watch mine") evolved with humans, and probably made it possible for us to survive on the African savannah. But real myths – such as "us versus them" – are adapted to very different circumstances in a zero-sum world that no longer exists.

These ancient myths and instincts make people easy to manipulate. As the scale of their societies increases, the quality of information degrades with time and space, forcing people to rely on jingos and jackasses, often with disastrous consequences.

&— CHAPTER 7 —&

Win-Lose Money

You shall do no wrong in judgment, in measures of length or weight or quantity. You shall have just balances, just weights, a just ephah, and a just hin [units of dry measure].
– Leviticus 19:35-36

✝·✝··✝··✝·

WHAT'S SO IMPORTANT about a "just" measure? In this chapter, we try to figure it out.

And continuing our Bible reading, we find this in Genesis 3:19:

> *¹⁹ By the sweat of your brow will you have food to eat.*

If you want money, in other words, you have to earn it. And earning it means satisfying a customer or a boss. It means giving something in order to get something.

If you want to get ahead financially, if we were to put it in terms of rules, we could list them as follows:

1. Work hard
2. Learn as much as you can
3. Save your money
4. Invest wisely in things you know.

Or hold up a liquor store.

There are always dishonest ways to get what you want, too. Less violent than robbing a liquor store is printing up counterfeit money. And laying on the ground in front of us like an unexploded bomb in a playground is another Bible quote, this time from Proverbs 21:6:

> *⁶ Wealth created by a lying tongue is a vanishing mist and a deadly trap.*

As long-term readers of our daily blog, *Bill Bonner's Diary*, know, we are connoisseurs of financial disaster. Give us a 1922 deutschmark – an excellent vintage! If you had bought a house in Berlin in 1921, you could have paid off your mortgage in 1923 for the price of a cup of coffee. Or how about a Zimbabwe dollar from 2006? That was a great year. Plenty of liquidity. We used to carry a 10 trillion Zim dollar note in our wallet, and we have a 100,000 deutschmark note on the wall of our office, too; both remind us not to trust paper money.

But the South American blends are good, too. Both Brazil and Argentina have produced some fine catastrophes. In Argentina, the inflation rate hit about 5,000% in 1989. The Argentines had tried to dodge their just desserts by replacing the discredited peso with a new currency, the austral, in 1985. By 1994, the austral had been discredited, and it was back to the peso. Meanwhile, one of our colleagues recalls what it was like living in Brazil in the 1980s:

> *When Dad got paid, we'd meet him at the office. And then, we'd take the money right over to the grocery store. We had to get there as soon as possible, because they marked the prices up all day long. If you waited, you'd get a lot less for your money. And there might not be anything left to buy.*

There are many different vintages of disaster. There are natural disasters, such as the explosion of Vesuvius, which wiped out the Roman city of Pompeii in the first century. There are military disasters, such as

Japan's attack on Pearl Harbor in 1941, or the French attack on Russia in 1812. There are political disasters, too, such as the French Revolution or the *coup d'état* in Russia in 1917. The financial disasters are more amusing. They're more comic than tragic, unless they lead to disasters of the other sort. And fraudulent money, or too much money that you didn't actually earn, is almost always the culprit.

And right now, a classic catastrophe is developing in Venezuela. The bolívar – the Venezuelan currency – lost about 99.99% of its value last year. In April 2018, the *Financial Times* reported that 5,000 people were leaving Venezuela every day. At that rate, the country would be completely empty by 2038.

Financial disaster, often spawned by counterfeit, win-lose money, usually leads to social, political, military, and health disasters. Were it not so, the coming U.S. financial crisis would be merely entertaining. After all, who cares if rich people lose money?

For poor people, though, the stakes are higher.

As if to demonstrate this, by July 2018, inflation in Venezuela had reached 82,766%. In other words, if you bought a pack of cigarettes for $5 in June, you could expect to pay $4,138 by the end of July. But by the end of the year, new estimates put the rate of inflation at 1,000,000%!

When the money goes, everything seems to go with it. The economy, the government, order, morality, right and wrong – all go into a twilight zone, where you don't know who to trust or what is going on.

The 2017 rise in oil prices was supposed to give Venezuela a little breathing room. Oil is the country's biggest asset and its main export. And the state-owned oil giant, PDVSA, was supposed to rescue the nation. But it was too late. The vernacular – the vast web of thoughts and deals that make up everyday life for everyday people – had been so corrupted and distorted that it couldn't react normally. Venezuela could no longer take advantage of opportunities or respond to crises.

Wages could not keep up with inflation. *The New York Times* highlighted the case of a typical rig worker, who stayed on the job for the entire month of May yet earned only enough to buy one chicken. No longer able to feed their children on their earnings, workers walked off the job. Or drove off. Trucks disappeared. So did wrenches and copper pipes. Even with a higher oil price, income fell for the company... the state... and the remaining employees. What was a man to do? Leave! The newspapers reported that Venezuelans were rushing the borders to escape, often taking little more than the clothes on their backs with them.

More than 1.5 million Venezuelan refugees already live in Colombia. They scrounge for food. They pick through trash for something they can eat... or use. They work at pick-up jobs or as prostitutes and sleep rough under bridges or in parks.

"We are dying of hunger," said a refugee to the *Financial Times*. "Three members of my family have already died of hunger."

Back in Venezuela, most hospitals have no medicine, and little or no running water. Lack of food, medicine, and sanitation makes people more vulnerable to illness – especially communicable diseases.

After a 40% drop in output, 90% of the Venezuelans still living in the country are said to be impoverished. "Extreme poverty" has tripled in the last four years. Law and order are breaking down, too, both in Venezuela and in neighboring countries.

Those who do manage to get across the border to Colombia or Brazil often find little hospitality. There are so many of them that local services are overwhelmed. Jobs are scarce. And few people are happy to have so many desperate refugees on their doorsteps.

But how do these crises happen? And why tell you about them? You don't live in Venezuela. Or in Zimbabwe. This isn't Germany in the early 1920s.

And no, we're not predicting that the U.S. is going to turn into Venezuela, Zimbabwe, or the Weimar Republic of Germany. But there are causes and there are effects in the financial world. And traps. And disasters. And they all follow familiar patterns. Everybody wants more money. And they want to get it in the fastest, easiest way possible. For a government, that means taxing, borrowing, and printing it.

At first – a process that can last decades – no harm is visible. Then, the spending continues to increase, and the debts mount up. In an effort to "stimulate" the economy and grow out of debt, governments spend even more. And borrow more. And print more, if they can get away with it. Soon, they are trapped by their own bad faith, bad money, bad debt, and bad spending. Nobody wants a financial disaster. But the easiest way out of the crisis at that point is to print more and more money... until the whole economy blows up.

An economic system is a natural thing. Like all natural things, it obeys laws that were never proposed by a legislature and that cannot be repealed by a majority vote. You can tell yourself that a dollar is a dollar, but there's a big difference between the pre-1971 U.S. dollar and the post-1971 buck.

Real money must be a "just" measure of wealth. That is, it must be connected to real things, especially to the least forgiving of real things – time.

Real money is a claim on real things. With it, you can buy the time of others. Or their stuff. It is easiest to think of it as a claim on something specific and tangible. When you give your car to a valet parking service, for example, you are given a ticket. That ticket, like money, is information. It tells the world that you have a claim on that car. If the valet service were to print up additional claim tickets and pass them around, the information content of those new tickets would be false. The tickets would say that other people had a claim on your car. But while the fraudsters could print more tickets, they couldn't create more autos. So, the whole picture would be distorted and confused by scammy information.

In Venezuela, again we see the consequences of unjust money. In August 2018, it took nearly 200,000 bolívar to buy a single egg. But because of government price-fixing, a liter of gas cost only one bolívar.

With one U.S. dollar trading for 3,500,000 bolívars on the country's black market, it would have been theoretically possible to buy nearly a million gallons of gas for one American greenback.

Nature does not disappear just because you act like a fool. Instead, she sneers and laughs. Nor does truth cease to exist because you deny it. Markets – based on voluntary, win-win exchanges – tell the truth. They don't set prices; they discover them. They provide new information. They surprise you by telling you something you didn't know.

Markets go up and down all the time – sometimes sharply. People never know in advance what things are worth. One person asks; another bids. Where they come together is the market-clearing "price." Collectively, through markets, prices impose order and reveal truth.

Of course, human beings tend to overdo it. They get overly optimistic or overly pessimistic... driving prices too high or too low... causing mini-booms and panics. In the U.S., between the end of the War Between the States and the Great Depression, there was the Panic of 1873, the Panic of 1884, the Panic of 1893, the Panic of 1901, the Panic of 1907, and the Depression of 1920-21. The pain and damage caused by these setbacks varied. But generally, they came and went.

Bidders and askers never know in advance what is too high or too low. But markets quickly adjust. Prices rise and fall. Companies flourish... and go broke. Entrepreneurs and speculators succeed and fail. And when they fail, others are ready to pick up the pieces... and get back to work.

Anyone can make a mistake. But if you want a real catastrophe, you need violence – to force people to do what they otherwise wouldn't and prevent them from discovering the truth or correcting errors. That is, you need government.

Before the stock market crash of 1929, the Coolidge administration cut taxes, ran a budget surplus, and paid off a quarter of the national debt. By the time the crash of 1929 came, Calvin Coolidge was already out of office. But his Treasury Secretary, Andrew Mellon, had been picked up by Herbert Hoover, and he brought the spirit of the Coolidge administration with him. So, when the stock market crash came, Mellon knew what to do – let the dead wood burn itself out. He knew that a limit had been reached… and that the crisis was simply getting rid of mistakes – bad debts and bad investments – so that the economy could begin again with fresh growth.

In the Depression of 1920-21, the feds stayed out of it and the economy quickly recovered. But by 1929, instead of letting the markets correct mistakes, the feds intervened. As economist Murray Rothbard demonstrates in his book, *America's Great Depression*, the authorities attacked with a barrage of wage, price, trade, and industry controls (aka win-lose deals imposed by force) that prevented the markets from clearing properly. The result was a depression that lasted, off and on, until World War II.

Instinctively, we know that you can't make people rich by giving them pieces of paper with green ink on them. We know that stocks aren't infinitely valuable… that we won't live forever… and that something always happens to prevent things from getting too far out of whack. Or, to put it another way, things get out of whack… but then, they always get back into whack somehow. There are feedback loops… corrections… and reckonings. There are alarms that go off, bells that sound the hours to tell us when we're staying up too late… and headaches to tell us when we've had too much to drink. There are bosses to tell us when we're doing a bad job… and priests to tell us when we are bad people. And what else are husbands and wives for? They remind us when we are acting like a damned fool.

There are limits. The biggest of them all is time. Credit is offered by the Fed and the banking system. It is used by Wall Street to run up asset prices. But it is paid back by the Main Street economy, where all the win-win deals are made. Debt is offered in dollars, yuan, yen, or euros. But it is paid back in time.

It's always time we run out of. We meant to save for our

retirement… We meant to stop eating so much… We meant to say something to someone we cared about, but time got away from us… We meant to spend more time with our parents when they were still alive… or more time with our children when they were still little. But we didn't have enough time. We ran out. We would have… we should have… we could have… But we ran out of time. Even the richest person in the world runs out of time, just like we do.

In a financial system, counterfeiters – including central banks – can put out an almost infinite amount of money… like those fraudulent valet parking claim tickets. And once an economy accepts fake money, the feds can keep it supplied, almost indefinitely. So what's the limit? What goes wrong? Where is the brick wall that we know, instinctively, is out there?

As you will see, of course, it's time.

"Can any one of you by worrying add a single hour to your span of life?" Jesus asks in his famous "Lilies of the Field" sermon. Of course, you can't.

Everything you do takes time. It takes time to make a car. It takes time to park a car. So, when money is created "out of thin air," it is a claim on time. Money can be used to buy a car or park a car. But if the money is borrowed, more time is needed to pay the interest on the loan. And it will take time – future time – to pay back the principle, too. So, when you are borrowing money, you are essentially borrowing time.

There is a way to estimate how much time you can borrow… before you run into a brick wall. By long tradition – which, remember, distills valuable experience – debtors are generally comfortable bearing debt equal to about 1.5 times their annual income… but not much more. Since time is money, a clearer way to put this is: You can afford to borrow one and a half hours from the future for every hour you work in the present.

But the ratio in the U.S. today is 1-to-3.4. Taken as a whole, and using GDP as a stand-in for hours worked, the economy owes 3.4 hours of future work for every hour of current employment. Or, assuming the typical citizen puts in 50 weeks on the job annually, he's on the hook for 170 weeks – 3.4 years of work – to pay off his share of household, corporate, and government debt.

That's why interest rates are so important. If you earn $100,000, net of taxes, and you owe $150,000 at a 2% interest rate, that means you will spend seven and a half days working just to keep up with the interest repayments. But if you make $100,000 after taxes, and you owe $150,000 at 5%, you have to work four weeks just to keep up. You're running out of time.

Time is what gets us all. We run out of it. Everyone in the world is running out of time. And it can't be stretched. It can't be printed. It can't be saved up, stitched up, or revved up.

The BBC reports that global income is about $70 trillion, with median household incomes of about $10,000… or about $5 an hour. Global debt may be as high as $250 trillion. At a 3% interest rate, that's $7.5 trillion per year of interest… or 1.5 trillion hours of work… or about 300 hours for every working adult. Or about two months of the year. Now, raise the interest rate to 5%… What happens is obvious. You're out of time… and out of luck.

1971 AND ALL THAT

Now, let's back up and look at the path on which we are now dependent. America's central bank – the Federal Reserve – was set up in 1913. Its ambitions were modest – to protect the currency and make sure the big banks made money. This it did cautiously at first, by, as Fed chief William McChesney Martin described it, "taking away the punch bowl" when the party started to get out of hand, or "leaning into the wind" when the storms blew up. Then, the Fed began making wind itself. And soon, it was the life of the party.

On August 14, 1971, Richard Nixon was worried. He was afraid of interrupting America's favorite TV show, *Bonanza*. But he had something important to say, something completely asinine and thoroughly appalling.

The following day, on the Feast of the Assumption, according to the Catholic calendar, he announced that henceforth, wages and prices would be subject to federal control, and that foreign central banks could no longer go to the "gold window" at the Fed and redeem their U.S. dollars.

It was hard to know which of these acts was the most shameful. Every economist worthy of the *métier* knew that wage and price controls wouldn't really contain inflation – which was running as high as 6%. They would just warp markets and distort prices, leading to shortages and mistakes. Though widely applauded in the popular press, it was such a silly thing to do that it got almost all the coverage. But it was so clearly absurd that the controls were dropped soon after.

The second part of Nixon's announcement was largely ignored. What did it matter? Foreign governments were perfectly happy to take U.S. paper dollars; gold seemed unnecessary and out of date. Besides, the greatest "conservative" economist of the time, Milton Friedman, was all for it. He thought he had cracked the code that would eliminate liquidity crises... and inflation, too. He thought it was as simple as controlling the money supply, with a steady rate of increase of 3% per annum. Friedman, a Nobel Prize-winning economist, was right about many things. But he was wrong about the thing he claimed to know best – money. Disastrously wrong.

We remember, vaguely, the argument from the early 1970s, when today's money system was put in place. There were the Hayekians – disciples of Austrian economist Friedrich Hayek – on one side, and the Friedmanites on the other. Simplifying, the "Austrians" thought government should have nothing to do with money. Hayek called the government monopoly over the issue and control of money "the source and root of all monetary evil."

But Friedman, normally so distrustful of government, was willing to trust it with our money:

The first and most important lesson that history teaches about what monetary policy can do – and it is a lesson of the most profound importance – is that monetary policy can prevent money itself from being a major source of economic disturbance.

Friedman was a student of the Great Depression. He and Anna Jacobson Schwartz wrote their great tome, *A Monetary History of the United States, 1867 – 1960*. In it, they came to the conclusion that the worst of the Depression could have been avoided by manipulating the supply of money.

Writing along the same lines in their memoirs, *Two Lucky People*, Milton and Rose Friedman say:

The Fed was largely responsible for converting what might have been a garden-variety recession, although perhaps a fairly severe one, into a major catastrophe. Instead of using its powers to offset the Depression, it presided over a decline in the quantity of money by one-third from 1929 to 1933. [...] Far from the Depression being a failure of the free-enterprise system, it was a tragic failure of government.

This view became known as "monetarism," in which government agents keep their eyes on prices, increase the supply of money when they are falling, and decrease it when they are rising.

In a severe downturn, borrowing comes to a halt, bankruptcies and defaults increase, and the money turnover – or the velocity of money – plummets. The correct procedure, said the Friedmanites, was to increase the supply of money so that the whole economy didn't get locked in a deflationary, depressionary slump. The hope of monetarism was that a steady increase in the money supply of about 3% per year would eliminate jolts of too much or too little credit.

At least, that was the idea. But during the last 20 years, the U.S. authorities have increased their monetary footings (their assets) at a

30% annual rate – far beyond anything Friedman ever imagined. And this is at the heart of the troubles we examine in this chapter.

We were alive at the time of Nixon's announcement. We were among the millions who saw something ugly afoot. But we didn't know what it was. We presumed it would be higher rates of inflation. Once freed from the golden hutch, we reasoned, the U.S. dollar bunny was free to multiply.

But it took us 30 years to understand (and still only partially and imperfectly) just how pernicious this new money system was. And it will take us more than 30 pages to explain it. So, let's back up, approach it from another perspective, and try to get a good look.

In a discussion with a colleague, we pointed out how the fake money system has robbed the middle and lower classes of trillions of dollars. By feeding the new, counterfeit currency into the asset markets, we explained, the relative wealth of the rich in the U.S. has increased by at least $30 trillion since 1980, while the middle and lower classes, who owned only their own time, have not gotten a penny.

"Well, if the system were so unfair," came the challenge, "how come it has lasted nearly half a century?"

It was then that we realized that the system has endured because it was unfair, not in spite of it. In any government, there are always some people who get control of the coercive power of the state and figure out how to use it for their own benefit. That was true of the Big Man in prehistoric tribes. It was true of the chiefs, kings, and emperors who dominated governments in early historic times. And it is true of the elites who dominate the U.S. government today. And no more cunning, more elegant, or more effective a flimflam has ever been developed than America's current money system.

Many of the people who gain from the system – probably the majority of them – are not even aware that they are participating in a fraudulent conveyance. They go to the best universities. They can talk about the Fed's "demand management." Or they simply invest alongside that great genius from the plains, Warren Buffett. Like everyone else, they come to believe what they must believe when they must believe it. They think they are making money because they are smart, unaware that they are really just short-changing ordinary working people with the hidden help of the feds' fake money system.

(We speak with some unaccustomed authority on this. We stumbled into the business of offering alternative investment ideas and economic commentary in 1979. For many years, an investor might have done well simply buying the Dow in 1982 and sitting tight; he didn't need us. Yet our business grew immodestly – far faster than GDP. Now, with offices in 10 foreign countries and thousands of analysts, writers, editors, and researchers working for us, how do we explain this remarkable – perhaps disproportionate – success? Unbeknownst to us at the beginning, we had the wind of the feds' fake money at our back. The more the feds disconnected Wall Street's asset prices from the Main Street economy, the more people wanted to know how it worked. The more counterfeit claim tickets the feds issued, in other words, the more people wanted to know how to get one.)

Many people got rich in the period from 1980 to 2018. The stock market, measured by the Dow, rose from under 1,000 to over 26,000 – a 2,500% increase. When looking at all U.S. stocks, approximately $27 trillion was created, not including dividends. As has been well documented, this new wealth went overwhelmingly to a small portion of the population – the upper 10%. Or the upper 1%. Or the upper 0.1%. The higher you went, the more disproportionate the gain. The rich got richer. And the richer they were, the richer they got.

But what kind of wealth was this? Was this win-win wealth, with a positive gain for society? Or was it win-lose… where the rich only got richer because the poor got poorer?

In the news in 2015 was a report from Princeton economists Anne Case and Angus Deaton, who sounded the alarm about the shocking increase in death rates among middle-aged white men. According to their figures, the death rate for a white man aged between 45 and 54 without a college degree was rising faster than for any other demographic group, while the death rates for Black and Latino men the same age continued to decline.

Forget terrorism and Mexican murderers. In America, a middle-aged white man is now much more likely to kill himself than to die at the hands of foreigners. "Deaths of despair" – from alcohol, drugs, and suicide – have more than doubled in the U.S. in the last 20 years. The Centers for Disease Control and Prevention tell us that the mortality rate in the U.S. has risen to almost 900 per 100,000. And we recall reading elsewhere that at least one county in West Virginia was so overwhelmed by these deaths that the funeral homes weren't able to keep up; they had to export cadavers to a neighboring county.

In our last visit to our father's hometown – Donora, Pennsylvania… a steel town that peaked out in the 1960s – we were shocked. Not that so many people had killed themselves, but that so many were still alive. We'd hit the bottle hard, too, if we had to live there. Empty buildings. Derelict houses. It might as well have been West Baltimore-on-the-Monongahela.

Economists, do-gooders, and social activists argue about the causes. Not enough spent on education and job training, says one. Globalization, charges another. No, it's the unequal distribution of income, announces a third. The decline of unions, guesses another. But we will show the real cause in this chapter. Not capitalism. Not greed. Not too little regulation. The real cause is money itself… or, more precisely, the feds' claptrap money. In 1971, the feds changed the money system. Donora has been going downhill ever since. And its time-selling working classes, compared to the asset-owning bourgeoisie, got poorer. And let's look at what has happened to the whole economy since the new, fake money was introduced:

- The Fed's "base money" assets have gone from $84 billion to $3.3 trillion.

- Stocks, as measured by the Dow, have risen from 839 to as high as 26,828.

- Productivity growth has declined from 9.3% per year in the 1960s to 2.5% per year in the 21st century.

- U.S. government debt was $397 billion in 1971. Now, it is $21.5 trillion.

- Total U.S. debt was $1.3 trillion ($786 billion private debt+$397 billion federal government debt+$159 billion state and local government debt) in 1971. Now, it is $69.6 trillion ($45 trillion private debt+$21.5 trillion federal government debt+$3.1 trillion state and local government debt).

- The gap between rich and poor has widened. In 1975, the top 10% owned 67% of the wealth. By 2016, they owned 77%.

Coincidence? Or causation?

We do not presume to say that the change in the economy was the only thing that happened as a result of the new money system. Many other things were going on. But the new, fake money played a large part in what has happened over the last 40 years.

The monied classes – including those who run the show – saw nothing they disliked in the new money system. Donald Trump, who described himself as the "King of Debt" (see more in a subsequent chapter), saw his own net worth go up from barely $200 million in the 1980s to what he claims is a $10 billion fortune today. Money was available. Those with access to it got it, in great abundance. Leveraged real estate speculators, such as Mr. Trump, used it effectively.

But the trail is so obscured by mythical economics and fake news, it's hard to follow.

MONEY AND THE DEEP STATE

Sometimes, a rich person is maligned, as in, "He only cares about money." Or money itself is dissed, as in, "It's only money." But money is more than "just money." It connects us to our fellow humans. It keeps track of our relative status and material accounts; it quantifies a hierarchy; it is a "way of keeping score in life," as American business magnate T. Boone Pickens used to say.

Most important, it tells us who owes what to whom. If the money is honest, it helps us maintain a sense of basic fairness... and keeps us "grounded" in the real world of resources, skills, information, and – crucially – time. Money is not something apart from us; it represents who we are... what we've done... what we know... how much we've done for others... how we've gotten along in the world so far... and what we hope to do in the future. It is choice. It is liberty, independence, and, at times, survival.

Imagine that you spend your entire working life saving money for your retirement. Is that saved-up money "just money"? It is much of your life. It represents the time you've spent working... and all the times you decided not to spend your money, but to save it for the future.

Now, imagine how you will feel if that money is taken from you. If you are held up on the street, you will be indignant... and want to see the criminal brought to justice. But what if the money itself cheats you? What if inflation turns your $1,000 savings into just $100... or only $10? Or imagine how you will feel when you see someone else... perhaps someone who has never worked a day in his life... get $1,000 for nothing.

Or imagine that someone is able to borrow $1,000 at no interest. How does that make you feel? What does that make of all your years working, saving, and scraping by? What are your life's savings worth if someone else is able to get the same amount of money for nothing? Does it feel like someone cut in line ahead of you?

In an idealized, honest economy, people give and get in more or less equal measure. You get paid for a day's work. If you put in more effort, you get more money. And if you are able to invent something that helps people save time... or if you are able to build a business – like

Walmart – that helps them save money... don't you deserve to get more?

Money was one of the most important innovations of all time. Like the wheel and fire, it was a technical breakthrough that opened the door to much further technical progress. And like language and writing, it was a social innovation that made the modern, civilized world possible. You could trade with people you didn't know... people from different cultures... people speaking different languages. Money allowed you to move wealth across space and time. If you were a farmer in the Roman Empire, and you had a ton of wheat that you wanted to exchange for a ton of tea from India, it would have been almost impossible – and extremely expensive – to transport your wheat to the Indus Valley and make the exchange.

But commerce got easier with the invention of money. You traded your wheat for a few gold coins... which then could be traded for tea from India. The seller didn't have to know anything about you. Or anything about your wheat. All he had to know was that the money was good. It was real money. Just money. It was honest money.

Imagine that you raised a crop of cabbages. These vegetables represented years of preparation, learning, and skill... along with many thousands of hours of field work. Your cabbages were your wealth. They were a vegetable form of your time. But in a few days, the cabbages would dry up and rot... and the wealth would disappear. Money, however, allowed you to convert your cabbage wealth into financial wealth. And with this new form of wealth – money – you could keep your wealth for weeks, months, and years. You could then enjoy the cabbage crop you raised in Tuscany in 59 A.D. even after your retirement in 71 A.D., perhaps in Spain. But the money had to be real. Otherwise, you would be misled or cheated.

Money is best compared to writing. You can communicate without writing. You can do business without money, too. Both writing and money are ways to pass along information, spanning thousands of years and thousands of miles. Today, we can still read about Diocletian's third-century cabbages, or about Emperor Claudius' proposal to the senate, bidding it proclaim corned beef and cabbage the world's most perfect food. A gold coin minted in Claudius' day will still buy a corned-beef-and-cabbage dinner, too. We don't know precisely, but it may even still cost about the same amount.

Both writing and money helped make modern civilization possible. Exchanging information and ideas across languages, cultures, oceans, and mountains... the rate of innovation, learning, and specialization sped up. Trade increased. And so did prosperity.

But as we will see, money and writing can lie, too. So, let's take stock of what we already know... Then, we'll move ahead.

Progress is cyclical. Win-win deals add wealth and move the society forward. But they depend on trust. As trust increases, deals are made more efficiently. People specialize. They learn. They become more productive. The society gets richer. And then... the temptation to cheat increases. This temptation, perhaps, deserves a fuller explanation. The theory of declining marginal utility means that the first dollar you earn is worth more than every additional dollar. You can easily see why this is so. The first money you earn may keep you from starving. It is extremely important to you. When you have earned a million dollars, on the other hand, an additional dollar makes very little difference. Like everything else in life, the scarcity of money makes it valuable; abundance reduces its value.

Logically, a dollar lost is more valuable than an additional dollar gained. So, a dollar taken away from someone must also be more of a loss for him than an additional dollar earned by you (assuming you are about equal to begin with). Since it is relative wealth that matters – it is a status marker, after all – you are better off stealing a dollar from a neighbor than earning an extra dollar yourself. And now that the stolen dollar is your property, and not his, it is actually worth twice as much as an additional dollar gotten honestly. He has one less. You have one more. The difference = two dollars.

Wealth cannot be created by win-lose transactions. But it can be taken away by them. To avoid this, walls and security cameras go up. Costs increase. Trust declines. Progress slows... or goes backward.

Money, honest money, is just a way of keeping everyone honest. Gold-backed U.S. dollars were trustworthy for nearly 200 years (setting aside Lincoln's phony "greenbacks"). People became so confident in the integrity of the dollar that they hardly noticed when the gold backing, for Americans, was removed by President Johnson in 1968. Nor did many people complain when Nixon followed up by removing the gold backing for foreigners in 1971. But that's the way trust works. The more trusting people become, the easier it is to rip them off. And the more successful they are, the more you want to.

As trust expands and win-win deals proliferate, it is inevitable that some people gain more than others. The typical Chinese day laborer makes seven times as much today as he did in 1999. But the typical American day laborer, in real terms, has gained nothing. In 1964, the average hourly wage for an American worker, in today's dollars, was $20.25. Fast-forward more than fifty years, and that worker now makes $23.18 an hour. In other words, the typical man has not had a significant raise in over half a century. His time – which he traded for money – has remained almost unchanged.

But the situation is substantially worse than it appears. Because the Bureau of Labor Statistics' figures reflect an abstraction, not the real cost of living. Even as his wages remained stagnant, it took the average working American more time to buy the basic conveniences. For example, the typical man must now spend twice as long working to buy the average pickup truck and the average house as he did in the early 1970s.

International labor competition and fake money made the American feel like a loser. Win-win allowed someone else to win. And now, he wants to go into reverse, to make America great again, with walls and win-lose trade barriers. He wants to turn the positive-sum game of global commerce into a zero-sum game in which he believes he will be a guaranteed winner.

But it wasn't really win-win deals that hurt him. It was win-lose money. Overseas, his competitors used America's cheap money to gain market share and take away his job. At home, the elite used the new, cheap money to pump up its stocks, bonds, and real estate. Meanwhile, the feds imposed their crony boondoggles, regulations, and win-lose deals – financed with fake money.

His medical care now costs him nearly 10 times more than it did in 1980. His household debt rose nearly 8 times since 1980. He blamed the Chinese, the Mexicans, the Liberals… the media… and the government. He wanted a change. But who would have guessed that he had been ripped off by his own government… and its untrustworthy money?

Who would have imagined that after 3,000 years, the civilized elite would have come up with a money that betrayed his trust… a "bezzle" so subtle that he didn't even notice?

MONEY AND CIVILIZATION

Before World War II scattered them around the globe, a group of intellectuals met regularly in "kreis" – what we would call "salons" – in Vienna, Austria. Philosophers, economists, mathematicians – the circle was small enough to allow for much cross-discipline discussion.

Out of these conversations, the economists among them – Carl Menger, Ludwig von Mises, Friedrich Hayek, Joseph Schumpeter, and others – developed the "Austrian school." But the Austrian school of economics was not at all like the academic discipline practiced by the modern celebrity economists of our time – Paul Krugman, Janet Yellen, Ben Bernanke, Thomas Piketty, et al. It was a broader view, based on insights about the way the world – and civilization – works. And it resulted in a rather humble view as to what an economist could do to make it better.

There's a reason Alan Greenspan, formerly a partisan of the

Austrian school, gave it up when he took the role of head of the Fed. The Austrians tried to understand the economy; they did not pretend to fix or improve it. And if they had seen someone recklessly experimenting on it – such as with Zero Interest Rate Policy (ZIRP), Quantitative Easing (QE), or the Greenspan Put (which assured investors that the Fed would come to their aid if the stock market sold off) – they would have been appalled, quickly pointing out why the experiment would only make things worse.

The Austrians saw that money was just a part of the complex fabric of civilization. It served a purpose beyond simply making people rich or poor. It brought them into the civilized world, where they could truck with people they didn't know… exchange vital information with people whose languages they didn't speak… and reward people they never met for making their lives better.

Money, real money, brought discipline and forbearance to the economic world, just as the Roman centurions imposed it on their Goth recruits. You could get richer and live better. But you had to submit to the disciplines and limitations of the civilized world. You had to understand that actions have consequences. And you had to respect time.

First, you had to earn money, by exchanging your time in the present for a reward that you would receive in the future. Second, if you wanted to make money from your money, you had to forgo the pleasure of immediately spending it. You had to save it. And saving it, you had to learn self-discipline. And you had to develop trust, depending on others not to steal it. Thus could you create investment capital… which you could build up… and use to create more capital. This was the foundation for the whole edifice of modern-day capitalism, upon which progress and our standards of living depend.

Real money reflected the reality of the world itself – with its limited quantities of time and resources. Real interest rates on real savings connected the present with the future, compensating for the uncertainties that the future inevitably holds, and restraining the desire to "spend it now." Real interest rates not only rewarded forbearance, they discouraged consumption (eating the seed corn that would increase the next year's harvest)... and thereby favored capital formation and material progress.

Alas, like some modern-day Vandal tribe unleashed on the civilized world, the feds, aided and abetted by cocksure economists, have been destroying capitalism with their fake money and fake interest rates. Instead of encouraging saving and civilized restraint, they discourage it by dropping interest rates below the rate of inflation and trying to stimulate the economy with trillions in debt that can never be repaid.

The whole spectacle would be funny if it weren't so dangerous. Without honest, fair, true money, growth rates fall. Bubbles get pumped up... and they explode. Debt grows. The rich get richer; the poor fall further behind. Societies are destabilized... and people turn savage.

Our guess is that none of the people involved in policy-making decisions today has even read the Austrians. None takes them seriously. None really understands money. Instead, they all continue along a bumpy road that leads, as Hayek and Schumpeter both predicted, to disaster. This is not just a monetary disaster, by the way. When the money gives way – as it did in Germany after World War I – so do the norms, values, and customs of civilization itself.

FAKE MONEY. REAL MONEY. WHAT'S THE DIFFERENCE?

Money is not made money simply because a government says so. It takes more than that. Otherwise, the people of Zimbabwe would still be using their Zim dollars. The government said they were legal tender. They handed out quadrillions of them. But they are worthless.

Real, durable money must be win-win money. It must be accepted by the people who use it. It may or may not be an "official" money, but it must be a vernacular money. It must be true. Or at least true enough. People are used to a little fraud in their money; they put up with it and adapt to it. But too much fraud is unbearable.

When money was first invented, nobody knew for sure what form of money would work best. All sorts of things were tried – shells, stones, beads, and "wampum." In the southern American colonies, for example, tobacco was a favorite form of money. It was transportable, packed into rolling "hogs' heads," and pulled behind oxen to the docks on the Chesapeake. If kept out of the rain, it did not perish. It was divisible; you could take out as many "hands" of tobacco as you needed. And people knew what it was worth. Anglican churches were built in Maryland with "tobacco tithes." Member families contributed a portion of their harvests to pay for their construction. In prisoner of war camps during and after World War II, a tobacco derivative, cigarettes, was used as money, too.

But over the centuries, one thing proved exceptionally useful as money – gold. It was not necessarily perfect money. But it was better than anything else people had ever tried. A cryptocurrency may or may not turn out to be an even better form of money. But for now, gold is still the "gold standard" for money.

People recognized long ago that gold worked as real money. There was only so much of it. You could carry it, bury it, lend it, save it… and so forth. And it was easy to see that it was real. Of course, there are always people who will try to cheat. Even with gold. Typically, they shave off some of the gold – that is, they "clip" the coins… or they substitute other metals. These techniques were fairly primitive and easy to spot. Paper money, on the other hand, provided cheaters with more opportunities. At first, it was "100% backed" by gold. Then came "fractional reserve" banking, in which bankers claimed they had enough gold to cover the usual requests for it, but often had not enough to survive a "run" on their banks. In the Great Depression, for example, 9,000 U.S. banks failed; they were unable to honor the claims they had issued.

After 1968, American citizens could no longer redeem their dollars for gold at a fixed, statutory rate. This was the era of President Lyndon

Baines Johnson, with his budget-busting "guns and butter" programs – war in Vietnam and the Great Society at home. Disconnecting the dollar from gold made it easier to increase the number of dollars and keep the spending going. However, the "gold window" remained open for another three years. This allowed foreign central banks to submit their dollars to the U.S. Treasury in exchange for gold. This "window" was slammed shut by Nixon on August 15, 1971. Since then, the U.S. dollar has been phony money. It's money that you can fiddle with – if you control it.

THE "BEZZLE"

Proverbs 11:1 tells us, "A false balance is an abomination to the Lord, but a just weight is his delight." It's easy to see larceny when it is carried out by an armed robber. The loss is sudden… and unambiguous. Even inflation does its work right out in the open. Your money loses value day by day. And there's an even-handedness to it: rich and poor are robbed proportionally.

But the larceny of almost unlimited, and almost always underpriced, credit is subtler. It is what economist John K. Galbraith described in his book on the 1929 stock market crash as a "bezzle." He observed that in any economy, there is an element of theft and fraud. But when the credit is flowing and markets are rising, the "rate of embezzlement grows, the rate of discovery falls off, and the bezzle increases rapidly." Not only that; the larceny is welcomed and rewarded. And its worst blackguards are feted as national champions. In 1999, for example, Fed chief Alan Greenspan, Treasury Secretary Robert Rubin, and Deputy Treasury Secretary Larry Summers were put on the cover of *TIME* magazine and heralded as "The Committee to Save the World." What they saved the world from, said *TIME*, was a meltdown from too much debt. But what they really did was add more debt. They goosed up the amount of credit (and debt), making the eventual unwinding worse. That debt began to unwind in the early 2000s… which was stopped by Mr. Greenspan on his own. Then, in 2007, the new Fed chief, Ben Bernanke, had to make the save. He, too, was celebrated, this time by *The Atlantic* magazine in April 2012, which dubbed him, simply, "The Hero." Mr. Bernanke seemed to like the description. He stuck with it as the theme for his hagiographic fantasy, *The Courage to Act*.

After the "Black Monday" Crash in October 1987 – the worst single-day percentage fall for U.S. stocks in history – Alan Greenspan's Fed slashed interest rates to backstop the market. And since then, the Fed has never stopped protecting speculators... and boosting stock prices. In 1987, when Alan Greenspan began backstopping the stock market, the Dow was at 2,200. In October 2018, it was over 26,800. Stock holders were up over 1,000%. Meanwhile, the rate of growth of U.S. industry declined, and the real value of the average worker's time fell. So non-stockowners got nothing. But the gains from owning stocks have increased. How is that possible? How could an economy slow... and its consumers lose purchasing power... but its enterprises still be more valuable?

This new, post-1971 dollar was like the old one in every respect, except the most important one. The old dollar was weighted down by gold. It could never get off the ground. If you wanted more dollars, you had to earn them the old-fashioned way – by providing goods or services. That was how the Main Street economy worked. It created wealth. Money went to the people who created it. You had to give to get.

The old dollar helped make America the biggest exporter in the world, with an unbroken chain of export surpluses reaching back more than a hundred years. But the new dollar could be gotten without selling anything to anybody. It was not earned on Main Street. Instead, it was created, by the credit industry, on Wall Street. Out on Main Street, people could borrow, too. But they had to pay the money back. Lenders looked to their ability to pay... to their output and their collateral... and usually gave the money out carefully.

On Wall Street, the game was very different. A large borrower could get money at preferential rates. He had none of the risk of building factories, starting new product lines, or trying to please difficult customers in a competitive market. He was speculating... often just by buying risk-free U.S. Treasury bonds. And in many cases, these preferential rates were well below the rate of inflation. Meaning that the "carry" – the cost of maintaining a speculative position – was free for well-connected speculators. Any trade that they thought might produce a profit or a trickle of income could be carried at no cost.

In an honest economy, there are only two sources of purchasing power – either you spend your own income (past or present) or you borrow someone else's savings. This naturally limits the amount of spending. People don't earn an infinite amount of money. Nor do they save an infinite amount. Credit (or debt) cannot exceed the amount of savings available (with an allowance for the elasticity of the fractional banking system).

And there is a further limitation. People lend their savings out carefully, at interest rates that give them a decent return on their money and protect them from the risk of loss. Pre-1971, the system was self-regulating. If consumers borrowed too much money, the pool of savings dried up. Interest rates rose. Lenders stiffened their backs. And consumers had to cool it. Internationally, the same feedback loop kept accounts in balance and limited debt. If Americans bought too many goods from overseas, foreign banks showed up at the Treasury demanding gold in exchange for their paper dollars. The Treasury dutifully honored its obligations, as it had done for at least six generations. But this reduced the supply of gold... upon which the dollar rested, in effect reducing the available money supply and forcing up interest rates. The resulting correction dampened consumers' appetites, shifted the trade deficit to a surplus, and allowed the money supply to recover.

But the new money system didn't need no stinkin' savings. Or caution. Or market-discovered interest rates. It was estranged from the real world of time and resources… and divorced from honest price discovery. The Fed could create as much new credit as it wanted and lend it out at (almost) whatever price it cared to put on it. This was a new, uncivilized money; it didn't respect the limits of the natural world.

This "financialization" yielded "wealth" that the economy could not produce; the banks – aided and abetted by the Fed – could create all the dollars they wanted by lending this new money, which no one ever earned or saved, at EZ rates. Since 1999, central banks worldwide have added some $20 trillion of this fake money to the world's monetary footings. And the economy has changed from one that produced wealth and rewarded work with real money to one that used fake money to extract wealth from the working classes.

EX NIHILO NILIL FIT

The "funny" thing about the extractive economy is that it appears so bountiful. Savings that came from nowhere, like manna from Heaven, are available for hire. Capital appears unlimited.

Scarcity – the real nature of things – imposes its own rules and disciplines. Trying to pretend that there is no scarcity – by flooding the system with fake capital – undermines the behavior of consumers, businesses, and the government. All are encouraged to spend money that doesn't exist and borrow from a future that will never come.

There are only so many hours in a day. Only so many drinks in a bottle of wine. Only so much air in the Earth's atmosphere… and only so many planets orbiting the sun. Without limits, where is your farm? Where is your neighbor's? Where do we stop and you begin? How much of that pizza are you going to eat? And how much will you leave for others? When was yesterday? Will tomorrow ever come? Without limits, the universe collapses in on itself like a wet cardboard box.

The total deficits, accumulated as federal debt, from 1980 to the present, toted to more than $21 trillion. Debt soared to the rafters…

and then went through the roof. Total U.S. debt rose similarly. From an average of less than 1.5 times GDP... debt has increased to almost 3.5 times GDP. Today's GDP is around $21 trillion. At the historic ratio, the economy should be able to support $31.5 trillion in debt. Instead, it has $69.6 trillion. This gives us a measure of how out-of-whack the whole system has become. And it also gives us a hint as to what lies ahead. About $38 trillion of debt... and debt-fueled asset prices... would have to disappear to bring the ratio back into its traditional balance.

This will have far-reaching effects. Excess debt, made possible by the fake dollar and the Fed's EZ-money policies, flattered and distorted prices throughout the economy. Corporate sales were fattened by $38 trillion of excess spending over the four-decade period. Corporate profits were favored even more. Typically, corporations earn money and pay wages. Their wages are what consumers use to buy corporate products and services. Wages are usually a major business cost. But this new spending came from neither savings nor wages. It came from borrowed fake money. Corporate profits rose as companies got extra income with no offsetting wage expense increase.

The boom just described – 1980 to present – was strange, untidy, and unjust. Investors didn't really make money by providing a service – funding America's win-win industries. Instead, their profits were speculative, and came from betting right (unwittingly) on the Fed's massive financialization scheme. Or, to put it differently, the money didn't come from being investors, funding real growth in real businesses. Investors were accomplices in the Fed's flimflam, stealing money from the Main Street economy and transferring it to the moneyed Washington and Wall Street-oriented elites.

THE FUTURE IN THE PAST

People do not naturally work, sweat, save their money, and lend it out to someone else for less than nothing. Sidney Homer and Richard

Sylla studied the matter. Their book, *A History of Interest Rates*, reaching back some 5,000 years, finds not a single instance where people hired out their money and paid for the privilege.

Five thousand years is a long time. The Ammonites, Sumerians, Hittites, Israelites – imagine the proto-Bernanke's of the first millennium B.C. – Ephraimites, Angles, Saxons, Britons, Franks, Vandals, Goths – you'd think that if negative interest rates were such a good idea, surely someone would have thought of them before now.

Negative rates are definitely an outlier. Interest rates signal a fundamental relationship between human material wealth and time. At 20% interest, it takes five years to recover a certain amount of capital. At 10%, it will take 10 years. At 2%, 50 years. And when the rate falls below zero? Then, the future disappears.

The future is *terra incognito* insofar as it is impossible to know what will happen there. But while it is a place you've never been before – that doesn't mean you shouldn't pack your old, familiar toothbrush and a warm sweater; it's usually not so different from home.

Aesop, the ancient Greek storyteller, wrote his *Fables*. The French have added to them with a few of their own. Here's one about the future:

Long ago, an old man decided to turn his farm over to his son and his daughter-in-law. "I have just one condition," he told them. "You have to let me stay with you as long as I live."

This was readily agreed. But the son's wife and the old man didn't get along. Finally, the wife persuaded her husband to throw him out. And so he did.

But taking pity on the old man, the younger man turned to his own son. "Go and get a horse blanket for your grandfather so that at least he'll have something warm to wrap around him."

A few minutes later, the young boy came back with a blanket. But his father could see that it was only half a blanket. "Why did you cut the other half off?" he asked. "Oh…" replied the boy. "That's for you when you get old."

All of a sudden, a pattern came into view. The future didn't seem so unknowable. Like a tall tree, the future casts its shadow backward over the present. If you think it will rain later in the day, you take an umbrella with you in the morning. If you think stocks will go up, you buy now. If you think you have only two years to live, there is no point buying a refrigerator with a 20-year guarantee. Either the evolution of money greatly increased man's interest in tomorrow, or the evolution of his interest in tomorrow greatly increased his interest in money. Either way, he saw the benefit of preparing for what was to come.

Savings are always a gift to the future. Debt is always a burden on it. Savings are a crop of cabbages that your father planted… but you can enjoy. Debt is a crop of cabbages you have to plant… to pay a loan that may have been taken out by your father or grandfather.

But suppose you were to plant black walnut trees. It could take 50 years for them to mature. It will be a gift to your children. What if a pest kills them? What if, half a century from now, people no longer want natural wood? What if you borrowed the money to plant them and the bank called in the loan before the trees were ready to harvest?

The further ahead you look, the more risks you can't see. Logically, the further out you go, the more you are likely to run into something that will upset your plans and ruin your cabbage wealth; the longer the debt term… the less likely you are to be paid back. Logically, too, the more debt there is outstanding, the more likely it is that some will never be paid back.

In this context – that is to say, the real world – negative interest rates are an absurdity. And yet, even on the last day of 2018, after deep cracks had spread throughout the entire capital structure, approximately $8 trillion of government bonds worldwide still traded at yields below zero. They are made possible only by the meddling of central banks, who presume to destroy time.

HAYEK WAS RIGHT

While the idea of managing the money supply seemed coherent and sensible, the people who ended up with their hands on the levers were neither. They had theories to test... axes to grind... careers to embellish... and Nobel Prizes to win. Leaving control of the money supply in their hands was asking for trouble.

We had lunch with Milton Friedman in the mid-1990s. At the time, our own views were so inchoate and callow, we could not hold a proper conversation with him. Besides, nobody had ever won an argument with Friedman; we certainly weren't going to be the first.

We only began thinking about the world of money when we started writing a daily blog in the 1990s. Before that, our brain had been focused on business, family, home repairs, and not much more. We were already over 50 years old when we began reading Friedman, Hayek, et al. seriously.

This was very late to begin puzzling out such complicated matters as monetary policy. But coming late to the party probably had some advantages. While most of the revelers were already drunk on Keynesianism or monetarism, we were just getting out of our car, sober as a Baptist schoolteacher in a dry county. They had studied the Phillips Curve in detail. They had invested their time in the Taylor Rule... hedonic adjustments to the CPI... seasonal gerrymandering of employment numbers... and the Paradox of Savings. Their heads were full of so much theoretical clutter that they couldn't make it across the room without falling down. Ours was nearly empty. All we had was the real-world experience of actually running a business for 20 years... the practical training of making payroll and trying to earn money... as well as the front-line challenge of raising a family of six children.

And what we saw was that Hayek was right; Friedman was wrong. As clever as they are, economists cannot create real money (for that would mean expanding time and resources). They can only create fake money. And with this fake money, they have misled the entire world economy. That is, this money does not represent new wealth. In this sense, it is not win-win money. It does not arise naturally and honestly. Instead, it is win-lose money; it is a dishonest claim on wealth that was already created and is now in someone else's hands.

This fake money only came into existence as it was lent out – first, by the central bank, and then, by member banks and other lenders. This meant that the money supply itself could only increase as debt increased. Debt – as a form of money – has a particularly serious flaw. Like a sleeper cell, or a doomsday code, it suddenly comes to life in a crisis and triggers a much worse disaster. Real money – along with the real wealth it represents – builds up, like bricks in a wall, each one laid on a firm foundation of real Main Street output... and each one contributing to making a solid, useful, and prosperous structure. But the new, fake money stacks up like glasses of champagne at a raucous wedding; it is just a matter of time before some drunk comes along and knocks them down.

Debt is subject to the credit cycle; real money is not. As debt increases in quantity, the quality of it declines. The more borrowers owe, the less able they are to pay. Fake money is really nothing more than I.O.U.s – claims on the wealth of others that may never be paid. And like any debt, it goes down in value as the issuer borrows more of them. As a credit-fueled boom develops, more and more marginal borrowers get more and more risky loans to buy more and more overpriced assets. The debt structure totters... then collapses. That is what happened in 2008.

When the credit cycle turns... and credit contracts – as it must, someday – the doomsday device will be triggered. The system itself turns into a deflationary nightmare. All the delusional claims on future output are suddenly marked to market as credit disappears. Stocks sink. Bonds default. The losses ricochet, like pool balls, from debtor to creditor to asset-holder to banks to businesses to employees to merchants... until the entire table has been cleared.

HIGH FINANCE FOR TODDLERS

In the summer of 2017, our young grandson, James, came to visit us in France.

One night, his mother tried to get him to go to bed at 9 p.m. But the little boy's internal clock was still on Baltimore time; it told him it was much too early to go to sleep.

Grandpa took over, drawing out the monetary system like a general spreading out a map on a field table. "Here is the enemy," he said gravely. "They have us completely surrounded. We're doomed."

James has a sunny, optimistic temperament. But now, he squirmed. And he resisted sleep… until we explained…

"Money is not wealth; it just measures and represents wealth…" we began. Then, we laid out the whole win-lose money bamboozle, explaining…

…that our post-1971 money system is based on fake money that represents no real time or resource, and that it measures wealth unreliably…

…that this new money enters the economy as credit… and that the credit industry (Wall Street) has privileged access to it. The working man still has to earn his money, selling his work by the hour. But Wall Street – and elite borrowers connected to the Establishment – get it without breaking a sweat or watching the clock…

…that a disproportionate share of this new money is concentrated in and around the credit industry – pushing up asset prices, raising salaries and bonuses in the financial sector, and making the rich (those who own financial assets) much richer…

…that this flood of credit helped the middle class raise its living standards, even as earnings stagnated. But it did so only by increasing debt levels throughout the economy…

…and that it allowed the average American family to spend money Americans never earned and buy products Americans never made… Instead, Walmart's shelves were stocked with goods "Made in China."

The middle class lost income as factories, jobs, and earnings moved overseas. Debt stayed at home.

"Okay so far?" we asked James, as his eyeballs rolled backwards and his breathing slowed.

But one thing must still puzzle him. How did the new dollar actually retard growth? Maybe it didn't make people richer... after all, how can you expect to make people better off by giving them fake money? But how did it make them worse off?

WHY STIMULUS DOESN'T WORK

Since 2000, the feds have added $4 trillion in new money, suppressed interest rates below zero for an entire decade, run deficits of $16 trillion... and still ended up with the weakest post-recession expansion in history. How was it possible? What's the matter with "stimulus" anyway?

Try this experiment at home. Tell your teenager that he will get $5,000 a month for the rest of his life, and a lifetime supply of marijuana. See how that stimulates him.

We went down to Argentina to study the evidence firsthand. Despite runaway budgets, out-of-control spending, and lusty, gaucho money-printing – that is, despite "stimulus" up the kazoo – in early 2019, the Argentine economy was shrinking at a 6% annual rate, with inflation estimated to be as high as 100%.

Why? Let us return to our formula. $TS = rv\ (w\text{-}w - w\text{-}l)$. Total Satisfaction equals the real value of win-win deals minus the loss from win-lose deals.

Our formula recognizes that money isn't everything. So, it focuses on satisfaction, rather than GDP or raw wealth.

It also recognizes that win-lose deals are negative – they subtract from total satisfaction because they force you to do something you don't want to do. When a stick-up man confronts you in an alley, for example, he takes your wallet and greatly reduces your satisfaction.

But the biggest win-lose deals are much more subtle. Most people don't even know they're being robbed. And yet, those hidden win-lose deals greatly reduce net satisfaction, which shows up in lower incomes, less growth, and poorer people.

Remember, win-lose is the opposite of win-win. In a win-win deal, wealth is created as people do things for one another. They work. They learn. They save. They take chances. They trade with one another. Not because they want to… but because they have to. And little by little, as they succeed at satisfying each other's wants, progress happens.

In a bakery, for example, the baker gets to work at 4 a.m… kneading his dough in the wee hours so that the sweet smell of freshly baked bread will draw in the customers at dawn. He would probably prefer to stay abed. But nobody's going to pay him to sleep in. So, he gets to work, and his customers have bread to eat.

But suppose something strange happened. Imagine that the Bakers' Union hired a particularly powerful lobbyist, who persuaded Congress to pass the Bakers' Income Enhancement Act. This law changed the win-win deal into a win-lose deal, requiring customers to pay the baker whether he baked any bread or not. The baker… a nice fellow… might still feel an obligation to put out a few loaves. Out of habit, he might fire up his ovens. But after a while, he would probably slack off. He's only human!

Well guess what. Capitalists… investors… businessmen… and speculators are no different. Imagine that, like the lucky bakers or the lucky teenager, they don't have to work so hard. Imagine that they can make a profit without risk. Imagine that someone gives them money without demanding any quid pro quo. Imagine that the feds force a win-lose deal on the whole country… in which a few people – the rich, the insiders, the elite – get money without having to give anything in exchange.

Would they still take long-term risks with their money in order to develop new products and services for consumers? If the stock market were rising at 10% per year, would they still invest their money in new plants, new equipment, and new lines of business that might earn them – if they work out – 5%? Is it because they are saints that they do the hard work of capitalism… or because they have to produce some real product or service in order to earn a profit?

We have the answer to these questions right in front of us. For the last 30 years, capitalists could take advantage of a special win-lose deal offered by the feds. In effect, the feds took money from the public – via taxes, artificially low interest rates, debt, and printing-press money – and gave it to the elite. The insiders could borrow fake money from the Fed at a rate near zero (after inflation). And then, they could buy stocks and watch them go up from Dow 2,600 in 1989 to Dow 26,000 in 2018. Or, they could do even better… with buybacks, mergers, bonuses, or special dividends, funded by the Fed's win-lose fake money.

With the feds' fake money available to them, capitalists didn't put their money and talents to work in win-win deals for the benefit of others. Because they didn't have to. Win-lose financial tricks were much more profitable. Corporate borrowing hit new records. So did stock buybacks and stock prices. And startups like Uber, Lyft, Wag, and WeWork hit multibillion-dollar valuations without ever earning a penny.

But net of inflation and depreciation, real capital investment – the essential ingredient in a modern economy – fell to zero.

James was quiet. Monetary theory was taking its toll. We set out in a new direction, opening up a philosophical front:

"As you sow, so shall ye reap," we said. "And when you put a lot of fake money into a society, you end up with a fake economy."

Just look at Argentina in 2001… Zimbabwe in 2006… or Venezuela now… When people discover that their money is fake, both prices and people go feral. It was the same way in Germany during the Weimar hyperinflation. People stopped producing. You might have had a billion deutschmarks in your pocket, but you couldn't buy a bar of soap.

"But wait… we know what you're thinking…" we imagined James pushing back. "Those are all hyperinflation stories. We don't have that now. Instead, we have much less inflation… prices are almost stable."

Yes… for now. The inflation is in the asset sector… and in credit itself… not in consumer items. But the phenomenon is much the same.

Fake money is giving grossly distorted information to everyone. In Manhattan, we are told that an ordinary apartment is worth $2 million. But in Geneva – where interest rates have turned negative – we are told that $2 million is worth nothing… you will have to pay one of the banks to take it off your hands.

Without honest money, real savings, and true interest rates, businesses and investors have nothing to guide them. They are lost in the woods. Few want to do the hard work and take the risks of long-term, capital-heavy ventures. With GDP growth sluggish… and consumer incomes stagnant… there seems to be little incentive to expand output. Instead, the focus shifts to playing the game for short-term profits.

What's more, artificially low interest rates provide fatal misinformation. They tell the world that we have an infinite supply of resources – time, money, energy, and know-how.

Then, without its back to the wall of scarcity, and with no need to make careful choices, capitalism becomes reckless and irresponsible with its most valuable resource – capital itself. It is destroyed, wasted, misallocated, and mal-invested. Growth rates fall because the fuel – real capital – dries up. The world becomes poorer.

And in Japan, there was talk of the ultimate absurdity… Look carefully, because we believe this straw may have "final" etched on it in tiny letters.

Japan was said to be considering a perpetual bond issued at negative interest rates.

"How does that work?" we can hear James asking.

"Well, it's very simple. You give your money to the government. And then, you pay the government every year, forever, for taking it from you."

James startled awake. Disturbed.

"What kind of a world have I tumbled into…?" he seemed to ask.

๛ CHAPTER 8 ๛

Government – The Ultimate Win-Loser

Society, however, cannot subsist among those who are at all times ready to hurt and injure one another. The moment that injury begins, the moment that mutual resentment and animosity take place, all the bands of it are broke asunder, and the different members of which it consisted are, as it were, dissipated and scattered abroad by the violence and opposition of their discordant affections. If there is any society among robbers and murderers, they must at least, according to the trite observation, abstain from robbing and murdering one another... Society may subsist, though not in the most comfortable state, without beneficence; but the prevalence of injustice must utterly destroy it.
– Adam Smith, The Theory of Moral Sentiments

✛ ✛ ✛ ✛

IN A SPEECH IN May 2018, Pope Francis called credit default swaps "a ticking time bomb." He was not the first to hear the tick-tock coming from derivatives. Maybe they will blow up. And maybe they won't. But how would Pope Francis know?

God's man at the Vatican used an old Ford Focus to get around Rome and prided himself on his humility. But what a remarkably arrogant and conceited idea – to think that he knows better than thousands of seasoned investors with skin in the game.

"What do you think of Pope Francis?" we asked an Argentine friend. "He's a Peronist," was the reply. Nothing more needed to be said.

Peronism is a political ideology with economic pretentions. Juan Domingo Perón described it himself in 1948:

> *Peronism is humanism in action; Peronism is a new political doctrine, which rejects all the ills of the politics of previous times; in the social sphere it is a theory which establishes a little equality among men... capitalist exploitation should be replaced by a doctrine of social economy under which the distribution of our wealth, which we force the earth to yield up to us and which furthermore we are elaborating, may be shared out fairly among all those who have contributed by their efforts to amass it.*

Perón's basic idea was that a free economy, with its "capitalist exploitation," should be replaced by a controlled "social economy," where fairness comes into play.

Pope Francis seemed to have the same idea. In 2017, he attacked the idea of "libertarian individualism":

> *I cannot but speak of the serious risks associated with the invasion, at high levels of culture and education in both universities and in schools, of positions of libertarian individualism. A common feature of this fallacious paradigm is that it minimizes the common good, that is, "living well," a "good life" in the community framework, and exalts the selfish ideal that deceptively proposes a "beautiful life."*
>
> *If individualism affirms that it is only the individual who gives value to things and interpersonal relationships, and so it is only the individual who decides what is good and what is bad, then libertarianism, today in fashion, preaches that to establish freedom and individual responsibility, it is necessary to resort to the idea of "self-causation."*

Thus libertarian individualism denies the validity of the common good because on the one hand it supposes that the very idea of "common" implies the constriction of at least some individuals, and the other that the notion of "good" deprives freedom of its essence.

In other words, the Holy Father is suggesting that individualism is not a worthwhile moral doctrine because, by elevating the needs of the individual, it necessarily lowers the desires of the group.

In these pages, if we preach anything at all, it is not the idea of libertarian individualism but that of libertarian collectivism. The common good, we believe, is unknowable. It is what you discover by sharing and respecting the basic rules of a civilized society – the evolved vernacular of manners, morals, and markets that makes modern life possible. You never know who gets what... or why. But your "amor fati" – your appreciation of honest fate – helps you accept it.

But the contrary idea – that you can recognize the "common good" (Pope Francis) and share wealth out more "fairly," (Juan Perón) – is ubiquitous. Even "conservatives" believe it. Here is British Prime Minister Theresa May:

We do not believe in untrammeled free markets.

In other words, she believes in markets (aggregated win-win deals) that are trammeled by government. She prefers "fair" markets: "True conservatism means a commitment to country and community; a belief not just in society but in the good that government can do," she concluded. Here, her counterpart in the New World has much the same idea. Donald Trump, speaking for neither professional politicians nor clergy, nor anyone with any visible ideology or studied philosophy, or anyone who's bothered to think about it, favors "fair labor laws," "fair trade," and a "fair tax system":

Protection [from free markets] will lead to great prosperity and strength.

And here's Martin Wolf, chief economics commentator at the *Financial Times*, and one of the leading lights of the worldwide Deep State, arguing that it is time to revise the idea of "free markets":

It is a legitimate criticism of the Reagan and Thatcher revolutions that they underestimated the enduring functions of states as insurers, as protectors, as funders of education and health, as providers of infrastructure, as suppliers of public goods, as managers of externalities, as regulators of monopolies, as stabilizers of economies, as redistributors of incomes and not least as the focus of political loyalties.

There they are – the great and the good... the Four Estates... Church, Elite, State, and Press... conservative and liberals – all lined up together. All in favor of the "good" government does. All opposed to "free markets." All confident that if the Establishment is allowed to continue working its magic... redistributing income... stabilizing the economy... regulating trade... protecting markets, workers, widows and orphans, cronies and zombies... and otherwise intervening in other people's business, as it sees fit... the world will be a better place.

And we don't doubt that it will be a better place for some people. Pretending to do good, you can do very well. As for the rest of us, there is no evidence that the *federales* make life easier, richer, or more satisfying. As we saw in the previous chapter, no economy has ever been made to work better after it was trammeled by the government. Trammeling takes up money, time, and resources. It must take them from somewhere. Logically, the only place it can get them is from those who have them... and who must have plans of their own for them. That is, government can only do "good" by undoing the good that was being done by the people who had gotten the money honestly.

Mr. Wolf speaks of "funding" education and health. But every penny has to come from somewhere else. The feds make no money of their own. They can only "fund" something by defunding something else, or by squeezing the taxpayers for more loot. To make a long story short, what they "fund" is what they want to fund. What they defund is what the rightful owners of the money wanted to fund.

And it is not at all clear that the feds eliminate more monopolies than they create… or stabilize the economy more than they destabilize it… or manage "externalities" in any way that is generally beneficial. On the contrary, the "externalities" managed by the government all appear negative, not positive. Wars, famines, purges, concentration camps, mass-murders – none of these things are the result of capitalist exploitation or libertarian individualism; they are the fruits of government, supposedly in pursuit of the "common good."

Of the virtues frequently claimed for government, almost all are fake, based on the feds' tendency to impose the will of some on all. In other words, there are always some people who actually want the government to do what it is doing.

Modern Monetary Theory, for example, supposes that government issues money, and thereby controls the monetary system and its own finances. But, as we have seen, government issues something that looks like money and is used as money – but only so long as it imitates real, vernacular money. When it no longer quacks like the duck of real money, it is no longer money.

This insight helps us understand some other achievements of government. The feds eliminated slavery, for example. But they did so only as slavery was going out of style anyway. So, too, do the feds build highways… which work only so long as they are highways – a useful, vernacular means of getting around – not because they express the wishes of the feds. And the feds promote handicapped access, feed the hungry, and so forth. These, too, are sometimes useful – often, they are counterproductive – but only inasmuch as they imitate services that the vernacular, free market would provide without them.

Without voluntary win-win deals behind them, and markets to price them correctly, you never know if you're getting your money's worth. Note, too, that since the feds do not have to raise money honestly – by getting people to give it to them voluntarily, as in an IPO in the stock market – or make sales or profits, or satisfy customers, they have much more latitude to undertake projects that are never going to be profitable. They can build pyramids and extermination camps, and keep at it, even in the absence of the aforementioned satisfied customers.

Curiously, though no proof is ever offered of the "good governments do," none is ever required. In every society, some group maintains – or attempts to maintain – a monopoly on the use of force. That monopoly, called "government," is backed by guns and bombs, not by evidence or argument.

It is also very profitable. In the United States of America, the government captures and spends nearly $2 out of every $5 of GDP, directly. It forces the economy to spend at least another $1.50, thanks to laws and regulations, bringing the total to over half of GDP. Naturally, such a rich source of lucre doesn't go unnoticed. Groups, families, and factions contest control of the government's monopoly... launching revolutions, civil wars, and elections.

In modern democracies, the foxes that end up in control of the chicken house are usually those that have the support of the most hens. And this is an important nuance, one that we think explains the attraction of today's democracies over other forms of government. It is not the fact that it is a democracy that makes it appealing, or even that it is government at all, but that it is a "consensual" system. The trend towards female political leaders, for example, is probably evidence of further feminization, favoring the consensual approach over its more masculine, brutal nature. That is, like the willing workers slaving away on the pyramids... or the eager volunteers signing up for the army in wartime... the win-lose deal that is at the heart of all government is hard to see. Thanks to the elites' skill at myth-making... and the masses' skill at myth-taking... the obvious scams of democracy are hardly noticed, barely resisted, and rarely resented.

Democracies encourage a persuasive campaign of PR and propaganda, convincing the poor voters that whatever program is offered will be in their best interest. They are told that, despite the evidence of their own eyes and experience, by voting, they control the government, and that the government "is all of us," as Hillary Clinton put it. Since they control it, and since it is "us," it must act in our interests... with every program somehow intended to promote the "common good."

It may be hard for the common citizen to find much common good in the feds' schemes. But fortunately for the government, he doesn't try very hard. His government, his church, and his newspaper all insist that it is for his own good, whatever it is. Who is he to argue with them?

And yet... as we have seen, Jesus had no faith in any of this bunkum. Instead, he made it clear that there is no such thing as the "common good." Good is uncommon... it is for each of us to find... and do... individually. We do not enter the Kingdom of Heaven by showing our voter registration cards, party affiliations, drivers' licenses, club memberships, or church attendance records. We get there one by one, on our own merits.

"Render unto Caesar that which is Caesar's" is one of His dicta. Typically clever, almost evasive, it left open a momentous question for roughly 2,000 years – what is Caesar's? Moral philosophers had been bedeviled by the question for even longer: If you want to do the right thing, can you just obey the feds... or do you have to figure it out for yourself?

Finally, in June 2018, like Moses coming down from Mount Sinai, legal and biblical scholar and then U.S. attorney general, Jeff Sessions – who had previously distinguished himself by sponsoring a bill to name September "National Prostate Cancer Awareness Month" – handed down the answer. At the time, news had broken that the U.S.

government was housing immigrants illegally crossing the Mexican borders in government facilities, often separating the children from their parents.

Mr. Sessions – explaining to the nation how it came to be that America separated young children from their parents and put them in cages at the border (despite no trial... no judge... no jury... no evidence of wrongdoing presented... and no court order or sentence) – cited chapter and verse.

The Bible says we can do it, was his reply. Specifically, he cited Romans 13 for his moral authority, in which the apostle Paul urges his correspondents to "obey the laws of the government."

TIT FOR TAT

We have seen that the private sector vernacular is a vast and intricately complex web of win-win deals: "I'll scratch your back; you scratch mine." "I'll say thank you to you if you say thank you to me." "I'll give you $3 if you give me a gallon of gas." Tit for Tat. To get, you give. The whole elaborate edifice of modern, civilized capitalism – its giant corporations, its swaps and debentures, its markets and supertankers – rests upon those very simple deals, in which single individuals make individual choices. A man buys a pack of cigarettes and sends a signal to a vast corporation – it, too, composed of thousands of individuals. In response, it may change the color, add more nicotine, or raise the price. Hundreds, thousands, millions, billions of little private deals create a huge global economy.

Of course, the public sector includes decent people doing decent things, too. It has real workers – teachers, firemen, doctors, builders – who do real work that people might otherwise pay for voluntarily. But there is one thing, and one thing only, that distinguishes, fundamentally, the public sector from the private sector. Every deal in the public sector, no matter how trivial, is backed by the threat of violence.

In the case of Mr. Sessions, he was merely defending a program that routinely used violence to separate young children from their parents and put them in cages. His boss, Donald Trump, had vowed to shore up America's southern border. Separating children from their parents, who were supposedly going to be charged with a misdemeanor, seemed like it might be an effective means of discouraging illegal entry. But seeing videos of crying children did not sit well with many Americans. What the feds were doing was probably lawful – they had no way of knowing. But was it right?

Citing Romans 13, Mr. Sessions was clearly not helping his argument – that whatever the feds say to do is the right thing to do. Because if you could go to Heaven simply by doing what the feds tell you, Jesus could have kept his mouth shut.

ORDERED TO SHOOT

The question was posed, perhaps most vividly, to the Reserve Police Battalion 101 from Hamburg, also known as the "Hamburg Policemen," in 1942. They were men in their thirties, a little old for front-line duties. But as the war in the East developed, they were called in to deal with the "Jewish Problem," which led to the children issue. That is, they were meant to take Jews to work camps or death camps. Or to camps where they could be worked to death. But children, the sick, and old people just got in the way. What to do with them?

Battalion 101 veteran Bruno Probst later testified that while no specific orders to shoot them were given, the officers made it clear that "nothing could be done with such people." By then, things were heating up on the Eastern Front. More and more captives – Jews and Poles – were coming into the Nazi grip. They needed to be "processed," removed, and resettled. On July 13, 1942, the real killing began in the village of Józefów, Poland. As many as 1,500 Jews were lined up. The Hamburg Policemen were given the task of killing them. As far as any of them knew, it was a lawful order. It came from officers, who got it from other officers all the way up to Germany's lawful head of state, the Führer himself.

The Hamburg Policemen were overwhelmingly Christian. They might have heard of St. Paul's instructions to the Romans. They probably didn't know that the letter was not written by Paul at all, but by Tertius of Iconium, as modern scholars believe. But it hardly mattered. They were given the order to shoot... and they had been taught to follow orders.

Besides, what higher authority was there than the Führer?

A few hesitated. Fewer still refused. At least one wrote home that he feared God would get even with them. But as the orders kept coming down, the killing became routine. Before they returned to Hamburg, they had killed some 38,000 people – mostly Jews. And yet, they were policemen. They had been trained to uphold the law and to protect people and their property. What was this strange new duty they had been asked to perform? And was it not contrary to their religious beliefs? They were supposed to love their neighbors; what kind of love was this?

Five hundred Hamburg Policemen had reported for duty in Poland. How many do you think refused... or were unable... to do as they had been ordered to do?

Twelve.

We are shocked. But we're not sure why. Did we expect more of them to have a stronger sense of what was wrong and what was right? Or are we surprised that any of them did? The whole episode is so shocking that every detail shocks. Who would give such an order? Who would obey it? And who, surrounded by 488 law-abiding, jack-booted, rifle-toting patriots, would dare to say "no"?

We don't know. We weren't there. We don't know what we would have done. The easiest thing to do is to always follow orders. You are safe. You have the authorities at your back. But at night... with no rifle in your hands and no uniform on your back... who knows what terrors haunt you? Will you be tormented, like Dostoevsky's Raskolnikov, by ghosts and demons? Will you toss and turn, and awaken suddenly in a sweat... cursing life, but fearing what lies beyond it?

Perhaps later, when the fever of life itself breaks, you discover that Hell was not just an idle threat after all… and that maybe a little independent thinking, and less reliance on government's "common good," was in order.

As we have seen throughout this book, government is always an instrument of win-lose deals. This has always been the case. As explained by Italian economist Vilfredo Pareto, it doesn't matter what you call your government; it will always be taken over by the "foxes," who figure out how to use state power for their own benefit. The foxes aren't dumb. And most people – as demonstrated by the Hamburg Policemen – are ready to go along with almost any leader, no matter how diabolical or predatory, if he establishes order and gives them a place in it.

Auschwitz is still available for a visit. There are vestiges of the gulag camps in Siberia and the killing fields in Cambodia. If you really wanted to do a Mass Murder Tour, you might include a trip to the villages of Ukraine, where Stalin's Holodomor (genocide by famine) killed as many as 15 million… or to the Templo Mayor near Tenochtitlán, where thousands of prisoners of war were butchered to satisfy the Aztec's gods.

None of these things were the result of private initiative. No individualism, no matter how libertarian, had anything to do with them. There were no IPOs; no shares in these ventures were sold to the public. None were the result of *laissez faire* capitalism. None of the great disasters of the 20th century were the product of win-win deals. None were the result of chasing profits. None came from having too little government or too much capitalism… or doing too little to enhance the "common good." Instead, every one was a product of state power directed by central planners on behalf of the common good.

SH*THOLE THEORY

Sh*thole Theory first emerged in January 2018, when President Trump allegedly referred to the poor, desperate, and hapless places where refugees come from as "sh*thole countries." When we first caught wind of President Trump's "sh*thole" comment, we were outraged. We thought he was talking about our hometown in Maryland. A family friend described the experience of driving into Baltimore through the neglected neighborhoods:

> *I couldn't believe it. You roll up your windows and lock the doors. And drive as fast as you can. There's just block after block of boarded-up houses and padlocked stores. It doesn't look as though anyone lives there. I don't see how anyone could live there.*

We were, of course, relieved when we realized that our president was referring to foreign sh*tholes… not those in the USA. But that's the problem with sh*tholes: They're all over the place. And they don't stay put. Ireland was a sh*thole for about 300 years, after Oliver Cromwell's army laid waste to the country. In the early 20th century, it was considered such a woebegone, poverty-stricken, benighted backwater – and its people so disagreeable – that efforts were made to keep the Irish from immigrating to the U.S. Now, Ireland is not so bad. Few people would call it a "sh*thole" today. China was a sh*thole when we first visited back in the 1980s. Nothing seemed to work. The roads were horrible. The people stared at us as though they were starving and we were a plump puppy. But when we went back years later, China didn't seem like a sh*thole at all. In many ways, it is now more advanced than the U.S. – with more skyscrapers, luxury autos, and super-high-speed trains.

And talk about sh*tholes – at the turn of the 20th century, the Philippines must have been one of the world's major sh*tholes. It came under U.S. control as part of the spoils of the Spanish-American War. Then, what to do with the faraway islands? Fortunately, God spoke directly to President McKinley and told him. Addressing a group of Methodist clergymen in 1898, he explained:

> *The truth is I didn't want the Philippines, and when they came to us, as a gift from the gods, I did not know what to do with them. I*

walked the floor of the White House night after night until midnight. And I am not ashamed to tell you, gentlemen, that I went down on my knees and prayed Almighty God for light and guidance more than one night. And one night late it came to me this way – I don't know how it was, but it came: (1) That we could not give them back to Spain – that would be cowardly and dishonorable; (2) that we could not turn them over to France or Germany – our commercial rivals in the Orient – that would be bad business and discreditable; (3) that we could not leave them to themselves – they were unfit for self-government – and they would soon have anarchy and misrule over there worse than Spain's was; and (4) that there was nothing left for us to do but to take them all, and to educate the Filipinos, and uplift and civilize and Christianize them, and by God's grace do the very best we could by them, as our fellow-men for whom Christ also died.

Alas, the Filipinos were ungrateful. Instead of graciously accepting the bounty of American rule, as ordained by God Himself, they resisted. The U.S. Army had to kill 200,000 of them to get them to say "thank you." An American general told his troops to kill everyone over the age of 10 – civilians as well as combatants – since they were all capable of carrying firearms. Whether this was what God had in mind or not, we don't know. But it helps understand what government is, how it works, and how it fits into our schematic of civilized life.

Sh*thole Theory suggests that there are some bad places with bad people we wouldn't like to have as neighbors here in the U.S. But like all "public myths," it suffers from distance and dishonesty. More broadly, it lacks useful substance. You could take issue with it by pointing to a recent study, for example, that suggests that when African immigrants move into an African-American community in the U.S., the crime rate goes down. And in London, African immigrants tend to earn more, and get more advanced degrees, than the native English population. "Sh*thole people," in other words, do not necessarily take their sh*tholes with them; they might just improve the places they move to.

But we do not live in a "country," or know "the people" who live there. Instead, we know specific individuals, and families in specific communities. We may talk about countries in generalized, statistical, public-information terms. It allows us to "groupify" people and places, to categorize them, and to formulate public policies to suit them. The "poor" ones will get foreign aid. Richer ones will get trade deals. But the particular – the real quality of life in a particular place at a particular time – defies generalization.

We've been visiting Nicaragua for nearly 20 years. The second-poorest country in Latin America, after Haiti... and ruled by a socialist government with lunatic tendencies (the wife of the president is widely considered to be a real witch)... it would easily qualify as a "sh*thole." Sh*thole Theory suggests that it is an awful place.

But in our experience, in the particular, it's not so bad. Just the opposite. The people are among the nicest anywhere we've been. And the quality of life on Nicaragua's Pacific Coast can be the highest in the world. One of the most felicitous scenes we've ever witnessed was in Nicaragua. Children had tied a rope to a tree leaning over a river. They swung out over the water and jumped into the river. No computers. No big screen. No admittance fee. The water was warm. The sun shone brightly. The kids were as near to being completely happy as any we have ever seen.

But there is no place in Sh*thole Theory for particulars. No room for quality. No space for specifics, nuance, or irony.

BACK TO CHARM CITY

West of Eutaw Street in Baltimore is a wide expanse of modest houses, built in the 19th and early 20th centuries to offer comfortable, fairly spacious, airy, and light homes to the city's proletariat. The ubiquitous white marble steps became an icon of Baltimore itself. It was a ritual of city life for housewives to scrub them clean; sloshing the wash water over them was a sacred civic duty.

But there are hardly any clean marble steps in West Baltimore today. And hardly any housewives. And hardly any husbands. And hardly any working people, either. Whole neighborhoods have turned into semi-abandoned slums, with boarded-up and/or burned-out houses, and trash scattered in alleys and vacant lots. As for the people who remain, they are like survivors of a catastrophic War of the Worlds, living amongst the ruins like rats, barely literate, barely numerate, and barely civilized. A child born here cannot even expect to collect Social Security; he will live only as long as someone in famine-plagued North Korea. His living conditions will be worse than in Nigeria. The poor kid has been born in a sh*thole.

Racists will say: "Well, what do you expect? That's the way those people are." But "those people" weren't that way before 1965. Between 1940 and 1960, the black poverty rate had been nearly cut in half. Blacks were gaining ground on whites – with a steady increase in black professionals, and a doubling of income for blacks in skilled trades.

The streets of West Baltimore were relatively safe, inhabited by families with two parents. In the 1880s, more than three-quarters of black families had both parents present. As recently as 1950, black women were more likely to be married than white women; only 9% of black children lived in single-parent homes.

Today, everyone knows that Baltimore's slums are hellholes of drugs, crime, and poverty. But how did they get to be that way? Simple. The feds undermined the fundamental win-win deals that make civilization possible – work... family... marriage... and "gentle commerce." In effect, they decivilized the city.

Win-win deals aren't necessarily easy. And they're not necessarily successful. But if you want to earn a living, your best bet is to get up in the morning, dress properly, mind your manners, and often do things you'd rather not do. You might prefer to sit in the shade drinking a beer. But the work world has its own plans, its own schedule, and its own rules. Whistles blow at factory gates. Clerks hustle to their desks. There are meetings to attend, targets to hit, budgets to keep within, and bosses to please.

Likewise, if you want to get married, you have to bring something to the deal. You're proposing a partnership. You need something to offer to your partner. And you must hold up your end of the bargain. Then, to make a lasting deal, you have to compromise. The other party wants someone who at least pulls his own weight. She doesn't want the man smoking in the house. He doesn't like the color pink. He snores. She whines. And yet, a form of marriage has proven such a big win-win that it is universally present – in every civilized culture we've heard of.

It's not hard to imagine why. Keeping a house, raising children, earning a living, dealing with life's challenges – it's not easy, even with two people on the job. Ideally, each party to the marriage brings something the other lacks. One earns money. The other is a good housekeeper. One can do math. The other does words. One is daring. The other is timid. One spends. One saves. Together, they succeed. The whole civilized edifice is made possible by just extending the division of labor. Marriage is the first, and most basic, building block.

And if they don't succeed, nothing does. As Daniel Patrick Moynihan, assistant secretary of labor under President Lyndon B. Johnson, noted in his landmark report in 1965, the disintegration of the family leads to the destruction of the whole community.

Intentionally or accidentally, federal War on Poverty programs, begun that same year, went to work on the family with torch and pliers. Its Aid to Families with Dependent Children program only gave money to women if "no man was in the house." A blog, citing reports by The Heritage Foundation and the Cato Institute, elaborates:

> *For the next few decades, means-tested welfare programs such as food stamps, public housing, Medicaid, day care, and Temporary Assistance to Needy Families penalized marriage. A mother generally*

received far more money from welfare if she was single rather than married. Once she took a husband, her benefits were instantly reduced by roughly 10 to 20 percent.

...FamilyScholars.org adds that "such a system encourages surreptitious cohabitation," where "many low-income parents will cohabit without reporting it to the government so that their benefits won't be cut." These couples "avoid marriage because marriage would result in a substantial loss of income for the family."

When the War on Poverty was announced, the out-of-wedlock birthrate was only 3% for the nation and 24% for blacks. Today, three out of four black children in the U.S. are born to unmarried women.

Avoiding poverty and staying out of jail are easy, say the experts. Just get married and stay married. Women seem to have a "civilizing influence," say the experts. But since the War on Poverty began, marriage rates have fallen and crime rates have risen. Poverty has increased. As to the precise cause-and-effect of these things – marriage, crime, and poverty – no one knows. But the links are undeniable.

And the feds didn't stop there. They also undermined the one thing that is probably the most critical element of civilization: the win-win deal. In a broad sense, the whole welfare system encouraged people not to work. "You get what you pay for," said Milton Friedman. The welfare system paid for idleness; it got plenty of it.

Minimum-wage laws also knocked the lowest rung off the employment ladder. It didn't make sense to hire people whose skills made them worth less than the statutory minimum. By the 1970s, the schools were failing as communities fell apart. This left young blacks with very low skill levels and, therefore, few ways to get a start in the win-win world of work. Various studies have tried to quantify the loss of jobs owing to minimum-wage laws. Some put the figure for unskilled black Americans as high as 21% (in New York). In 2000, researchers Richard

Burkhauser, Kenneth Couch, and David Wittenburg concluded that minimum wage increases "significantly reduce the employment of the most vulnerable groups… young black adults and teenagers…"

Not satisfied with the destruction thus wrought, the feds went further. In 1971, the Nixon administration announced a "War on Drugs." Since drug use was already heavily concentrated in black communities, the body count in West Baltimore was bound to be high. Many of the people shot dead in Baltimore today, for example, are victims of the drug war. The illegal drug industry cannot turn to the cops or the courts to settle disputes. By definition as well as practical necessity, it operates "outside the law," leading it to collect debts with violence, fight for market share with street battles, and resolve differences with gang warfare.

Many observers – such as Steven Pinker – come to the conclusion that the problem is a kind of failure of the state; that these areas have become effectively state-less, and thus do they slip back into pre-state lawlessness. But the real problem is that the feds had replaced gentle commerce with a nasty combination of illegal drugs and welfare, operated with various degrees of indifference and incompetence. If drugs were legal, for example, the excess profits would evaporate and the industry would soon operate like every other win-win business. Dealers would have to fight for market share in the traditional way – by trying to please customers. Instead, nationwide, more than a million people a year are charged with drug offenses – mostly trivial ones. These people then have police records, further alienating them from the win-win world of work and marriage.

But then, in 2018, the president of the United States had a plan. He wanted to inflict further government on the hapless people of America's inner cities. He wished to make dealing drugs a capital offense. "Trump backs death penalty for drug dealers," was a big headline in March 2018.

If we just increase the penalties, goes the logic, the dealers will go into law or politics, and leave the drug market to the professionals at Novartis and Sanofi. Would that help? The occupation would surely become more hazardous. But wouldn't this make the price of drugs go up, fattening profit margins for those who stay in the business? And what kind of person would continue dealing drugs in the face of the death penalty? Let us guess… the hardened criminal, the desperado with nothing more to lose, and the seasoned crony with fixer-friends in high places.

WHY GOVERNMENT DOESN'T WORK

But wait, you're probably thinking… democratic governments express the "will of the people." Isn't that so? Leaders are voted into office. They pass laws. The laws imposed on the people are the laws the people want. They are meant to protect us… and to promote our general welfare. What is wrong with that? That is the myth that makes consensual democracy relatively benign; the win-lose deal behind it is not so obvious.

As we know by now, the only way to truly promote the general welfare is with win-win deals. But government, by definition, is win-lose. It only gives by taking from someone else. In the past, this truth was out in the open. Let an Attila lead an army onto Times Square… or a Tamerlane put up a tower of severed heads on the White House lawn… and you have no trouble understanding what is going on. There's no subtlety. No mystery. No jaws pumping out dulcet lies. Instead, the politics of it are right out in the open, where everyone can see what is going on. No surprises. No hidden agenda.

Modern democracy, on the other hand, appears to be more civilized and tolerable – mostly because the prevailing myths make it seem more consensual than it really is. Internally at least, it hides its bloody swords and amalgamates the interests of competing groups. Thus is the wickedness of raw, political power clothed in pantsuits, endless pow-wows, and platitudes.

Still, the vital force of government is violence. Government, and government alone, claims the right to force people into win-lose deals. And as our formula, $TS = rv$ $(w\text{-}w - w\text{-}l)$ – total satisfaction is equal to the real value of win-win deals minus win-lose deals – shows, the more win-lose deals you have, the worse off you are. As we've seen, small communities naturally limit the number of win-lose deals they are willing to put up with. The people are too close to the facts to stomach much nonsense. It is not so with large-scale governments, which force win-lose deals on people far away with no real consensual feedback to limit the damage.

The first problem with large-scale central planning is a lack of good information. In a large community, you can't know things in a direct, personal way. Central planners begin with a huge handicap. They cannot know current conditions; that would require an infinite amount of information. It would require, as British philosopher Samuel Bailey wrote in 1840, "minute knowledge of a thousand particulars which will be learnt by nobody but he who has an interest in knowing them." The knowledge needed to make good decisions is dispersed, not concentrated. This leaves elite planners with nothing but a body of public knowledge, which, as we have seen, is little more than myth, claptrap, and statistical guesswork.

Another problem is that while an individual… or even a smallish group… can benefit from a win-lose strategy – with its imposed rules, lies, and larcenies, all backed by violence – it is very hard for a large group to get ahead that way. As the size of the group increases, mathematically, it becomes harder and harder to win by taking things from others. Unlike a win-win society, which becomes richer as it expands, the more people follow the win-lose approach, the less effective it is. Eventually, as former British Prime Minister Maggie Thatcher said of socialism, "you run out of other people's money."

A third, major problem for large-scale planners is the temptation to corruption. In a large community, planners and policymakers are a small minority – often culturally, or even racially, distinct from the people they rule over. Fewer than one out of four adults voted for Trump. Fewer than one out of 1,000 are actually in a position to bend public policy in their direction. These people usually have an agenda that is far different from what the majority would want. Their myths are different; so are their economic interests.

An elite is inevitable. Some people are just faster, smarter, stronger, more cunning, or simply better connected. As society becomes more sophisticated, it needs more people with more skills – priests, professors, generals, engineers... rich people, persuasive people... people who know how to make the plumbing work. These people invent things... they are artists, poets, entertainers... they launch new businesses, write books, and win Nobel Prizes. They are the lead dogs of civilization... exploring, guiding, and experimenting... setting fashions and standards... building schools and insane asylums... and dragging the bulk of mankind forward.

But as the scale of a society grows, the elites acquire more power, which they inevitably use for their own benefit. Thus conflicted, their plans tend to twist, imperceptibly at first, then brazenly, in their own direction. Even the information flow, which they control, is bent to flatter their programs, myths, and prejudices. They sound the alarm about a foreign enemy – and gain the glory of conquest. They show the need for a massive infrastructure project; their brothers-in-law get the contracts. They stir up a rebellion... and they become the new rulers. Typically, whether it is a war on poverty or a war on terror... the elites get the benefits while the commoners pay the price.

As time goes by, the elites get farther and farther away from the average citizen. They live in different zip codes. They work in finance, communications, technology, and government... not in Main Street industries, such as manufacturing, farming, and retail. They get richer... while 90% of the population loses ground financially. Then, the powerful federal falcon no longer pays any attention to the voting falconer. And why should it? The masses have no idea what is going on... how the game is played... or how they are being ripped off.

As the scale increases, a big gap opens between the "leaders"and the "people"... between public policy and private consequences... between real news and "fake news." The elite insiders – in business, government, academia, religion, and the media... left and right... whether it is the centralized government of Louis XIV or the post-World War I USA... Republican or Democrat – become parasites.

A parasite is less lethal than a killer. The parasite wants his host to live, not die. Pinker points out that homicide rates fell as government became stronger. We don't doubt it; modern government has a keen interest in the welfare of its citizens. But it is more like the interest of a good slaveowner than a good parent. The good parent wants his children to grow up to be strong and independent. The good slaveowner wants to keep his slaves as healthy as possible for as long as possible, but only so he can exploit them.

After slavery was abolished in the U.S., many former slaves were said to have missed the order and predictability of life on the ol' plantation. And most citizens of today's democracies find their fetters tolerable... even comfortable. People are easy to deceive, especially when they only have access to "public information." Out of range of the herald's voice, they have no more idea what is going on than the planners. They are encouraged to believe that the collective plans are beneficial. Often, they go along with the gag – for decades – even as the evidence of their daily lives contradicts its premises and undermines its promises.

Even worse – typically, when the elites' frauds fail and their myths give way, they do not simply give up. They do not say, "Ok... We won't rip you off anymore." They turn to force. Consensual governments become less consensual and more confrontational. Then, to encourage compliance, ruthless planners – think Lenin, Hitler, Stalin, Mao, Pol Pot, Kim Jong-il – begin purges, cleansings, regulations, famines, deportations, disappearances, tortures, drone attacks, and mass murders. The planners argue that the people must make sacrifices for the greater good. As Lenin is believed to have said, "You can't make an omelet without breaking some eggs."

People go along with breaking a few eggs (particularly if they belong to someone else) for a while, but the omelet never makes it to the table. No "workers' paradise" ever appears. The War on Drugs (or Poverty... or Crime... or Terror... or Trade) ends in a defeat, not a victory. And if any of these grand programs "succeeds," it does so at a cost that is far out of balance with the reward, and almost always as a result of countermanding some previous planners' programs.

In short, large-scale central planners fail because they claim three things that aren't true: First, that they understand the current conditions (wants, desires, myths, hopes, capabilities, and resources) of the community they are planning for. Second, that they know what the community's future ought to be. And third, that they are capable of creating the future they want.

None of those things is more than an illusion. Together, they constitute what Hayek described as the "fatal conceit that man is able to shape the world around him according to his wishes."

Life on Earth is not so rational that it lends itself to simpleminded, heavy-handed intervention. Bridges are designed. So are houses. And particle accelerators. Economies are not. Nor are societies or families. Instead, they are products of vernacular civilization, in which most of the transactions, most of the time, are the result of evolution, not intelligent design.

Of course, humans can achieve a certain kind of imposed future. If the planners at the Pentagon, for example, decided that a nuclear war would be a good thing, they could bring it about. The effects would be huge. But this is the only kind of alternative future that planners are capable of delivering – one that pulverizes the delicate fabric of evolved gentle commerce and civilized life. Less dramatically, they stretch it out, stain it, and rip it in countless ways.

Win-win is the commonly accepted way to get what you want and need in life. Only crooks, cads, and governments operate on a different model. But we end this chapter by referring to a thought put forward in our last book, *Hormegeddon*. That is, we wondered if large-scale government was simply a transitional institution, like slavery, rather than a permanent feature of human life. Slavery was a win-lose system, too. And for thousands of years, slavery was considered "natural" and inevitable. Even Jesus apparently couldn't imagine life without it. But in the space of a single generation, slavery practically disappeared from the civilized world. Perhaps, someday, that will happen to government, too.

ஃ— **CHAPTER 9** —ஓ

The Deep State

For those who live inside a myth, it seems a self-evident fact.
– John Gray

✛·✛·✛·✛

CHARLES DE GAULLE KNEW how to rally the troops. In April 1961 – almost 16 years after the last gun of World War II had blasted its last shell, and de Gaulle had hung his gold braid and epaulets in the closet – the French president put on his old uniform and went on national television. He told the people of France that their beloved Republic was in grave danger. A *coup d'état* was underway in French Algeria. He called on them to help him stop it.

"Help me!" he said. And they did. The coup was stopped. The leaders were arrested. The country went on with its business.

A friend was involved personally in that coup attempt:

> *I really didn't know what I was doing. I just got caught up in right-wing politics. I thought de Gaulle was ruining the country.*
>
> *My job was to seize a small airport. I drove out in the night, with a small group. It was a small airport. We expected to take out our guns, wave them around, and announce that the airport was now under the control of the new government, which would be formed in the next few days, after de Gaulle resigned.*

I wasn't even 20 years old. It was all very exciting. De Gaulle had agreed to give independence to Algeria. But Algeria was a part of France. We were protecting the nation.

And I was very lucky. We just sat in the car listening to the radio, waiting for the signal to take action. When we heard that [army units that were supposed to be on the side of the putschists] had surrendered, we just quietly drove home. The leaders were arrested and given prison sentences. I was never identified.

De Gaulle was no stranger to insurrection, insubordination, and treason. He had rebelled against the lawful government of France in June 1940 after the French had signed an armistice with Germany. He fled to England, deserting his post as undersecretary for war, and encouraged the French people to resist occupation. Two months later, he was condemned to death by a court martial. Had he been caught and tried, he would have gotten the firing squad.

Now, the shoe was on the other foot... and the old general knew what to do with it: kick. His television address made no mention of it, but later, the word was out: The coup in French Algeria concerned not only the French but Americans, too. Rumor had it that de Gaulle believed the CIA was behind the coup attempt... and that the notorious intelligence agency was not under then President John F. Kennedy's control. In effect, de Gaulle believed the CIA had gone rogue... and was targeting the elected government of France.

Was that true?

We don't know. But later, Charles de Gaulle said something even more remarkable. After attending JFK's funeral in 1963, he told aides that he believed the CIA had gunned down Kennedy. This detail was published in 2002 in a book, *C'était de Gaulle*, written by Alain Peyrefitte, de Gaulle's minister of information. As far as we know, this comment was not reported in the U.S. press.

Was that true?

Again, we have no way of knowing. Are we being too cynical? A book by David Talbot, *The Devil's Chessboard: Allen Dulles, the CIA, and the Rise of America's Secret Government*, suggests that we're not cynical enough. In January 1961, outgoing President Dwight Eisenhower warned the nation that the "military-industrial complex" was getting too big for its britches. And according to Talbot, JFK was trying to bring it under control.

Most people will say that this is a "conspiracy" theory... as if conspiracies never occurred in fact. Raise the possibility of a "coup" against JFK at a cocktail party, and people edge away from you. The Warren Commission said it wasn't so. But the Warren Commission was dominated by ex-CIA chief, Allen Welsh Dulles, who, says Talbot, was the very person who wanted JFK out of the way.

People conspire all the time. There must be plenty of conspiracies involving political leaders, assassinations, corruption, and treachery.

Boston College professor Lindsey O'Rourke estimates that the U.S. clandestine forces played a role in at least 72 different foreign regime changes between 1947 and 1989 alone. They carried out or assisted in the assassination, or attempted assassination, of foreign leaders hundreds – likely thousands – of times. Fidel Castro alone was targeted 638 times by the U.S. government, according to some estimates. Would it be so surprising that these same people took charge of a regime change in the U.S. too... where they had more at stake?

We can rarely know what actually happens and what motives lie behind the story. Besides, it is hard enough to pull off a complex and controversial operation with the full knowledge and straightforward cooperation of all the participants. Imagine what happens when most people don't know what is going on, and, of those who do, you're not sure who is really with you and who is not. Conspiracies are difficult and often take unexpected (non-conspiratorial) directions.

And why bother with conspiracy anyway? Why bother with

assassination? Killing people seems like an unnecessary provocation. The Deep State doesn't need to kill anyone. And it doesn't need to conspire, at least not in the usual way.

When people talk of the Deep State, they are generally referring to the permanent government run as a collusion between the elite of corporate America and the national security industry. They think of the "military-industrial complex" that General Eisenhower said we "must guard against" in his farewell address in 1961. The concept of a powerful group of insiders – mostly unelected – controlling government policies is hardly original to us. As explained elsewhere, everybody knows that lobbyists, special interests, rich people, non-profits, and corporations exert an influence far beyond their numbers. Recent studies have shown that government policy is much more likely to be affected by these groups than by voters. In other words, the government that is supposed to be "by, for, and of" the people is actually a government of inside operators and privileged elites.

Probably the best book on the subject is Mike Lofgren's *The Deep State: The Fall of the Constitution and the Rise of a Shadow Government*. He shows how little Washington really cares about what voters want. Instead, it regards voters much like a bartender views his drunks. He wishes them a long, happy, and healthy life, but he has no interest in seeing them sober up.

The term "Deep State" was first applied to countries such as Turkey and Egypt. These are places where military/police/security insiders put screws to your thumbs, forcing you to do as you were told. Elections, often rigged, changed ruling parties and their leaders. But the real power was elsewhere.

Mike Lofgren popularized the use of the term in the U.S. But he had a much broader view of the Deep State:

> *The Deep State... is the story of our time. It's the thin red line that runs through the war on terrorism, and a militarized foreign policy.*

Also the financialization and deindustrialization of the economy, and a social structure that has given us the most unequal income distribution in almost a century.

Lofgren worked as a congressional staffer with "top secret" clearance for decades. He noticed that business went on as usual, regardless which party won the White House. Gradually, he came to see that the public spectacle we see on TV and call "politics" is only a small part of the governing system. The important decisions are made by the "foxes" – bureaucrats, lobbyists, campaign contributors, and crony businesses. It was no accident, for example, that not a single member of Congress even bothered to read the Obamacare legislation – a sweeping program that affected almost everyone and altered one-seventh of the nation's GDP. Nor did they bother looking too carefully at Trump's $1.5 trillion tax cut. They knew there was nothing they could do about it.

The Deep State is big... diffuse... and adaptable. Lofgren calls it a "hybrid association of elements of government and top-level finance and industry." It is respectable – even prestigious – including university professors, think tank analysts, lobbyists, and contractors. And it is international. It doesn't care which passport you hold, which party you vote for, or what you think. It includes liberals and conservatives, Republicans as well as Democrats, Platonists and Aristotelians, Catholics as well as Jews.

Internally, these different interests compete for money and power. Traditionally, the "conservatives," for example, want to direct more of your money to the military/security industries. The "liberals" want to favor cronies in the social welfare industries. Even within sectors, there is competition. The Navy may want more ships. The Air Force may want more planes. The Army may want more tanks. Most of the news you hear focuses on these battles within the Deep State to see who will get the most of your money. Elections shift the favors from one crony industry to another. The faces change. Budgets are adjusted, marginally.

But the major goal of the insiders remains: to keep the power and money headed in their direction.

The headlines can rant about a victory for the Right or a defeat for the Left. But behind the scenes, the real winner is almost always the same: the Deep State itself. That's why, though President Obama and President George W. Bush were very different personalities with very different ideas, they kept the major programs going in the same direction for 16 years: war abroad and entitlements at home. And even now, with the "Great Disrupter" in the White House, what's new? Stylistically, much. Programmatically, little.

"Avoid foreign entanglements" was advice given to the new nation by its "father," George Washington. But more than two centuries later, there is scarcely a foreign power anywhere in the world – no matter how insignificant – with which the U.S. doesn't want to tangle... and no messy war, clumsy trade deal, squirrelly treaty, or wasteful foreign aid program it doesn't want to get entangled in.

The wars are rarely "won" in a conventional sense. It is almost impossible to win them. And there is no real interest in winning anyway. What works for the Deep State is what doesn't work for others. In the War on Drugs, for example, the more the feds try to stop drug-taking, the more the profit margins for illegal distributors fatten, attracting more dealers and more drugs. And in the War on Terror, it is unlikely that victory is even conceivable. Terror is a tactic, not an enemy. It is not going to disappear. As recounted earlier in this book, primitive tribes committed horrible atrocities, intending to terrorize their neighbors, perhaps to drive them off... perhaps as a deterrent against attack.

But as senseless as these wars appear, there is a hidden motive. Wars are profitable – for the Deep State and its war industries. The wars provide justification for shifting wealth from the real economy to the war economy, from people who engage in win-win transactions – trading goods and services with each other to make each other's lives better – to the win-lose economy of guns, prisons, and artificial legs.

Even the War on Poverty has its generals, consultants, and suppliers – none of whom have any interest in actually defeating poverty.

Empires love wars, even – or maybe especially – fake ones. In America's foreign wars, there is little real danger from the enemy. Not one of America's enemies from the past half-century was capable of invading the U.S., stealing our money, ravaging our women, or defeating our armies. These fake wars were simply a way of transferring money and power – from the people who earn them to the foxes in the war-fighting sector, including the Pentagon. Win-lose, in other words.

Major General Smedley Butler, who served in the Philippines as well as in World War I, was, at his death, the most highly decorated Marine in history. He summed up his role:

> I served in all commissioned ranks from Second Lieutenant to Major-General. And during that time, I spent most of my time being a high class muscle-man for Big Business, for Wall Street, and for the Bankers.

"And for the politicians and the Deep State," he might have added.

No matter what the voters want, the Deep State gets what it wants. And what it wants is more of your money… and your liberty. It controls the police, the Pentagon, the departments of health, education, and welfare, and much, much more. Readers are reminded that this Deep State is not a conspiracy, and it is not confined to the U.S. It operates right out in the open and across borders, languages, currencies, and governments. Organizations such as the UN, the IMF, the World Bank, and Goldman Sachs all contribute to the Deep State infrastructure. Of course, those are only token names. There are thousands of institutions, groups, families, businesses, and political parties involved.

The Deep State works cooperatively with its international allies to keep the ruling elites fed, clothed, and housed in the style to which they have become accustomed. Its leaders all worship the same gods (manna and Mars)… speak the same language (international business English)… and work together for the betterment of mankind, or themselves, whichever comes first.

It is impossible to understand the policies of the U.S. government, or of central banks around the world, without understanding the Deep State and its real motives. What it cares about most, of course, is its own survival and aggrandizement. This is hardly an original thought. Our contribution to this genre of thinking is merely to connect the Deep State thighbone to the post-1971 financial system anklebone that funds it. But let us put some more flesh on the bones. Here, we introduce some of the people Eisenhower warned us about. Two of them were in the graduating class of 1974 at West Point.

HERO OF THE SURGE

According to the popular press, former United States Army General David Petraeus was the hero of the "surge" in Iraq. According to famed tank commander Colonel Douglas Macgregor, the heroics were "a remarkable piece of fiction." Petraeus was awarded the Bronze Star for combat valor, but, says Macgregor, "[He has] never pulled a trigger… and has never been in direct fire combat."

In fact, one of the toughest scrapes of Petraeus' life was probably with his own mistress, Paula Broadwell, to whom he divulged national security secrets. Broadwell was writing a biography of Petraeus at the time. As then director of the CIA, you'd think he would have been more careful with his secrets and his alliances, especially his secret alliances.

Asked to resign by Barack Obama, he moved on in 2012. In addition to academic posts, he took the route that has become routine for retiring (even disgraced) generals. He went to Wall Street. In 2013, he joined private equity firm Kohlberg Kravis Roberts, where he heads its "Global Institute." Wall Street has become a stop, usually the last one, on today's *cursus honorum*.

When Eisenhower left the White House, he and his wife Mamie went back to live on the family farm near Gettysburg, Pennsylvania, only a few miles from where his father was born. There is no record of his ever lifting the telephone to urge or cajole a senator for any purpose... much less to lobby on behalf of a defense contractor. There is no record of his ever even visiting Wall Street, let alone taking up employment there. In Eisenhower's era, power and money were separate. The cronies and the capitalists worked in different cities for different goals. Now, they are united in the service of a single master: the Deep State.

Another person Ike might have warned us about is Keith Alexander.

Like Petraeus, Alexander went to West Point and then spent his military career in various "intelligence" roles, where his biggest threats were back-stabbers and paper cuts. By 2010, he was head of the NSA, pushing the "all-the-information-about-everyone" doctrine that has become the substitute for real intelligence in the industry.

But in 2013, while compiling a zillion true facts, Alexander appears to have found not a single one that would suit his purposes. Asked what he was up to, none of the facts on hand was what he wanted, so he invented new ones. No, the NSA did not collect data on U.S. residents, he told Congress, a fact that we now know was untrue.

In addition to apparently lying to his overseers in Congress, he was also where the buck stopped when the biggest breach of government intelligence in U.S. history occurred. In June 2013, one of his own contract employees made off with enough real facts to show that Alexander was giving out phony ones. And when the fibs were revealed by the leaker, Edward Snowden, Alexander resigned.

Again, you might wonder about the value of such a man on the open market. Over 60... untrustworthy... arguably incompetent... Even when he wasn't lying, he was speaking blah-blah. Here's a sample:

As our dependence on information networks increases, it will take a team to eliminate vulnerabilities and counter the ever-growing

threats to the network. We can succeed in securing it by building
strong partnerships between and within the private and public
sectors, encouraging information sharing and collaboration, and
creating and leveraging the technology that affords us the opportunity
to secure cyberspace...

And what hath he wrought? The NSA's budget is classified. But
according to documents leaked by Edward Snowden, the agency spent
$10.5 billion in 2014. Headcount is also classified, but reports estimate
that it employs 40,000 intelligent men and women. And yet... there is
no record of any useful "intelligence" coming out of the NSA. For all
the money and all the invasions of privacy, the nation doesn't seem to
have been made any safer. We shall return to Mr. Alexander shortly...

THE "PIMPOCRACY"

The Deep State is not all of us. It is only some of us. And some who
are not us at all. It is a curious group; some of its main components are
not even American citizens. For example, Israel, a foreign government,
occupies an important position in the Deep State hierarchy. Through
its billionaire political donors – Haim Saban, Paul Singer, and Sheldon
Adelson (who is the top contributor to both Donald Trump and
Israeli Prime Minister Benjamin Netanyahu) – and its lobbyists at the
American Israel Public Affairs Committee (AIPAC), and other well-
funded organizations, Israel may exert more influence on U.S. foreign
policy than 200 million American voters.

Many international corporations, global organizations, and supra-
government agencies are also part of the Deep State. And overseas banks
with foreign owners are major beneficiaries. Together, they – along with
favored domestic industries, the bureaucracy itself, special interests, and
cronies of various stripes and persuasions – run the U.S. government and
control the police, the armed forces, the financial industry, the medical
industry, the education industry, and other major parts of the economy.

Today, we still have the same apparent structure of government in the U.S. that we had 200 years ago. George W. Bush said it was the "world's oldest democracy." And maybe it is. But it's not what it used to be. The words are the same. The form is the same. The myth has been preserved. The country is still called a constitutional republic. People believe in it and use the writings of the Founding Fathers to help them make their arguments.

But under the hood, the motor and drivetrain are completely different. As our old friend, investor and author Jim Davidson, puts it, the U.S. is now a "pimpocracy" (the feds offer favors... someone else is forced to provide them). People still go to the polls and imagine that they are deciding the fate of the nation. But it isn't true. An analysis by Princeton and Northwestern universities showed that "economic elites and organized groups representing business interests have substantial independent impacts on U.S. government policy, while mass-based [i.e., pluralist] interest groups and average citizens have little or no influence." In other words, the U.S. government actually functions more like an oligarchy than a democracy.

In a study of 1,779 proposed policy changes between 1981 and 2002, the researchers found that even when 80% of the population favored a particular policy change, the desired change occurred only 43% of the time. Hence their conclusion: "When a majority of citizens disagrees with economic elites or with organized interests, they generally lose."

By contrast, economic elites, representing the top 1% of the population, were able to push through the policy changes they wanted as much as 70% of the time, according to Princeton professor Martin Gilens.

"He who pays the piper calls the tune," is the old expression. But it costs remarkably little for the Deep State to call the tune of U.S. government policy. A research project by the Sunlight Foundation probed the darkness between 2007 and 2012, tracking 200 of America's most "politically active corporations":

> *After examining 14 million records, including data on campaign contributions, lobbying expenditures, federal budget allocations and spending, we found that, on average, for every dollar spent on influencing politics, the nation's most politically active corporations received $760 from the government.*

On these numbers, no other investment comes close; the best thing a corporation can do with its money is not build new factories, undertake research, add employees, or develop new products and markets. The best thing it can do is join the Deep State and further corrode the political process.

As time goes by, more and more people – usually in loosely organized groups – find ways to join up and exploit the system. They use the "government" to gain an advantage or privilege. As this happens, the system retains its outward appearance, but it is corrupted from the inside out. It gradually ceases to serve the common interest that made it so successful in the first place, and begins to serve, primarily, the interests of those who actually control it.

In *The Wealth of Nations*, Adam Smith explained that...

> *People of the same trade seldom meet together, even for merriment and diversion, but the conversation ends in a conspiracy against the public, or in some contrivance to raise prices.*

Mancur Olson, a professor at the University of Maryland, provided more insight two centuries later. He explained how "distributional coalitions" gradually capture the machinery of politics and use it for their own advantage. The cronies, he added in his book, *The Rise and Decline of Nations*, "obtain policies that favor themselves and work in different ways against the interests of the larger unorganized groups in the society, thereby making the distribution of income far more unequal." This process shifts wealth from those who earn it to those who control the government. It also reduces output overall, since it interferes with capital formation, decision making, and investment. As Olson put it, it creates a "perverse policy syndrome... [that] promotes inefficiency and stagnation as well as inequality."

Inefficiency and stagnation reduce wealth and lead to dissatisfaction... which leads to a loss of faith. The magic fades. The myth erodes. Defections increase. And those who control the system find they have to come down harder and harder on the lemon to get out the same amount of juice.

BIGGER AND BADDER THAN YOU THINK

We lived in France for 20 years, and still own a house there. In France, the size of government is notoriously about 60% of GDP, compared to about 20% for the U.S. This made us suspicious. Because it always seemed as though the feds had about the same reach in both countries.

For example, we once went to the hospital in Poitiers for an emergency procedure. As near as we could tell, it functioned just like hospitals in the U.S., with the same protocols established by the medical industry and the government, and similar third-party, mixed private/public payment systems. It even looked and smelled like a hospital in the U.S., despite the fact that medical care in France is a government activity, and in the U.S., it is private.

Intrigued by the comparison between the French and American healthcare systems, we took a closer look. And what we found was what we expected: there ain't much difference. Both the French and the U.S. health systems are mixtures of the medical care industry, the insurance business, politics, and bureaucracy. Neither can be said to be "private," although both have private sector elements that are more or less heavily regulated. In both countries, medical care should be considered a quasi-government activity.

In both countries, medical care is expensive. In the U.S., it is outrageous. Costa Rica, for example, has a higher life expectancy than the U.S. Yet its costs for medical care average only about $1,400 a year per person. That is only about one-seventh the average in the U.S.

Likewise, our children also went to "private" schools in France. Similar to the private schools in America, there was heavy government involvement in the curriculum and the school finances. This was worthy of extra study, too. In both systems, there is a mix of public and private funding. And in both systems, the feds are so deeply involved – as owners, supporters, or competitors – the whole activity should be considered "quasi-governmental."

The "quasi" covers a lot of ground. The feds do not control everything that is taught in the schools, nor every doctor and his prescriptions. They don't control where you live, either. But in all cases, tax breaks, zoning rules, licensing requirements, building codes, public road access, public transportation, and energy prices (as influenced by subsidies and penalties to the energy industry) will have a big impact on your decision. The feds do not directly control what food you eat or what drugs you take, either. But the choices you have are restricted and channeled by the authorities.

Since 1970, the number of U.S. doctors has tripled. But the number of "administrative employees" has gone up 3,000%. The same is true in education. Teachers provide real value for money; administrators play politics. Since 1970, the number of teachers has risen about 60%. The increase in the number of non-teaching administrators is more than twice that.

You can see the same trend in the military, too. The military is pure politics, in a sense. It is meant to be a win-lose business, and it is intended to use violence. And yet, even the military can be undermined and diverted from its real mission – by Deep State politics. The ideal fighting force is "lean and mean." Fighting men need to be young and vigorous. So, as they aged, the Pentagon used to say it was "up or out." Old soldiers were dead wood... unless they were destined for the top.

And dead wood at the top was fatal. They slowed down decision-making. They wanted to "fight the last war." They got in the way. There was only one officer for every 10 enlisted men when the U.S. won World War II. Now, there is enough dead wood for a forest fire – twice as many officers and four times as many generals... and we haven't won a war since.

Even in industries that are otherwise untainted by government bamboozles, the effect of public money could play a bigger role than it seems. A business could book $100 million in software sales, for example, but only make a profit on a $10 million federal contract. Were the feds to go away, so would the entire business. Likewise, a private college could depend on revenue from student loans for the decisive part of its budget. So could a hotel depend on the custom of federal employees, even though it is not the bulk of its revenue.

What is the effect of so much money, so many rules and regulations, and such deep roots into the economy? As President Reagan's chief budget advisor, David Stockman, foresaw more than 30 years ago, we are seeing the final "triumph of politics." The Mises Institute gives us the bottom line: If you add up all the regulations, rules, payoffs, bribes, subsidies, and transfers required by law, the U.S. actually has more "government" per person than France.

TEN THOUSAND COMMANDMENTS

The U.S. is supposed to be a nation of laws, not of men. But since the 1960s, it is a nation of regulations, too... rules imposed by unelected apparatchiks, on and off the federal payroll, who are becoming bolder and more prolific. While it is impossible to accurately measure how much control over the U.S. economy and our private lives these insiders have, we can look at the pages of the Federal Register for an indication. The register is the official journal of the federal government. In its pages, you will find every rule, regulation, and claptrap agency dictum the feds have to offer.

In 2013, the 20th anniversary edition of *Ten Thousand Commandments*, the annual report from the Competitive Enterprise Institute, documented 81,883 new regulations during the two decades that had passed since the first edition. Flash-forward to 2019 – that number is 101,380.

On average, a new regulation – often with criminal or civil penalties attached – appeared at the rate of one every 2 hours and 9 minutes. In 2013, the total annual burden on the economy was estimated at $1.8 trillion, an amount that has surely jumped over the $2 trillion mark by now.

The number of specific regulatory restrictions recorded in the Code of Federal Regulations (CFR) is far greater. In 2010, the number topped 1 million. But in 2010, the regulators were just getting started. By the time Barack Obama left office six years later, regulators and lobbyists were at work on an estimated 4,000 more rules covering everything from e-cigarettes to energy efficiency to sugar in cranberry juice.

In 2014 alone, 224 new laws were enacted by Congress. But 3,554 new rules were issued by unelected officials, bringing the total over the last 20 years to more than 100,000. Each of these new rules required some measure of action or forbearance that ought to be included on the government side of the ledger rather than as a part of private enterprise.

The Competitive Enterprise Institute totes the bill:

> *If one assumed that all costs of federal regulation and intervention flowed all the way down to households, U.S. households would "pay" $14,976 annually on average in regulatory hidden tax. That payment amounts to 23% of the average income of $63,784 and 29% of the expenditure budget of $51,100. The "tax" exceeds every item in the budget except housing. More is "spent" on embedded regulation than on health care, food, transportation, entertainment, apparel and services, and savings.*

Economist George Stigler went on to propose a general theory in which "every industry or occupation that has enough political power to utilize the state will seek to control entry. In addition, the regulatory policy will often be so fashioned as to retard the rate of growth of new firms."

That insight may be useful; it helps explain how government retards growth and concentrates wealth in the hands of those who are already wealthy. But it is not cynical enough. Industry regulation may be more than just an opportunity for private interests to use the feds for their own benefit. It is an opportunity for the feds to use industry, too... to extend their reach beyond the laws of the land... and for them both to conspire and collude against the public.

FOLLOW THE MONEY

A government needs money to function. It is the ability to withhold funding that, in theory and in fact, allows people to control their local governments. The Magna Carta Libertatum, for example, was grudgingly accepted by King John of England, largely because he needed money. His son, Henry III, reaffirmed it twice – the second time clearly in exchange for new taxes. And his son, Edward I, did so again, this time making it part of England's "law of the land."

It was access to money that led France's Louis XVI to convene his parliament, too. He needed the assembly to consent to levying taxes. This assembly ran away from him, asserting its own authority – ultimately costing Louis his head.

The American Revolution began as a tax revolt. Then, the U.S. Constitution put the power of the purse clearly in the hands of the people's representatives. Congress approves the budget. Congress raises money. Congress can cut off funding for whatever project it chooses.

The founders of the American republic were well versed in Greek and Roman history. They knew how democracies degraded into dictatorships. They counted on "checks and balances" to keep power under control. They admired the Roman Republic. It is not by accident that the United States and the Republic of Rome both consist of three branches of government, each applying a restraining force on the other.

On the other hand, the American founders saw the Roman Empire that followed as despotic, evil, and ultimately, ruinous. And they saw how powerful, charismatic generals were always a threat to civilian government. That was why Caesar was forbidden from leading his troops across the Rubicon. He could come to Rome himself, but not at the head of his army.

In the American Constitution, the power to make war was taken away from the chief executive. Only Congress had the power to declare war. And then it, and only it, had to find the troops to fight it and the money to pay for it. There should be no question of "forever wars" and open military budgets. The security industry – government and private – should always be under the congressional heel.

But since the Korean War, U.S. armed forces have gotten used to entering into action on the president's say-so alone. "On paper," a declaration of war is still a requirement. But the whole country has gotten used to a new form of government.

Bankers, or more broadly, money men, have always been drawn to government. Regardless of how they make their money, they typically turn to the police power of the state to protect it... and enhance it. Often, they finance wars, too. This is always a risky thing to do. Wars are lost as well as won. And sometimes, it is easier for a king to extinguish a creditor than a debt.

But the post-1971 system is something new. No more did the lenders have to worry about getting their money back; it wasn't their money in the first place. It is a new system, based on credit. Since it requires no savers, neither does it require any earners. Nor does it require any additional tax on earnings. Congress need not raise taxes in order to finance a war in Iraq or Afghanistan. It simply issues more debt. Nor does Congress need to call up additional troops (though it may). The

Deep State has both money available and a permanent, standing army. Congress gets all the benefit of a war – military contracts, lobbying, flag-waving, campaign contributions, post-congressional sinecures – with none of the costs.

Tax revenues, too, are a feature of easy-money financing. Over the last 30 years, stimulus policies – otherwise described as "financialization," aka shifting wealth from Main Street to Wall Street – have added trillions to U.S. asset prices. The Deep State has been a major beneficiary. Cronies, contractors, and government hacks have enjoyed increased revenues, bonuses, and capital gains, as well as low financing costs.

In the crisis of 2008-2009, tax revenues collapsed, along with the stock market and GDP. The central bank swung into action. But for whom? Who gained? The newspapers said it was Wall Street. Or "the one percent." Or "the rich." But the real winner was the Deep State.

EVERYBODY'S A TARGET

Bill Binney worked for the NSA for 32 years. It was he who "created the agency's mass surveillance program." Now, that program collects 100 billion emails per day… and 20 trillion communications altogether.

Washington's Blog, reporting on Binney's comments on mass surveillance, writes:

> *If anyone gets on the government's "enemies lists," then the stored information will be used to target them. Specifically, he notes that if the government decides it doesn't like someone, it analyzes all of the data it has collected on that person and his or her associates over the last 10 years to build a case against him.*

And another post from *Washington's Blog*:

> *All of the information gained by the NSA through spying is then*

shared with federal, state and local agencies, and they are using that information to prosecute petty crimes such as drugs and taxes. The agencies are instructed to intentionally "launder" the information gained through spying, i.e., to pretend that they got the information in a more legitimate way... And to hide that from defense attorneys and judges.

Which brings us back to Keith Alexander, the geeky "intel" officer put in charge of the NSA in 2005, whom we mentioned earlier. He wanted to put into service bigger, faster, better information collection systems. It was expensive, but this investment heightened his own power and prestige. Not only that, it made him very useful to the info-tech industry and the Deep State.

"Old soldiers never die," said General Douglas MacArthur in his farewell address. "They just fade away." MacArthur had been in three major wars. He had been a target at close range at least half a dozen times. He had been stabbed by a bayonet and gassed. He survived the Veracruz expedition and World War I. In World War II, he led U.S. forces to a successful conclusion against Japan, with relatively few casualties on the American side.

Keith Alexander was a soldier, too, or so it says on his résumé. There is no record of Alexander ever coming into contact with live ammunition, but he had plenty of contact with live money. So, it seemed natural that after presiding over the biggest security breach in U.S. history, and after lying to Congress, he didn't fade away.

Like Petraeus, he went to Wall Street. "Thank you for your service," said the Street. According to a report in the press in early 2014, the Securities Industry and Financial Markets Association offered to pay his firm, IronNet, $600,000 a month for advice.

What has Mr. Alexander done to deserve such generous compensation? What contribution could he have made to our country? For starters, he was a strong proponent of the Utah Data Center in

Bluffdale, Utah. Completed in 2014, the facility cost $1.5 billion to build, plus another $2 billion for electronic components. It consumes about $40 million worth of electricity each year and uses 1.7 million gallons of water each day to cool the massive rows of data servers it houses.

The data center is overseen by the NSA. Its official purpose is classified. But everybody knows it collects data from emails, phone calls, text messages, and online chats on the scale of several exabytes a year. For reference, one exabyte of data is equivalent to one hundred thousand times all the information stored in the Library of Congress.

You don't put that kind of hardware in place just to snoop on a handful of woebegone terrorists. Instead, the idea is to keep records on everyone, so that at any time, the Deep State can find out what it needs to know about anyone. *Wired* magazine wrote about "the country's biggest spy center" in 2012:

> *"[T]his is more than just a data center," says one senior intelligence official, who, until recently, was involved with the program. The mammoth Bluffdale center will have another important, and far more secret, role that, until now, has gone unrevealed. It is also critical, he says, for breaking codes. And code-breaking is crucial, because much of the data that the center will handle – financial information, stock transactions, business deals, foreign military and diplomatic secrets, legal documents, confidential personal communications – will be heavily encrypted.*
>
> *According to another top official also involved with the program, the NSA made an enormous breakthrough several years ago in its ability to cryptanalyze, or break, unfathomably complex encryption systems employed by not only governments around the world, but also many average computer users in the U.S. The upshot, according to this official: "Everybody's a target; everybody with communication is a target."*

Keith Alexander said so himself in September 2013:

I believe it is in the nation's best interest to put all the phone records into a lockbox that we could search.

Who's "we"? If Generals de Gaulle and Eisenhower were right, "we" means the people with a dull, professional interest in protecting the nation... and a keen personal interest in protecting themselves. They will be the ones with the key to the lockbox.

Keith Alexander is probably the biggest single figure in the Deep State machinery. But there are thousands more whose names and faces are not known. In July 2010, *The Washington Post* carried an article by Dana Priest and William M. Arkin headlined "Top Secret America: A hidden world growing beyond control." The reporters found some 1,271 different government organizations and 1,931 private companies working on terrorist-related projects. They were installed in as many as 10,000 locations across the U.S., with 854,000 people – more than the entire population of Baltimore – holding security clearances.

Eight years later, the Intercept found that the NSA had established giant "spy hubs" in eight U.S. cities:

The secrets are hidden behind fortified walls in cities across the United States, inside towering, windowless skyscrapers and fortress-like concrete structures that were built to withstand earthquakes and even nuclear attack. Thousands of people pass by the buildings each day and rarely give them a second glance, because their function is not publicly known. They are an integral part of one of the world's largest telecommunications networks – and they are also linked to a controversial National Security Agency surveillance program.

Who are these people? What are they doing that is useful or worthwhile? Does anyone know? Apparently not. The reporters could find no one in any agency or organization who was aware of what the other groups were up to. *The Washington Post* sums it up:

> *The top-secret world the government created in response to the terrorist attacks of Sept. 11, 2001, has become so large, so unwieldy, and so secretive that no one knows how much money it costs, how many people it employs, how many programs exist within it, or exactly how many agencies do the same work.*

This is the heart of the Deep State. It is a combination of government and private businesses, working arm in arm to take advantage of the public. But what is the significance of it? How does the Deep State really affect us? There is no way of knowing for sure. But like government itself, it is not at all bound by the civilized rules, goals, or financial restrictions that limit the rest of the society.

The Deep State functions according to the codes of the security industry, not the securities industry. It is a throwback to a zero-sum world, no stranger to conspiracies… secrets… assassinations… manipulating public opinion… blackmail… or double-dealing. It becomes bolder and more powerful every year. And it has the will and the way to control public policy.

We have also seen that it depends on the easy-money system administered by the Fed and other central banks. And we can guess that since it controls the U.S. government, it will make sure that the easy-money system continues. "Whatever it takes" is what it will do to keep the credit flowing.

GÖTTERDÄMMERUNG FOR DEMOCRACY

In 2013, the Associated Press may have given us a disturbing look into where this is headed when it reported that the Department of Homeland Security bought 1.6 billion rounds of ammunition, including ammo specifically designed for snipers. What was it going to do with all that firepower? *Forbes* comments:

> *[A]t the height of the Iraq War, the Army was expending less than 6 million rounds a month. Therefore 1.6 billion rounds would be enough to sustain a hot war for 20+ years.*
>
> *Add to this perplexing outré purchase of ammo, DHS now is showing off its acquisition of heavily armored personnel carriers, repatriated from the Iraqi and Afghani theaters of operation.*

We doubt that all this military hardware will be necessary. Now, there are better ways of keeping the sheep in the pasture. Elections, for example. They serve three important ends.

First, like any poll or survey, they provide important information. They tell the insiders how far they can go… how far they can push the public… and what they can get away with.

Second, they make the public complicit in whatever the insiders want to do. Voters feel responsible for what happens and assume that it is their fault. "Hey, you voted for the bum," they say to one another.

And third, elections provide a cloak of legitimacy and respectability to the government. As long as the elected windbags in Congress and the White House are out in front, Deep State insiders can do almost whatever they want behind the scenes.

The nature of government is always "conservative" – in the sense that it is used by the people who control it to protect their positions. But, as the source of wealth changes, government turns to face the new enemy. Today, the world's developed countries – especially Japan and those in Europe – are little more than huge, underfunded, and irresponsibly managed pension/insurance programs. That is part of what makes them seem so consensual; they mimic real win-win insurance companies. They take in payments from citizens and they pay out pensions and medical care benefits.

For the last 150 years, the Welfare State has been a fairly good deal for most people. They paid their taxes… and they were likely to get more back than they put in. That can be easily explained. A "mutual" insurance system functions a bit like a tontine. People pool their money. Those still alive share the wealth of those who passed on before them. The losers don't complain. Meanwhile, growing populations put more and more money into the system, which could then be paid out to the fewer older retirees. Economic growth and technological progress, too, have generally made the future richer than the past, making it easy to increase benefits beyond what has actually been contributed.

None of these things are still working. People are living longer, putting additional strain on payouts. Populations are stable… or in some cases, falling. And growth rates are slowing to near zero. This leaves the rational, typical citizen to wonder what benefit he actually receives from his Welfare State. A private insurer could function more efficiently.

If the world's developed countries were private insurance carriers, for example, they would have been pronounced insolvent long ago; they don't have enough assets to cover their liabilities. But since they have the power both to change the terms of the insurance "contracts" as well as to force people to pay into the system, they remain in business. Eventually, however, the benefits that have been promised will have to be trimmed. This will not be a simple debt default or business failure. It will be a political default. The people who were promised benefits will feel cheated, not by a private company, but by their own government. This will call into question the whole system and its premises. Founder of *The Automatic Earth* blog, Raúl Ilargi Meijer, explains:

> *It's over! The entire model our societies have been based on for at least as long as we ourselves have lived, is over! That's why there's Trump.*
>
> *There is no growth. There hasn't been any real growth for years. All there is left are empty, hollow, sunshiny S&P stock market numbers propped up with ultra-cheap debt and buybacks, and employment*

figures that hide untold millions hiding from the labor force. And most of all, there's debt, public as well as private, that has served to keep an illusion of growth alive, and now, increasingly, no longer can.

These false growth numbers have one purpose only: for the public to keep the incumbent powers that be in their plush seats. But they could always ever only pull the curtain of [The Wizard of] Oz over people's eyes for so long, and it's no longer so long.

That's what the ascent of Trump means, and Brexit, Le Pen, and all the others. It's over. What has driven us for all our lives has lost both its direction and its energy.

In the past, "conservatives" – like the old patrician families of Republican Rome – would have kept Welfare State costs under control. Traditionally, they take the long view and are suspicious of change. Conservatives cherish the vernacular habits and myths that create a civilized society; they distrust rule-breakers.

Every group probably benefits by having some people who are eager to try the suspicious mushroom and others who are not. Most innovations fail. What exists now is the result of hundreds of thousands of years of evolutionary trial and error. What "might be," but is not, includes an infinite range of possibilities that have already failed… and millions of dead people.

In a tribal setting, some people had to be willing to try new things; some people had to resist. Without both types of people, a tribe probably had an evolutionary disadvantage.

They might all try to eat a new form of mushroom, for example, and all die from the poison. Or they might all resist the new thing and die of starvation. Either way, from the standpoint of collective genetic survival, it is probably a good thing to have a few conservatives in a group. But the straitlaced, stiff-collared "conservatives" of the past have disappeared from America. We are all eating the mushrooms now!

Why?

Our hypothesis is this: As the new, fake money became available in greater and greater quantities, the need for tough political choices diminished. Why oppose a spending bill if the funds were readily at hand? Why stop nuisance legislation if the economy could easily afford it? Why accept trade-offs... why resist inefficiency and waste... why care if the cronies got sweetheart deals? There was plenty of capital for everyone. Why bother with "horse trading" in Congress if the nags were free for the taking? In other words, there was no reason to not let the Deep State grow... and grow.

Elsewhere in this book, we show that it is the scarcity of capital, not the abundance of it, that leads to progress, growth, and wealth. There are always limits – time, especially. Recognition of these limits is an essential element of civilization. Like everything else in nature, capital obeys the law of diminishing marginal utility. A little is definitely a good thing. A lot may not be so good. If whiskey runs down from the mountains, who's going to build a distillery? In Eden, who needed a spam filter?

The effect of scarcity on politics is similar, but even more perverse. Government doesn't produce wealth. It consumes it. So, government is naturally limited by how much wealth the economy produces. And politicians are limited by how much they can steal. Generally, a poor society can afford little government. A rich society puts up with a lot of it.

What happened to the old conservatives? They were replaced – along with the old money – by new, fake ones. The old conservatives recognized limits. They saw that it was a bad idea to spend too much, or borrow too much, or pass too many laws, or start too many wars. Why? Because time and resources are limited. You can't afford to waste them.

If you knew you would live forever, you wouldn't bother "using your time wisely." Instead, you could waste hours watching presidential debates. You could fritter away whole days playing video games. You could spend as much time as you wanted goofing off… lying around… going to dinner parties… and paying no penalty for it. It is only because life is short and time is precious that the expression "to waste time" makes any sense.

Likewise, "conservativism" only makes sense when you have something you need to conserve. If you knew you could afford to do anything, there would be no need to make choices… no need to carefully balance the risk/reward ratios… no need to wonder if a project really "pays off." There is no need to conserve time, energy, traditions, and institutions when "there's always more where that came from."

That was true in the economy. It was true in politics, too. The prudent, wary, suspicious, and skeptical "conservatives" disappeared when there was no longer any need for them. The new conservatives were a different breed. They no longer saw the government as an institution that had to be restrained… making tough choices about where to spend the people's precious tax money… avoiding waste and corruption… suspicious of new programs and ambitious new projects. The new conservatives realized that they were not confronted by scarcity, but by abundance. The new money made resources available to them that had never even existed before.

How could a politician say "no" to a spending program when the money for it was not only available, but free? No, better than free – lenders (backed by the miracle of central bank money creation) provided it… and paid for the privilege with money borrowed at negative real rates. Who could turn down a new bridge – for free? Who could say "no" to more money for the poor when the money came at no expense? Who could oppose more "defense" spending… more snooping… more mall cops and assault amphibious vehicles for the county police… when the cost was less than nothing?

Not only would the public get these great new services at no cost, it would also help revive the economy and provide jobs. Nobel Prize-winners Paul Krugman and Joseph Stiglitz said so. So did former

Secretary of the Treasury Larry Summers… and Martin Wolf, chief economics commentator for the *Financial Times*. Who could argue with them?

Being a real "conservative" was a bad career move for almost everyone. The money was flowing freely. The music was playing. Free drinks were being poured. This was no time to be a party-pooper.

Decivilizing America

*As democracy is perfected, the office of President represents,
more and more closely, the inner soul of the people. On some
great and glorious day, the plain folks of the land will reach
their heart's desire at last, and the White House will be adorned
by a downright moron.*
– H.L. Mencken

✢ ✢ ✢ ✢

BY 2016, BALTIMORE'S acerbic wit was becoming a prophet. And the win-win world that had made America great was giving way to a win-lose world of "us-versus-them," zero-sum competition.

The heyday of the American republic was the interwar period between Korea and Vietnam. The economy was booming. The U.S. had the biggest trade surplus... the strongest manufacturing sector... the strongest currency... and the highest salaries in the world. New York was the world's most dynamic city. California was its Shangri-La. And the debt from World War II was being paid down.

In the arts, too, America was on top of the world. Motion pictures were the leading artform; Hollywood dominated the industry. As for the plastic arts, nobody did it better than the auto designers of Detroit who, with their sparkling glass and dazzling chrome, created the finest works of art of the century.

Elected in 1952, Dwight Eisenhower ended the Korean War,

balanced the budget, reduced U.S. debt as a percentage of GDP by 16%, and reduced government spending as a percentage of GDP from 20% to 18% (not even Ronald Reagan was able to do that). He cut defense spending by nearly 30%. The Dow doubled, and personal incomes rose 35%.

Eisenhower also resisted the temptation to throw his weight around overseas. When Israel invaded Egypt in 1956, with the United Kingdom and France eagerly joining in, he refused to take part. But Eisenhower teamed up with the Soviet Union and threatened to sell British bonds if the UK failed to withdraw. He was no saint. But the hallmarks of his two terms were peace and prosperity, with relatively fewer win-lose deals imposed by the feds.

We should mention that Eisenhower was also ably served at the Fed by William McChesney Martin. Martin was a Latin scholar from Yale, who joined the brokerage firm A.G. Edwards after graduation and made full partner two years later. He gave such a good showing of himself that he was elected to head the New York Stock Exchange at age 31. Then, when World War II broke out, he was drafted and served as a private.

McChesney Martin had a simple and modest idea of his mission as chair of the Fed. He sought neither full employment, nor Dow 30,000, nor 2% consumer price inflation. He neither appeased nor sucked up, neither to Democrats nor Republicans. Today's Fed model – based on "dynamic stochastics" – would have been Greek to him... or perhaps merely ridiculous claptrap. Negative real interest rates... quantitative easing... and a $4.4 trillion Fed balance sheet – all would have been regarded like a quack hair-growing elixir – with faint hope and much suspicion.

As we've mentioned in earlier pages, the 1950s Fed chief saw his role as simply to "take the punchbowl away" when the party got out of control or to "lean into the wind" when the seas got choppy. That is to say, McChesney Martin sought to loosen the money when the economy was lagging and tighten monetary policy when the economy was running hot. (Richard Nixon blamed McChesney Martin's "tight money" policies for his loss in the 1960 U.S. presidential election.)

Looking over our shoulders, back to when we were still riding a two-wheeler, whatever Eisenhower and McChesney Martin were doing, it seemed to work. GDP rose from $281 billion in 1950 to $540 billion in 1960. The rich got richer. The poor got richer, too. Jobs were plentiful. And an ordinary man with an ordinary job could support an ordinary family in a perfectly ordinary way.

So, you'd think that if you were serious about making America great again, you'd want to emulate Ike Eisenhower rather than George W. Bush or Barack Obama. You'd want to end wars, not start them. You'd want to balance the federal budget, not run some of the biggest deficits in history. You'd reduce federal spending and cut the Pentagon budget, not increase them. You'd want less government, not more. And less debt, too, not more of it. That is, you'd want to do the exact opposite of the Bush and Obama administrations.

But when we look out on the comic splendor of the USA today, we see neither Dwight Eisenhower reincarnated in the White House nor William McChesney Martin redux at the Fed. Instead, what we see is another thing Eisenhower warned us against on January 17, 1961:

> As we peer into society's future, we – you and I, and our government – must avoid the impulse to live only for today, plundering for our own ease and convenience the precious resources of tomorrow. We cannot mortgage the material assets of our grandchildren without risking the loss also of their political and spiritual heritage. We want democracy to survive for all generations to come, not to become the insolvent phantom of tomorrow.

What is today's nearly $22 trillion national debt? It is exactly what Eisenhower urged us to avoid – plundering the future… and mortgaging the precious assets of our grandchildren. But the old general didn't stop there. He also saw the Deep State taking shape:

> *In the councils of government, we must guard against the acquisition of unwarranted influence, whether sought or unsought, by the military-industrial complex. The potential for the disastrous rise of misplaced power exists and will persist. We must never let the weight of this combination endanger our liberties or democratic processes. We should take nothing for granted. Only an alert and knowledgeable citizenry can compel the proper meshing of the huge industrial and military machinery of defense with our peaceful methods and goals, so that security and liberty may prosper together.*

Why did George W. Bush make up the "weapons of mass destruction" fantasy and attack Iraq, after he had promised voters a more "humble" foreign policy? Why did Barack Obama continue the Middle East military misadventures, even after he had pledged to end them? How come Donald J. Trump – who repeatedly criticized America's losing wars in the Middle East and promised a new, "America First" foreign policy – got fully on board with the entire Bush/Obama program?

Why did the Trump government run $850 billion deficits… in peacetime, during an economic expansion… anticipating total debt of some $30 trillion to $40 trillion within 10 years? Why was the Fed being run by a disciple of Bush/Obama-era Fed chiefs, Bernanke and Yellen, rather than someone in the McChesney Martin tradition? And why would the Pentagon budget be increased, when it could be cut in half and probably still improve the safety of the Homeland?

Why? Because Donald Trump was such a genius that his methods were nearly divine… mysterious… inscrutable… beyond the comprehension of mere mortals? Did he (and apparently many of our blog readers) see something we couldn't? Or did General Eisenhower, who saw more clearly than any of us?

Our working hypothesis in this book is that General Eisenhower was right. He identified two big temptations for the American Republic of the 1950s; subsequent generations gave in to both of them. They spent their children's and grandchildren's money. Now (April 2019), the country has a national debt of nearly $22 trillion. That's up from $289 billion ($2.4 trillion in today's dollars) when Ike left the White House. And they allowed the "unwarranted influence" of the "military-industrial complex" to grow into a monster. No president, no matter how good his intentions, has been able to stop it.

PROFESSIONAL WRASSLIN'

When Donald John Trump entered the White House in January 2017, the decivilizing process was already well underway. America was engaged in military operations in 177 different countries. There was also a War on Poverty that had been going on since 1964. And a War on Drugs that had been going on since 1971. The U.S. bombed, droned, and bullied its way from the Levant to Detroit and all places in between. The cost: maybe $1 trillion... per year, all in. And maybe a million dead people in the 21st century, so far. But the Middle East wars have been a great success – for Northern Virginia. Gleaming new towers for military suppliers... and the proud new McMansions of the generals... prove it. They wanted power and money; the wars were a way to get them.

Meanwhile, anti-poverty forces have been pounding poor areas of America for the last 54 years. We know that war has been a great success, too. Just look at West Baltimore. Bombed-out houses... burnt-out stores... bummed-out people – Mission Accomplished!

And the War on Drugs deserves its victory parade, too. Yes, there are more people dying from drugs. Yes, there are more people addicted to drugs. And yes, there are more people taking mood-altering drugs now than there were when the first atomic bomb was dropped. But now... they're mostly legal drugs! And yes, two million people (five times as many as when the drug war began) are in the hoosegow, most of them on drug-related offenses. And rates of violence, especially in areas where the illegal drug industry thrives, are back to levels last seen hundreds of years ago. Yes, war is the health of the state, as writer Randolph Bourne put it. Especially a phony war.

And we hardly stuck our neck out when we guessed that Trump's Trade War would be every bit as successful as the other wars; it would continue the sordid trend, started on false pretenses: ripping off the public to reward insiders and cronies under the cover of a fake war.

Phony wars are scripted and staged. Like professional wrasslin', they're intended to amuse the fans with an evolving mixture of truth and fantasy... and take their money. It's too bad the elite political commentators don't watch World Wrestling Entertainment (WWE); it, more than the Constitution or the Declaration of Independence, could help them understand the government as it really is. Professional wrestling is a vulgar, crazy world... with cartoonish characters, such as Gorgeous George, Haystacks Calhoun, Hulk Hogan, "Stone Cold" Steve Austin, Paul Bearer, Ric Flair, The Iron Sheik, and two who will figure later in our story – The Undertaker and Mankind, aka Mick Foley.

These performers are trained at camps to do the maneuvers that wow audiences without seriously injuring each other. The camps are a bit like the training camps for gladiators who fought each other during the Roman era. Those combats, too, were staged for the spectators... and intended to shift wealth from fans to owners, promoters, and sponsors. The bestiarius fought animals. The dimachaerus fought with a sword in each hand. The retiarius used a net to snare his opponent. In the Colosseum, of course, gladiators fought for their lives. In the WWE, they fight for money. And fame.

But even phony wars have casualties. The actors miss their cues. Someone puts live ammunition in their guns. They forget to tell the soldiers that it is all supposed to be fake. And sometimes, the pressure is just too much. Mr. Perfect, Crash Holly, Malice, Ravishing Rick Rude, and many other WWE stars died young. Bogus battles, scripted wars, make-believe skirmishes – sometimes, something goes wrong... and then, things blow up.

END OF HISTORY

The history of civilization... and of wealth creation... is largely a boom-and-bust pattern. The booms were marked by expanding trade; the busts happened when trade shrank. Looked at through our own $TS = rv \ (w\text{-}w - w\text{-}l)$ – total satisfaction equals win-win deals minus win-lose deals – prism, we see that the good times were those that allowed win-win deals to flourish. The bad times were marked by win-lose deals, funny money, and war.

The Pax Romana, the relatively peaceful time following the establishment of the Roman Empire, for example, allowed free-flowing trade across Europe, the Near East, and North Africa. After they were conquered, those who survived were relatively prosperous... and safe. Then came the Barbarian invasions and the Dark Ages. It became difficult to travel. Trade collapsed. People retreated into walled towns for safety, where they lived in misery and poverty, relying on a local warlord for their lives and livelihoods.

It took more than 1,000 years for the prosperity of the Roman era to return. It did so when win-win deals once again proliferated. Over time, territories won by the sword congealed into kingdoms. A new empire – notably, the Holy Roman Empire – took shape in Europe. Of course, there were major setbacks. Typically, wars, pogroms, massacres, and crusades not only killed people and destroyed property, they also sent merchants scurrying for safety, reducing trade and increasing poverty.

The 19th century, after the Napoleonic Wars, was a long period of relative peace and growing prosperity. Money was gold; and it was solid and honest. Property rights were generally respected. The British Empire and its former colony, the U.S., created a huge area of more-or-less free trade. That stalled in 1914... with a period of war and trade contraction that lasted until 1945. That was followed by another big episode of expansion… especially after China joined the world economy in 1979 and Russia followed suit in 1991.

This new era was described by political scientist Francis Fukuyama as the "end of history." What more was there to fight about? Western commercial civilization had triumphed. But it wasn't the end of history, was it? Instead, history was just cleaning its weapons… preparing for another fight. As we said, sometimes, things go wrong. Again, professional wrasslin' lends perspective…

HELL IN A CELL

In the legendary 1998 WWE match known as "Hell in a Cell," two professional wrestlers faced off: the Undertaker and Mick Foley, aka "Mankind." The idea was for the two to do their usual three-stooges stunts – poking, whacking, tossing, and grappling with each other – in a metal cage. And then, in a crescendo of *allegro fortissimo*, they would climb on top of the cage, where the script called for the Undertaker to throw Foley down onto a ringside table that had been specially rigged to break his fall.

But something went wrong. Foley hit the mat so hard, the fans nearby thought he had died. There was blood coming from the side of his mouth. His eyes were fixed, staring blankly, like a dead man. The announcer said: "Good God almighty! Good God almighty! That killed him! As God is my witness, he is broken in half!"

Also unscripted was the announcer's follow up: "Stop the match." He thought Foley was severely injured… and possibly dead. It wasn't all acting. Foley had a concussion, a dislocated jaw, a dislocated shoulder, a bruised kidney, a cut lip, one tooth knocked out, and another broken.

Yes, professional wrasslin' is make-believe. But real stuff happens. And it is a good model to help us understand America's Swamp Wars. They, too, are staged. And like professional WWE wrestling, they are partly scripted, partly improvised… and often, unintentionally funny.

We've seen that periods of prosperity are generally marked by win-win deals. Merchants and consumers decide for themselves with whom they will truck... and on what terms. They may not like the way Canada treats its baby seals, for example, and may decide not to buy Canadian plywood. Or they may think Chinese companies steal intellectual property... and choose to work with the Japanese instead. In a win-win world, it's up to them. Trade happens between individuals, not between governments. And it is always positive sum (even when the parties lose financially, they learn something valuable).

But wait... Given an opening, the feds jump in... in the name of truth and justice, of course. They lull the lumpen into thinking that the government is fighting for "us" against "them." The "us" is encouraged to feel it is getting ripped off... and that now, it has a chance to get even. The "them" finds it useful, too – distracting the public from its many failures with a phony battle. Then, action begets reaction. Soon, you've got a "trade war." Then, things can get out of hand.

In the Bubble Era, 1987-2019, Americans spent money they didn't have on things they didn't need. The Chinese made things nobody really needed and sold them to people who really couldn't afford to buy them anyway. The fake money went from America to China... and then back again. China lent its earnings back to the U.S... where it lowered interest rates by buying massive amounts of U.S. Treasuries and helped Americans continue their borrowing spree. Then, China built more factories to satisfy the new demand for its products! Cumulatively, U.S. trade deficits over the 30-year period toted to about $20 trillion (in today's dollars).

That was the underlying fraud of the whole three-decade boom. It was based on bad money, not bad trade deals. Without the fake money, none of it could have happened. As soon as U.S. consumers spent more than they could afford, dollars would have piled up overseas and would then have been presented to the Treasury. Foreign governments would have asked for gold in exchange for their paper dollars – as promised.

This would have reduced the U.S. base money supply... forced up interest rates... and put a stop to the whole whirligig.

Without the fake money system, U.S. households, businesses, and governments could never have gone so deeply into debt. China could never have taken so many U.S. jobs. The U.S. stock market could never have risen 12 times, in inflation-adjusted dollars, from 1982 to 2018. And America's middle/working classes wouldn't have felt so betrayed... and most likely, wouldn't have elected Donald J. Trump as their champion. For it was they who had paid the price. Wages, bonuses, and wealth may have soared in the financialized economy. But in the heartland's work-a-day economy, they had been flat for 40 years. The rich really had gotten much richer; the poor had gotten, relatively, poorer. That was why Mr. Trump was elected – to Make America Great Again.

The former reality TV star, now performing in the West Wing, asked his trade representative to consider body slamming China with $100 billion more in tariffs. It was "easy to win a trade war," he told the nation. Hours later, China let it be known that two could play this game. China's *Global Times* revealed its position:

> *If the trade war happens, China will show that it has just as many reserve plans as the U.S., if not more. Chinese experts suggest that China could even take actions to weaken the strength of its currency. Since China is the world's largest trading economy and the largest buyer of commodities like oil products, China could use its influence to push its own currency, RMB, in global markets to reduce the dominance of the U.S. dollar. That would be a heavy blow to Washington.*

In the developing trade war, both sides were delusional. Donald J. Trump saw every public policy issue as an opportunity for a tough "art of the deal" negotiation. Remarkably, the Chinese leader, Mr. Xi Jinping, believed things equally absurd. He thought his country could get rich by taking America's fake money in exchange for real products made in his vast new factories.

But wait, maybe the whole thing was just another stunt to keep the ratings up. In his fight with Canada, The Donald ranted and raved against an unfair trade deal with the U.S.'s northern neighbor, insulted Canadian premier Justin Trudeau, and then quietly allowed trade to go on much as it had before. In this respect, it might have been a little like the maneuvers leading up to the "Hell in a Cell" wrasslin' extravaganza in June 1998.

Promoters gin up interest with a long warm-up of phony feuds and ersatz confrontations. You'll recall that the match in the Pittsburgh Civic Arena pitted The Undertaker against Mankind. But two years before that, the build-up began. Mankind would appear at Undertaker matches – such as the one at "In Your House 8: Beware of Dog," where he ambushed the Undertaker, costing him the championship title. Thereafter, the two brawled on stage and off, taking the fight into the stands… and creating the kind of tension that gets the fans eager to see what happens next.

The culmination of this tension – the cathartic release – was scheduled for the aforementioned match in June 1998. Fighting in a metal cage, the two stuntmen went at one another, The Undertaker in his familiar black dirge get-up, Mankind with his white shirt hanging down and a tie loosely knotted around his neck. Reaching for an ever-more-intense climax, the fighters climbed on top of the cage to continue the mock combat.

Everything was going according to the script… until…

Well, until it didn't.

That was when Mankind got tossed off the top of the cage but didn't go where he was supposed to go. Instead of hitting the table, which was meant to cushion the fall, he hit the floor. And he fell onto it so hard that he was knocked out. It was while thus unconscious that a metal chair, that he and the Undertaker had used to batter each other on top of the cage, fell and hit him in the face, knocking out one tooth, breaking another, and dislocating his jaw.

Today, like pro wrestlers, the world's two most powerful leaders entertained the folks in the cheap seats with their "Mongolian chops"… "body avalanches"… and the always-popular "spinning elbow corkscrew drops." Pretending to do battle, both were really on the same team… and had the same aim – to separate the fans from their money.

FOLK TALES

In the 13th century, a remarkable folk legend developed in what is now Germany. Emperor Frederick II was thought to be still alive, even though he had died years before. The common people saw destruction, chaos, and violence all around them. The Mongols had attacked and massacred the population of Breslau. Rival princes and warlords fought for control of the countryside, with one laying waste an area and then another doing the same thing. Knights, sworn to protect the weak of Christendom, had become bandits. And the whole country was ruled by "fist law," where the strong took whatever they could.

The people were sore afraid. And they imagined the good, just Emperor, Frederick II, sleeping in an enchanted place deep within the Kyffhäuser mountains. His long, red beard was said to have grown right through the stone table at which he sat. Once a year, the sleeping Emperor was said to awaken and ask his page if the ravens were still circling the mountains. If the answer was "yes," he went back to sleep for another year. When it was "no," however, he would rise, take up his sword, put on his shining armor, summon his troops, cleave the mountain in two, and march out. Then, he would quickly bring order and justice back to the empire.

This was a "myth." Frederick II never appeared again. As far as we know, he was not sleeping, but as dead as any other medieval doornail. But the myth had power. It connected to the soul of the people; they wanted to believe.

By all accounts a gifted, intelligent emperor, Frederick had grown up in Sicily. He charmed almost everyone he came in contact with, spoke six languages including Arabic, and was widely regarded as a "stupor mundi," a wonder of the world. When challenged by Pope Gregory IX to undertake a new crusade to liberate the Holy Land, Frederick hesitated and dilly-dallied. The Pope was annoyed and excommunicated him four times. Finally, and reluctantly, Frederick undertook a crusade. But he went about it in an entirely unorthodox manner. Instead of assembling a great army of knights and attacking the Arabs, Frederick sat down with the Ayyubid sultan, Al-Kamil. The result was an astonishing win-win deal. The Arabs maintained control. But the Christians were free to visit unmolested.

Frederick was perfectly happy with the arrangement and crowned himself King of Jerusalem. But the Pope was madder than ever. He accused Frederick of collusion with the Muslims. Some said he had become a Muslim himself. Pope Gregory called him the "anti-Christ."

It would be impossible to confuse Frederick II with Donald J. Trump. Frederick was a learned genius. Even by the short standards of American politics circa 2016, Donald J. Trump was a midget. Ignorant, possibly illiterate, vulgar, perhaps charming in his own way, but completely lacking in grace or dignity – he seemed an unlikely candidate for president. With more than 200 million adults to choose from, he seemed far from the best Americans could do. Still, in 2016/2017, something remarkable was taking place: Donald Trump was growing a long, red beard.

We mentioned it first in our blog, *Bill Bonner's Diary*. In it, we took a look at the plans, programs, and promises made by the Trump team. We noted that there was not much swamp-draining going on. Instead, government spending was set to increase... government debt would rise by more than $1 trillion a year... there would be no significant cut in "entitlement" spending... and the win-win trade deals that were essential to economic progress were being threatened with tariffs and other barriers.

These were not political comments. They were just economic and investment-related observations. But readers took great offense, as if we had invaded their place of worship and were burning their sacred relics. Rarely did they challenge the observations themselves, but they were extremely critical of your author... and, often, his mother!

Even when we tried to congratulate the president, albeit with a bit of back-handed sarcasm, readers were up in arms. We tried to explain that...

> *"The Donald" understood better than the professional politicians that democratic politics is basically a form of entertainment. It's a low-bred part of showbiz – all hocus pocus... suspension of disbelief... and performance art – closer to nude mud wrestling than* The Crown.

At the end of 2017, the press still didn't get it. In an article that appeared in *The Washington Post* in August 2018, reporters had tallied 2,140 "false or misleading claims" the president made during his first year in office, and 4,229 in total. We were surprised; we thought he had made more than that. And why not?

No one expects a standup comic to tell the truth. No one checks Beyoncé's lyrics for factual errors. And who worries about accuracy while watching *Buffy the Vampire Slayer?*

Another article at the time told us that Trump is "mocked on social media for bragging" about his nuclear button. At the time, the president was in a spat with the leader of North Korea. Taking to Twitter, POTUS declared that his nuclear button was "much bigger."

Of course, that's not what President Eisenhower would have done. But these were not Ike voters. And this was not Ike's Old Republic. Voters had lost faith in the system, with its solemn deceit and counterfeit dignity. And they were happy to hear someone speaking in a language they understood – the down-market media patois of Howard Stern, the

Kardashians, and the "Big Dog" himself, WWE champ Roman Reigns.

Trump, a lifelong celebrity, sensed that the role of president has little to do with geopolitical facts, mastery of the federal budget, or knowledge of history. It's more like a reality TV show or a WWE wrestling match – with put downs... posturing... and fake fights. In other words, it was right up his alley.

Mr. Trump understood, too, that he could leave the real task of government – bossing people around and ripping them off – to the Deep State, the cronies, the elite, and the lifers in D.C. He knew he couldn't beat them. All he could do was make the deal of his lifetime – allowing him to pretend to be the Champion of the Common Man of Flyover America... while not rocking the insiders' boat.

And so, the boondoggles continued at home. The phony wars went on overseas. And it was all still funded by a fake-money system. Mr. Trump brought together, like a gang of desperadoes meeting up to pull off a bank robbery, the major talents needed for the White House. He illustrates, too, the major currents of our discussion:

- He relies on the vestigial myth – "us versus them" – for his modus operandi.

- He favors the use of violence and bullying tactics (defection) over cooperation.

- He illustrates the conceits and deceptions of large-scale democracy.

- He makes no distinction between fake news and real news; truth, fiction, fantasy, and lies are all tossed into the same blender.

- He has no interest in the manners, arts, sciences, and other features of civilized life.

- He is an archaic win-lose guy, not a civilized win-win guy.

- He is the self-described King of Debt, not the King of Saving or the King of Equity.

- He is the object of a myth-based following.

- He is a defector.

- He is the perfect president for his time; he is a decivilizer.

Mr. Trump understood that the "fans" – the voters – were fed up with the elite. He guessed they would flock to a candidate who seemed to talk straight... pledged to stop losing wars... and promised protection from foreigners with walls, torture, and trade barriers. Many Americans felt that America was losing its place in the world and that they were losing their place in America. To whom? To "them." And Mr. Trump promised to put "them" in their place.

The pros – too circumspect and timid to stoop to teasing up the masses in such a low-rent way – no longer got the mob excited. The *hoi polloi* wanted someone to "tell it like it is." They wanted a brazen liar who wasn't afraid to tell the truth: that the system was rigged against them... and that the riggers filled the Capitol, the government bureaucracies, Wall Street, the media, and big business, too.

And if he could get the people on his side, in his words, he "could stand in the middle of Fifth Avenue and shoot somebody... and not lose any voters." Trump was right on all counts. Even the guy he gunned down would probably vote for him, if he could still pull the lever. The president probably still doesn't understand how the system is rigged. But he has the knack of a showman... an instinct for lizard-brain psychology... and a well-developed skill at crowd manipulation.

Posing as a friend of the little guy, Mr. Trump proved to be the perfect big-guy president – cutting taxes for the big guys on Wall Street... increasing spending for the big boys in the Pentagon and their industry cronies... helping to stifle real reform of runaway entitlements... teaming up with Democrats to keep the debt ceiling going up, with no limit on deficits… and bringing trade and technology under the Big Top, too.

What a show!

And everybody had a phony part to play. Even the liberal media had a role: guardian of democracy's faux virtue. The press pretended to be after the president for plotting with the Russians to defeat Hillary. Every day, it banged the drum of "Russiagate," knowing full well there was nothing there worth investigating. Everyone tried to influence the 2016 election; the Russians were probably among the least successful at it. But never was feigned outrage so profitable. The media never had it so good. People tuned in every day just to hear what dumb, outlandish, absurd, or pathetic thing the president did next. The media loved him; they knew he was good for ratings. The Deep State loved him, too; they knew his mock combat was protecting their scam. The rich and the insiders loved him; he continued to shovel money in their direction.

And we loved him, too. In early 2018, we got a note from our chief financial officer. He calculated that the GOP tax cuts would shave our tax bill by 22%. We were happy about that, and also grateful to The Donald for making 2017 an entertaining and instructive year. More than any candidate before him, he showed us what a greasy and disgraceful business government really is.

But it was the outsiders… the poor… the little guys… the lumpen electorate… whose affection for Mr. Trump was most surprising. He did nothing to ease their burdens. He cleaved no mountains and righted no wrongs. Instead, he stabbed them in the back. He took their money – directly and indirectly – and handed it to the elites. He took their sons and daughters and wasted their lives in cockamamie, phony wars. And yet, they loved him. They liked the way he talked. And they would tolerate no cynicism or mockery towards him.

"Laugh and know," said the Roman poet Martial. You can understand the pretensions… the foolish contradictions… and the absurd fantasies… only if you're able to laugh at them. Specifically, we were laughing at the way The Donald had bamboozled his own base. He talked their talk. But he walked the walk of the Deep State. And as a helpful dear reader reminded us, quoting Frank Zappa, "politics is basically the entertainment arm of the military-industrial complex."

We would add that it serves the social welfare-Wall Street complex, too. Trump – veteran reality TV star and professional wrasslin' fan – drew a crowd. Elite insiders stole credit cards and passwords.

And yet, not only did our dear readers disagree; they thought there must be something wrong with us for saying so.

Here's one piece of feedback from our *Diary* mailbag:

> *Mr. Bill Bonner, you are quite smug, and disrespectful to our president. Maybe you're just so jealous of his success – in spite of detractors like you, pretending to be hidden away in some remote area – that you, too, are part of the misinformation media trying to extract money from the ignorant. Go hate yourself. You deserve it.*

And another:

> *You've tried again and again to put Donald Trump down, and you have lost all the time. Maybe he is not an intellectual like you, but he is doing what he can with morons like you and others (Dems, media, GOP insiders, etc.) and still, he is getting better results than your pal Barack.*

> *You are a nobody who believes you are successful, but forgets that success is not to have money, but to have real friends, a good family, and also decency and honesty, not abuse the system. Because a lot of people are like you (losers). It is easy to throw rocks at everybody and believe that you are over and above everybody.*

Of course, our critics may be right. We reserve the right to be wrong... and exercise it frequently. And maybe sometime in the future, we will see that we were wrong about "The Donald" all along. Perhaps he will commit some redemptory act of grace and courage... maybe even intelligence. Or maybe, Melania's memoir will reveal the genuine charm and sweetness of the man's soul, behind the role he plays on TV. Then, we will doff our cap... sing his praises... and apologize.

But we've been laughing at public figures for many years; never have we seen one who had risen to a high level of power who was not, at least in some way, a scoundrel or a fraud. Our only regret about most of them is that we didn't laugh harder. We doubt that Mr. Trump will prove to be an exception.

Trump's fans, meanwhile, wanted nothing to do with laughter... or mockery. Even after two full years of Mr. Trump in the White House, they were convinced – against all evidence – that the man was performing near-miracles. And there was nothing you could say to convince them otherwise. Rarely did they have specific arguments about why a policy or a proposal might be good or bad. Their connection to the man was deeper than that. He was their Frederick II sleeping under the mountain. He was going to set things straight... and anyone who opposed him was a bad person. If you found fault with their hero, Trump fans attacked you the way Trump attacks his enemies – *ad hominem*... Here's a dear reader's reply to our note on The Donald's trade restrictions of March 2018:

Stop being such a moron!... you old, decaying, ignorant slime.

The phenomenon is not new. Washington, D.C. mayor, Marion Barry, had a rap sheet that stretched for many pages – drug addiction, corruption, traffic tickets, and dereliction. Barry was a scalawag. Caught on camera smoking crack cocaine with an ex-girlfriend in an FBI sting operation, he replied, "Bitch set me up. Goddamn bitch." But the voters kept electing him, even after he got out of prison.

Leon Festinger, a psychologist, explained the phenomenon:

> *Suppose an individual believes something with his whole heart;*
> *suppose further that he has a commitment to this belief, that he*
> *has taken irrevocable actions because of it; finally, suppose that he*
> *is presented with evidence, unequivocal and undeniable evidence,*
> *that his belief is wrong; what will happen? The individual will*
> *frequently emerge not only unshaken, but even more convinced of the*
> *truth of his beliefs than ever before. Indeed, he may even show a new*
> *fervor about convincing and converting other people to his view.*

One of the curiosities of modern government is that the worst leaders in history seem to develop the most loyal, uncritical followers. Millions wept when Stalin died. Millions still supported Hitler as the Soviet troops approached Berlin. The Peronists still win elections in Argentina after 60 years of wrecking the country. In Venezuela, Hugo Chávez is still regarded as a hero by many.

All of these leaders had one thing in common: all favored win-lose over win-win. And as win-lose bears its inevitable fruits – poverty, misery, slaughter, and meanness – the fans find someone to blame. Whites… Jews… counter-revolutionaries… the U.S. – failure is always someone else's fault. That, too, was a regular refrain from our own readers; they blamed us!

If you would just get off his back and give him a chance…

A community needs its elites. The plain people have neither the time nor the training to understand all the complex matters that come their way. If a town needs a power plant, for example, it turns to an engineer and hopes he knows what he is talking about. It trusts its lawyers to battle it out between themselves and establish a rough justice. It counts on its artists to draw forth the beauty of its surroundings, on its architects to elevate its dwelling places beyond mere hovels, and on its poets to remind it of what is great and good.

But by the 21st century, much of the American public felt it had been betrayed. Its elites were not working for the common man, but against him. We will pass over the cultural issues – the transgender bathrooms, the "deplorables" epithet, and the campus censorship. Much more fundamental was the money. As you saw in a previous chapter, the U.S. government used its control of money to redistribute wealth. It pumped up asset prices for the rich, but not the hourly wages of the middle classes. The robbery was so subtle that not one person in 10,000 understood what was going on. But all 10,000 felt cheated, and many lost faith in the entire system and in the people who run it.

As we explained earlier, the ultimate resource is time. A slave is a slave because his time (and, of course, his body) is owned by someone else. In the space of a generation, the fake money system had put America's working people into a new kind of soft slavery... forced to spend their lives servicing student debt, credit card debt, mortgage debt, car debt, and a never-ending list of installments, subscriptions, and other monthly payments. The phenomenon had many causes and explanations, but whatever else it was, it was also a transfer of wealth (time) from the working classes to the asset-owning elite.

Along came Mr. Trump, a straight-talking rabble-rouser. He had an explanation suitable to the professional wrasslin' fan he was. It was "us versus them," he said. We will not add much to the readers' knowledge or amusement by further exploring the Trump phenomenon. Editorialists, psychiatrists, and political analysts have bent to the task for years... and given themselves headaches and back pain chronicling it or trying to understand it. We merely aim to put it in context.

"The King of Debt," as he called himself, was the product of a very special time. Credit was unusually plentiful and abnormally cheap. And it was bogus. The fraudulent credit that helped make Mr. Trump rich was the very same fraudulent credit that made the poor and working classes relatively poorer.

But it didn't matter. By the time the Trump weed was rooted in the popular mind, there was no pulling it out. He was the hero of what had begun to see itself as a victim class. As we discovered in our daily blog's mailbag, his base had become immune to the ordinary weedkillers – humor and logic. Day after day, we poured on the Roundup: He was in league with the insiders, we pointed out; he had invited representatives of the two major Deep State wings – Goldman Sachs and the Pentagon – into his cabinet. He betrayed the principles of conservative budget control with his debt-ceiling increases and budget-busting tax cuts. His trade barriers were anathema to Republicans, and would only make things worse for heartland industries, not better.

When logical declamation failed to break his bones, we resorted to name-calling. Even his closest associates in the White House said he was a moron. He was an imbecile, a charlatan, a jackass. Ever since the beginning of the 2016 election campaign, the most alluring question in politics concerned Mr. Trump: Was he really an idiot? Or was he just pretending to be an idiot to get the idiot vote? By the middle of his first year in office, it had become clear that the president's intelligence, such as it was, was of a very special sort. Most people were capable of "thinking fast and slow." Mr. Trump never downshifted.

But it didn't matter what we said. We were dissed and dismissed by Trump's true believers. They claimed their man was "brilliant," "a real businessman." "Finally, someone willing to drain the Swamp… if they'll let him."

Every asinine remark was "telling it like it is." Every presidential blunder was "not his fault." Every double-cross was The Donald "working in mysterious ways."

BLOND MESSIAH

In the second decade of the 21st century, Americans were asked to which religion, if any, they belonged. Seventy percent said they were

Christian. By our rough math, this puts the number of self-identified Christians in the U.S. at approximately 230 million.

At about the same time, a Christian prayer group in one of the southern states was visited by a reporter. He wanted to know what the group thought about America's president, Donald J. Trump.

Mr. Trump, of course, was credibly accused of paying a porn star to keep silent about his affair with her. Nineteen women, in total, had come forward to complain about Trump, saying he was known for ungentlemanly conduct. Meanwhile, *The New York Times* did a thorough job of reporting on Mr. Trump's habit of bearing false witness, as well as many tax and business practices that might have put other people in jail. But Mr. Trump denied all the charges and claims. And religious leaders – some of the least cynical of them, surely – said that it didn't really matter anyway, because The Donald had found redemption in Christ.

But it wasn't the president's sex life or business affairs that made us wonder. Civilized people can get up to whatever private adventures they want. But there are some things they can't do. Mr. Trump famously believed – and still does – in an "us versus them" world. He tweets against the National Football League one day. He sets his jaw against a TV newscaster the next. And then, even on a Sunday, he will send out a tweet calling out a Republican Senator.

He is not ashamed of this bellicose behavior. He is as proud of it as a boxer is of his left hook or a card shark is of his false shuffle. Mr. Trump is a fighter. And if you're going to be a fighter, you have to fight with someone. If you are Muhammad Ali, you need George Foreman. If you are Boris Spassky, you need Bobby Fischer.

In December 2015, *The New York Times* analyzed Mr. Trump's campaign rhetoric – 95,000 words of it. Then, Mr. Trump was a novelty. The *NYT* didn't know what to make of him. Was he a serious candidate? Did he have a chance against well-financed career politicians?

The New York Times didn't know. But it noticed that his speech patterns and word choices were different from those of most candidates:

> *The dark power of words has become the defining feature of Mr. Trump's bid for the White House to a degree rarely seen in modern politics, as he forgoes the usual campaign trappings – policy, endorsements, commercials, donations – and instead relies on potent language to connect with, and often stoke, the fears and grievances of Americans.*
>
> *The New York Times analyzed every public utterance by Mr. Trump over the past week from rallies, speeches, interviews and news conferences to explore the leading candidate's hold on the Republican electorate for the past five months. The transcriptions yielded 95,000 words and several powerful patterns, demonstrating how Mr. Trump has built one of the most surprising political movements in decades and, historians say, echoing the appeals of some demagogues of the past century.*

Not surprisingly, the fighter used fighting words. "Attack" was a favorite. He also promised to "bomb the hell" out of his enemies. And to hit back "ten times as hard" when he was attacked.

So were fighting words used to describe his political opponents. He called Republican adversaries "horrible," "stupid," and "weak." He famously mocked them, too – as "low-energy" Jeb Bush, "lil' Marco" Rubio, and "lyin' Ted" Cruz.

We bring this up not to criticize President Trump. His campaign techniques were splendidly effective. We only mention it to ask America's Christians: What are they thinking? Here's *The New York Times* again:

> *"His entire campaign is run like a demagogue's – his language of division, his cult of personality, his manner of categorizing and maligning people with a broad brush," said Jennifer Mercieca, an expert in American political discourse at Texas A&M University. "If you're an illegal immigrant, you're a loser. If you're captured in war, like John McCain, you're a loser. If you have a disability, you're a loser. It's rhetoric like [1960's Alabama Governor George] Wallace's – it's not a kind or generous rhetoric."*

"Love thy neighbor," was absent from Mr. Trump's *oeuvre*. So was "turn the other cheek." Nor was there any hint that the "meek will inherit the Earth." Mr. Trump was the opposite of meek. Instead, he was in-your-face proud, vain, and rich. He was a winner; at least he said so.

What, then, did the members of the Christian prayer group think of their president? They were fully behind him. "He was doing the best job he could. And he would do a lot better if the people in Washington would let him get on with it. Like building that wall so we protect ourselves from all those illegal aliens. We'd be a lot better off if they'd let him drain the swamp."

By the summer of 2017, "us versus them" had replaced Christianity in many of the nation's churches. There were terrorists who had to be killed. And bad people with bad trade deals that had to renegotiated. And football stars who "should be fired" for "taking the knee." And mad dictators – such as the Rocket Man from North Korea – whose country of 25 million people might have to be "totally destroyed."

It was one battle after another. It was "us"... whoever we were... against "them"... whoever they were. And the battle lineups changed almost daily. The Republicans were heroes in 2016 – they had won both houses of Congress... and the White House, too. But wait... then, they were bums. The Trump White House made common cause with Nancy Pelosi and Charles Schumer – two archliberals – in December 2017.

But there was one enduring enemy – one unfailing "them" of the period – someone the Pentagon could sink its teeth into... and the Deep State could use to drive trillions of dollars its way. And this "us versus them" had a patina of respectability about it, like a cheap prostitute with a Louis Vuitton handbag. Based on the paranoid delusions of Harvard professor Samuel Huntington, Mr. Trump could claim not to be just fighting with rival TV celebrities. Instead, this was a "clash of civilizations."

We have already mentioned Fukuyama's "end of history" hypothesis. It stated, broadly, that the world was bound for peace. The capitalist/democratic ideals of the West had "won out." What was left to discuss?

But in 1996, Huntington put forth a very different outlook of the future in his book, *The Clash of Civilizations and the Remaking of World Order.* He predicted that, with the fall of the Soviet Union, global struggles would be waged, not by sovereign states with differing philosophies, but by different cultures. Specifically, it was the West (the United States and Europe) that would inevitably clash with the Islamic world.

The clash part is easy enough to understand. Like Donald Trump's other martial confrontations, it is a fight. If you want to sell newspapers or win the White House, start a fight. A fight gets ratings. Fights get spectators. Fights force people to take sides. And fighters get elected.

But having make-believe scuffles with athletes and politicians is very different from a fight between "civilizations." It brings us back to the heart of this book. If we're right about the nature of civilization, a fight between them is impossible.

Donald Trump traveled to Warsaw in July 2017. There, he gave a speech that echoed Jan Sobieski, who rode out with a small group of Polish knights to break the siege of Vienna in 1683. President Trump urged the nations of the West to "summon the courage and the will to defend our civilization." He went on to say that the U.S. welcomes immigrants who "share our values and love our people," adding that we are united with other European nations by "bonds of history, culture, and memory."

Huntington, who, unlike Trump, actually knew some history, saw it as basically a battle between "us" and "them," too. He seemed to want to turn Americans into a tribe and recreate the tribal world of the Old Testament. The obvious question in a fight is, "Whose side are you on?" Huntington believed the question answered itself. Just ask yourself, "Who are you?" he advised.

US VERSUS THEM

Good question. Who are you? With whom do you belong? Which

"us" includes you? The folks who speak English? The folks who worship Muhammad? Or Mary? The folks who shop at Walmart and fill their shopping carts with garbage? The folks who vote for imbeciles? The folks who dress in silly clothes… talk in incomplete sentences… put pictures of Che Guevara on their t-shirts and tattoos of snakes on their arms… watch daytime TV… are undereducated, overweight, and couldn't explain transubstantiation if their lives depended on it?

The problem – or one of them – with "us versus them" is that the "us" group is almost always a group that smart, cultivated, civilized people would be ashamed to join. Whether it is a lynch mob, a political party, or the Wehrmacht, put a bunch of people together with the right to do violence to others, and they almost invariably misbehave.

Besides, "us versus them" and "whose side are you on?" are strange and inappropriate for a nation of 230 million Christians. There is no room for "us" or "them" in the Nazarene Creed. There is just the individual… who is urged to love his neighbor, no matter how much of a jerk he is. Which tribe, nation, or "civilization" he belongs to is beside the point. That's what a universal faith is all about; groups don't matter. There are laws, principles, and codes – but they apply to everyone equally. That is also the core principle of the civilization we are meant to protect… and the foundation creed of the United States of America. "All men are created equal…" Mexicans, too.

That is the trouble with Huntington's *pensée*. He doesn't know what civilization is… and confuses it with culture. It is a common failing among the intellectually active. They see themselves as "civilized." They also like café latte. Therefore, they believe that liking café latte is what civilized people do. If Huntington had liked foot massages, they would be the *sine qua non* of Western civilization. His other book, *Who Are We?*, makes it clear; he thinks it's culture that counts. Universalism was out the window. There was no attempt to understand or appreciate what real civilization is. Instead, Huntington fell back on "us versus them." He claimed it was "us versus them" even from the beginning:

Would America be the America it is today if in the seventeenth and eighteenth centuries it had been settled not by British Protestants but by French, Spanish, or Portuguese Catholics? The answer is no. It would not be America; it would be Quebec, Mexico, or Brazil.

The political and legal institutions the settlers created in the seventeenth and eighteenth centuries embodied in large part the institutions and practices of England's late-sixteenth-century and early-seventeenth-century "Tudor constitution." These included: the concept of a fundamental law superior to and limiting government; the fusion of executive, legislative, and judicial functions and the division of power among separate institutions and governments; the relative power of the legislature and chief executive; the merger of the "dignified" and "efficient" functions in the chief executive; a two-house legislature; the responsibility of the legislature to their local constituencies; a legislative committee system; and primary reliance for defense on militia rather than a standing army.

And it was not just political institutions that settlers brought with them:

The Protestant emphasis on the individual conscience and the responsibility of individuals to learn God's truths directly from the Bible promoted American commitment to individualism, equality, and the rights to freedom of religion and opinion. Protestantism stressed the work ethic and the responsibility of the individual for his own success or failure in life. With its congregational forms of church organization, Protestantism fostered opposition to hierarchy and the assumption that similar democratic forms should be employed in government.

He was right, of course. The culture of the country... and its foundational institutions... had to come from somewhere. *Ex nihilo nihil fit.* But couldn't anyone come to the U.S… benefit from its free institutions… and contribute to the American dream? Apparently not…

> *There is only the American dream created by an Anglo-Protestant society. Mexican-Americans will share in that dream and in that society only if they dream in English.*

Which just makes you wonder about tenured professors at Harvard. Millions of immigrants came to the U.S., worked hard, saved their money, and made the country what it is today – while dreaming in their native languages. And if you break the American dream down into its component parts – liberty, prosperity, equality under the law – there is no part of it that is language-dependent.

Huntington worried that Mexicans couldn't be good Americans because they not only didn't dream in English… they suffered from the "*mañana* syndrome." By reputation, they were always willing to put something off until *mañana*… tomorrow. Presumably, this made it impossible for them to get things done.

Of course, these "lazy" Mexicans are the very same people President Trump and the other English-speaking Americanos wanted to keep out because "they're taking our jobs." They're the people you see flipping burgers for $10 an hour… pouring concrete in 90-degree heat… and trimming the hedges of small villages all over America. Somehow, these *mañana*-lovers are out there today, working their butts off.

Culture is not the same as civilization. A civilized person is one who respects the rules of civilization: he doesn't kill, he doesn't steal… he is capable of communication… And, most important, he obeys the No. 1 rule: he does win-win deals. That is what makes civilization possible – voluntary win-win exchanges between people who, generally, don't give a damn about the other's culture.

It doesn't matter which language you speak, let alone which one you dream in. It doesn't matter who you vote for… or whether you wear a kilt or a chādor. It doesn't even matter how lazy you are. None of those cultural trappings matter to Christianity. Or to civilization. There is no "us." No "them."

The appeal of the United States of America, *ab initio*, was that it didn't care either. It was the first Christian country to accept Jews, for example, with no strings attached. Come to America and you could be left alone to speak your own language, worship your own gods, and earn your own living. You would either make it or not make it; it was up to you.

But that was then. Now, many generations later, many God-fearing, native-born, English-speaking Americans – apparently enough to elect a president – want nothing to do with the American dream. It's too risky. Instead, the very people Huntington (and Trump) hold up as the epitome of the American race are weak, timorous, sniveling flag-wavers. Who else would be afraid of competition from people who have no training, no skills, no education, no visa, no driver's license, no Social Security number, and who don't even speak English!? Who else would be afraid of imports from people who only joined the world economy 40 years ago?

There's a reason that all democratic governments tend toward tyranny, incompetence, vulgarity, and claptrap. That's what most people want! They throw their support behind the shyster who makes the most fantastic promise; then together, the chiselers, the cronies, and the clods force onto others the win-lose deals that lead to the doom of a free, open, win-win society.

In a matter of weeks following the attack on the World Trade Center, for example, people began talking about the "homeland" and standing in line while silly goons felt up old ladies and young girl scouts at airport security. No one seriously believed any of them posed a threat to air traffic safety, but no one dared protest.

"You can't be too safe!" they said to themselves.

And now, nearly two decades later… with no evidence that this exercise in inconvenience and time-wasting has done a thing to make the skies safer... it still goes on. Americans strip down... walk through X-ray machines... and follow orders for no other reason than they are told to do so.

And the typical American feels better about it. He likes to follow orders. He craves the regimentation of the gulag. He knows his elites are scalawags and grifters, but he goes dumbly along with them, like Napoléon's grenadiers marching to Moscow. The only fight worth having is a fight to keep others from telling you what to do. And yet, that is exactly what the "us" wants to do.

In 2007, the Center for Immigration Studies took a look at which groups have made the most of their new lives in the U.S. Guess what? The two leaders were the Indians and the Japanese – neither of whom had anything to do with Huntington's "us" – Anglo-Protestant, European settlers.

And guess which group, overall, has been most successful in America? Jews, of course. They devoted themselves to career, family, and education, and benefited because of it. Closer analysis of other immigrant patterns shows that almost all groups arriving in the U.S. do better than the native population. Black, white, Asian – it doesn't seem to matter. Nigerians get more advanced degrees. Lebanese earn 30% more. Cubans are among the most prosperous groups in Florida.

Why? Who knows. Maybe it is the smarter, more aggressive, and more ambitious ones who emigrate. Then, perhaps unsure of their position in the new country, they urge their children to feats of learning and entrepreneurship that locals can't match. The native-born parent tells his child: "Don't worry... you're great... you'll be fine." The Chinese immigrant has a different message: "Work harder... longer... better... or you'll end up driving a trash truck."

But here is the curious nuance. After three generations, the local culture takes over. In a study of Chinese immigrants, researchers found a huge performance gap in the second generation, with the Chinese doing far better in almost every category. But by the third generation, they were just as dumb and shiftless as the locals, with little gap between them and other Americans.

Go figure.

Every substantial immigration threatens the existing culture. And every one brings out the patriots, eager to protect what they've got. Huntington saw it coming:

> *One very plausible reaction would be the emergence of exclusivist sociopolitical movements composed largely but not only of white males, primarily working-class and middle-class, protesting and attempting to stop or reverse these changes and what they believe, accurately or not, to be the diminution of their social and economic status, their loss of jobs to immigrants and foreign countries, the perversion of their culture, the displacement of their language, and the erosion or even evaporation of the historical identity of their country. Such movements would be both racially and culturally inspired and could be anti-Hispanic, anti-black, and anti-immigration.*

He was right about that, too. Threatened by people who work harder, and who have better habits and morals, the native mob doesn't try to pull up its socks; it becomes nasty and intolerant. Then, closing the doors to new immigrants, it cuts off the flow of the people who made the country great. The Apple Computer Company was founded by the son of an immigrant from Syria. Henry Ford, John Kennedy, Ronald Reagan – millions of Americans have Irish Catholic roots. And imagine America without Blacks, Hispanics, Jews, or Muslims. Or recent immigrants, still dreaming in their mother tongues.

What do you have left? Us.

This is the context in which Donald J. Trump was elected. A long period of stability had given elite insiders an opportunity to capture the political system and use it to take advantage of the masses. After the Eisenhower administration, entrenched special interests – aka "The Deep State" – gathered more and more power and money unto itself. By 2016, the Old Conservatives were gone. Both liberals and the new conservatives had come to the same general view: the government could do almost whatever it wanted, funded by low-cost debt. Then, using control of the fake money system, it was able to capture nearly 100% of the financial gains of the entire 21st century. This left the common man with a feeling of unrequited resentment, perhaps tinged with envy, leading to the election of Donald J. Trump.

But two years into his reign, opinions were still sharply divided. Approximately a third of the general American population regarded him as a fool, an idiot, and an ignoramus. Another third saw him as a natural genius, and the only hope for national resurrection. The final third didn't know what to think.

It is probably the third group whose vision was clearest. Not knowing what to think of Mr. Trump is not a sign of stupidity or ignorance; on the contrary, it signals a keener awareness of the world Mr. Trump comes from and lives in. It is a world where nothing is quite what it seems, neither as true nor as fictitious, neither as real nor as fake. It is a world in which Trump fans can see him as a stand-up straight shooter, simply because his world includes neither truth nor falsehood. The typical politician chooses his words carefully, not wanting to be caught in a lie. Mr. Trump is more honest; every tweet and every thought, no matter how fleeting or foolish, is as genuine as the last.

Trump's world is the world of the mob… the masses… the great, unwashed lumpen – and the super-rich, too. It is a world of confusing, contradictory myths. It is disorienting. It is destabilizing. Everything is distorted, even the lies, so that they come out like the whimpers of a spoiled child – earnest and innocent, even when they are unfounded. It is a win-lose world, in which winners and losers can switch overnight… on the whim of an egomaniacal imbecile.

But Mr. Trump did the world a great favor. He showed the world that U.S. politics had no more real solemnity or authenticity than WWE's WrestleMania.

Many people thought WWE's peculiar brand of entertainment was washed up in 1989. That's when Stephanie McMahon admitted to the New Jersey Senate that the whole thing was a spoof. New Jersey had rules governing sporting events; the WWE was not in compliance. Of course not, McMahon told the senators; it's not a real sport.

But instead of turning on McMahon and wrasslin', the fans doubled down. Like America's voters, they were way ahead of the New Jersey lawmakers; they knew the whole thing was fake. And they also knew it wasn't fake. Wrasslers were human. They got hurt. They bore grudges. They had wives and girlfriends… and they had real-life struggles, which professional wrestling seemed only to amplify… and make even more real.

Stephanie McMahon is the daughter of Vince McMahon, ringmaster of the whole circus. Part of her schtick was to get together with Paul Levesque, a pro-performer also known as "Triple H." The script called for them to be bad guys, pretending to marry and then trying to steal the family business from her father and brother. Then, in real life, they did get married and had three children.

Now, Triple H is a good guy. And in the April 2019 WrestleMania extravaganza at MetLife Stadium in New Jersey, he was going to work on his opponent, Batista, with hammer and tongs. He attacked him with a sledge… and then tried to pull his nose rings out with a pair of pliers.

It is not hard to see where Mr. Trump, a longtime pro-wrestling fan, learned his trade. Not from reading the Federalist Papers. Nor from studying Adams or Eisenhower. Instead, he was watching the Kardashians and hanging out with Vince McMahon. And now, he's taken fakiness to a whole new level and turned the U.S. government into a kind of state-sponsored WrestleMania. Fake wars, fake money, fake news, fake heroes, fake villains, fake truth, fake lies, fake myths –

like reality TV, it provides the public with a counterfeit world where it can believe any damned thing it wants.

A WORD ABOUT ROME

The Roman Empire was "civilized." Looking at it more closely returns us to the oxymoron at the beginning of this book – civilized warfare – and helps us understand the phenomenon of "civilization" more fully.

The Roman Empire was a going concern as long as the empire expanded. New kingdoms and dominions were conquered. Loot and slaves were captured. Empire was a paying proposition. Then, around the end of the first century, the limits were reached. This left a huge, more-or-less-free trade zone from the tip of the Iberian Peninsula to the upper reaches of the Nile, with a system of roads, police protection, a common language, and a common form of money. Win-win deals flourished. Gentle commerce encouraged people to try to please customers. This led them to become more civilized, gaining status not only by gaining wealth, but also by taking up the refined manners, language, arts, philosophy, literature, and customs of the empire.

Generally, at least before the Barbarian invasions began, Roman citizens enjoyed a quality of life that was substantially different, and more advanced, than that of the unconquered world. Roads, schools, trade, dwellings, decorations, food, sculpture, public architecture – it was all finer, much more sophisticated, and more elaborate on the west side of the Rhine than on the east side.

This civilized life was probably made possible by the empire's business model; it used violence to create the space, the time, and the rules that gave civilization a chance to develop. But there always was, and still is, a contradiction between force and cooperation. You can take by conquest. But you can't make or create cooperative, civilized life that way.

As time went on, the elite grew larger and more corrupt. In *The*

Collapse of Complex Societies, historian Joseph Tainter tells us what Rome had become by the fifth century:

> *The empire that emerged under Diocletian and Constantine was administered by a government that was larger, more complex, more highly organized, and that commanded larger and more powerful military forces. It taxed its citizens more heavily, conscripted their labor, and regulated their lives and their occupations. It was a coercive, omnipresent, all-powerful organization that subdued individual interests and levied all resources toward one overarching goal: the survival of the State.*

And *The Cambridge Ancient History* captures the next phase:

> *The full rigor of the law was let loose on the population. Soldiers acted as bailiffs or wandered as secret police through the land. Those who suffered most were, of course, the propertied class...*
>
> *In connection with all this, compulsion and state-socialist regulation had established themselves more firmly...*
>
> *Arrest, confiscation, and execution hung over their heads like a sword of Damocles...*
>
> *If the propertied classes buried their money, or sacrificed two-thirds of their estate to escape from a magistracy, or went so far as to give up their whole property in order to get free of the domains rent, and the non-propertied class ran away, the state replied by increasing the pressure...*

At the time of Odoacer's final assault, the empire had already been under attack and greatly destabilized for more than 100 years. Rome had been sacked in 410 by the Visigoths and again in 455 by the Vandals. Between the bright day of civilization and the dark night of Barbarian control lay a long and turbulent crepuscule. Civilization had been so weakened that by the time the last flickers of daylight disappeared, there were probably many people who were relieved.

By then, the Barbarian raids, incursions, and invasions – not to mention the open warfare between Rome's own leading generals and rulers – had created such anxiety, turmoil, and suffering that many people were ready for a change. Slaves, army deserters (many of them from Germanic tribes), displaced families, remnants of other broken-up armies, tribes, and cities went over to the invaders. They might not have expected better lives, but they were desperate, many on the edge of starvation. By then, the pleasant and productive life within the Roman Empire had been largely destroyed by taxes, regulations, corruption, rebellions, power struggles, epidemics, and invasions. As Salvian, the fifth-century writer from Gaul, put it, "They preferred to live freely under the appearance of slavery than live in slavery under the appearance of freedom."

Of course, it's been a long time since the Roman Empire's demise in 476. And we saw in our discussion of Fake News that the information value of what we know from the period has been greatly degraded by time and distance. So, our analysis is derived more from abstraction, theory, and guesswork than from actual "history." Still, we will make a feeble effort to deconstruct the apparent contradiction between a successful imperial strategy based on conquest, loot, and tribute (win-lose) and a successful civil society, which, we maintain, can only work on a win-win basis.

First, we point out that there is no such thing as a pure win-win civil society. There are always some pickpockets and parasites; and the richer, more trusting the society, the more confident the defectors become. Nor could a pure win-lose society exist. Parasites need hosts. Thieves need marks. Killers need victims. Always and everywhere, both strategies exist.

Second, the Roman Empire only began with Caesar Augustus in 27 B.C. And it reached its apogee only about a century later. After that, the character of the empire changed. Instead of conquest, Rome's remarkable martial talents were directed towards ambitious engineering projects – roads, aqueducts, and bridges – providing about 300 years in which win-win deals could flourish under the shelter of the Roman Imperium and its infrastructure.

During this period, even the nature of Rome's foreign policy shifted, after Trajan, from aggressive growth to get-along, go-along maintenance of the status quo. The Roman Empire, of course, maintained garrisons all around the frontiers. Soldiers were still trained for war. They were still ready to fight, but they fought less often, and only when diplomacy failed. As Scipio Africanus put it after annihilating Carthage, "The Roman people will never be the first to violate [a treaty]." Not historically accurate, but it foretold a tilt toward a win-win, tit-for-tat strategy.

Third, what made the empire such an attractive target for Barbarians was that its win-win deals were so successful. Made possible by a vast area of more-or-less free trade, a common, written language (Latin), common money (the aureus, solidus, and the denarius were generally and usually reliable forms of money, based on gold and silver), and a common court system, which presided over the expulsion, or even crucifixion, of defectors (law-breakers), far more win-win deals were done during the Roman Empire than had ever been done before.

Historian Michel de Jaeghere, too, explains that Roman society was based on vernacular, win-win arrangements:

> *The reciprocity of exchanges wasn't regulated by law; it was subject to social pressure which made ingratitude shameful.*

And it was governed, he says, by two Roman-era concepts: *fides* and *pietas*. "Fides" means reliability or faithfulness. Romans were, and should be, fides. To each other. They could count on one another. In business and in war. By contrast, they knew they couldn't trust the Carthaginians. "Punica fides" meant untrustworthy.

As we've seen, trust reduces the cost of win-win deals. Less "due diligence" was needed before the deal was concluded. Less monitoring was necessary while it was ongoing. Less enforcement of the terms was required. And there were fewer disasters of misunderstanding or ill-will at the end.

There was also a common myth that bound Romans one to another and gave them a sense of national purpose. Virgil laid it out for them in the *Aeneid*. Aeneas from Troy escaped the destruction of his native city. He wandered hither and yon, carrying his father on his back, with his young son, Ascanius, by his side. But he washed up on the shores of the Tiber, and there, founded Rome. The story was embellished by its author and accepted as a noble lie. Neither true nor untrue, it gave Romans a common narrative and connected them to those of the past and to those yet unborn.

Naturally, as the empire expanded, the connecting tissue stretched... and then broke. The Pax Romana – the peace and prosperity enjoyed by people within the empire – had greatly expanded the "us" beyond a single tribe. Many were the peoples within the empire, speaking many different languages and worshipping many different gods. Not all were Roman citizens. But all shared in the "universalist" promise: all could benefit from both the vernacular and the fiat rules.

Then, scarcely 100 years after the empire peaked under Trajan, Caracalla granted Roman citizenship to all free people within the empire. Intended to give them all a chance to share the noble lie, instead, it cheapened the common bond – citizenship. By then, the internal rot was already well advanced. Win-lose deals, in which the government played an essential role, proliferated.

Thus weakened by insiders, the wealth of the empire was vulnerable to outsiders; Barbarians took it away as soon as they were able.

Finally, it was alleged, by Voltaire and eighteenth-century historian Edward Gibbon, most famously and remarkably, that while the empire perhaps did not stop win-win deals... win-win deals stopped the empire! Or, more specifically, Christianity – with its "love thy neighbor" creed – undermined the Roman's fighting spirit. The Early Christian writer Tertullian, for example, tells us that religious pacifists refused to do military service for the empire. (They were excommunicated after the Council of Arles in 314.)

But it is one thing to refuse military service where there are plenty of Goths ready to do the job for slave wages. It is another when the Goths are at the gate! Then, after the invasions began, people did what they could to fight… or get away… regardless of their religious views. The problem was perhaps that win-win deals had been too successful. The typical citizen was neither trained nor organized to fight. Instead, the fighting (an essential win-lose occupation) had been outsourced to the foreigners. Part of the reason for this was that the population within the civilized world was falling… for obscure and hotly contested reasons. Manning the frontiers was just the kind of work – like picking vegetables in the San Fernando Valley today – that was easy to give to foreigners.

That said, there is some truth to Gibbon's charge, which was outlined in *The History of the Decline and Fall of the Roman Empire*. But not in the way he meant. For all the reasons given in this book, win-win makes people stronger, economically. This gives them the capacity to finance more sophisticated weapons and to support standing, well-trained armies.

But there is no guarantee that you will be able to enjoy your wealth in peace just because you obtained it in peace. Fat animals attract predators.

Win-win is the best way to play the game. But it's not the only way. As wealth grew, so did the temptation to take it away. Mentioned above, the frontier garrisons were composed more and more of Germanic or other non-Roman outsiders, who were fine fighters, but less committed to defending the empire to the death.

In 354, an offensive against the Alamans was undermined by high-ranking Barbarians in the Roman forces. In 357, Julian was betrayed by deserters, who passed vital information to the enemy on the eve of the

Battle for Strasbourg. Constance III watched his Visigoth allies walk off the job as he fought the Vandals in Spain in 420. As the empire weakened, the treason got worse. In the campaigns of Theodosius, Valens, and Magnus Maximus, over and over, the Barbarians deserted or betrayed their Roman commanders.

As the population of the empire decreased, so did the amount of land in production, which was the source of Rome's tax revenues. The result: fewer loyal soldiers and less money to pay them. The foreign mercenaries were relatively cheap, but as we have seen, they were not completely reliable.

There was also an evolution in the myths that held an empire together. On that score, too, Gibbon may have a point. At least many people at the time thought so. Gone were the old gods; the Christians had thrown them into the trash bin. Perhaps Rome's gods were having their revenge?

Yale professor Ramsay MacMullen, among others, believes much of the blame for the collapse of the Roman Empire lies in the fact that the bonds of civility that held it together had loosened over time, and were replaced by a new, short-term, exploitative morality. He believes the old bonds of reciprocity, honor, and obligation gave way to corruption and get-it-while-you-can money exchanges. That is, he too believes win-win deals played a role in Rome's decline and fall.

But the argument can be recast in our own terms. The cynical, commercial transactions criticized by historians like MacMullen often involve criminal or administrative authorities. One gets paid a bribe because he has some power over the other. One needs a document, a license, a pass, or a permission; and he is ready to pay for it. The parties come to terms. Money changes hands. It looks like a "capitalist," or a win-win, market deal. But this is hardly a civilized exchange. Behind it is a lopsided power relationship, with more and more people drawing on the government's police power to get what they want. By the late fourth century, corruption was so common that, as Cyprian of Carthage tells us: "Don't be surprised that they don't punish criminals [here]. There's nothing but criminals."

Salvian added, "What is the life of a businessman? A collection of frauds and perjuries. The clergy? A long iniquity. The public sector? A bunch of lies. Soldiers? A series of plunder."

In other words, Rome suffered from the phenomenon that author Walter Scheidel, mentioned in an earlier chapter, tried to measure. The insider elites used violence to extract wealth and power from the rest of the society. Then, after the Barbarian incursions began, the weaknesses caused by these win-lose deals were exposed; the returns to the Barbarians shot up, while those to the doomed resistors fell sharply.

WIN-WIN VERSUS WIN-LOSE

The details change. The patterns often don't.

For at least 2,000 years, public life has been dominated by a largely unnoticed struggle. On the one side were the takers... the parasites... and the Barbarians, ready to use violence to get what they wanted. On the other were the everyday people who had to get along and go along... give to get... and cooperate with one another to make their lives more agreeable.

It was win-win versus win-lose, with the battle generally going in the win-win direction, subject to epic corrections. The success of win-win was probably not brought about by a moral awakening or changing fashions. More likely, it was just better suited to a modern world. Win-win creates wealth. Those who have wealth are also able to use it either to produce more abundance, or for win-lose purposes (sustained, armed warfare, for example). Win-win wins, in other words, even at win-lose.

At the time of Romulus Augustus, the last emperor in the West, property was still either portable or seizable – if you had the force. You could invade – like the Vandals or the Huns – and steal everything you could grab, and then return back across the Rhine to enjoy your plunder. Or you could invade and settle, like the Visigoths or the Lombards, using your new lands to produce crops, the leading wealth of the time. Either way, you came out ahead. And you could also enslave whatever peoples fell into your hands. These slaves could be sold or used on your own lands.

Today, theft and slavery are less rewarding. It's almost impossible to steal stock in a publicly listed corporation. Bitcoin is difficult to purloin, too. Even portable goods, such as cars and antiques, are readily traceable and recoverable, so that their value drops sharply after you steal them. Imagine that you lead a group to seize the fertile farmland of Northern New Jersey... or a big swathe of its suburban homes. After the theft, the market value would drop so sharply that it would hardly be worth the effort.

Slavery, too, is much less profitable than it used to be. Hiring wage slaves is much cheaper, for almost any job you can imagine. Even digging the Lake Pontchartrain Canal in the mosquito-ridden swamps of Louisiana in 1832 was more economical with cheap, Irish wage earners than with slaves. The slaves had a capital value that would be lost if they died. The Irish worked on a pay-as-you-go basis. When they died, they were easily replaced. In the entire Bible, there is famously no condemnation of slavery. Presumably, it was still profitable and taken for granted. Our guess is that moral outrage rose as the net market value of slave output fell.

Today, only the feds dare to use win-lose violence publicly, and often proudly. But even they are often cagey about it. Tax rates in the U.S. have come down since the 1950s. Politicians prefer to rip off voters with fake money and public debt, rather than confront them directly with taxation. Embezzlement is more popular than armed robbery. Fraud has generally replaced force. But fraud only works until the fraud is discovered; then, the AK-47s come out.

You can't design or build a civilization. But you can destroy it. And sometimes, destroying a civilization is the best way to win. Because wealth is ultimately relative. Imagine that you have 10 pigs and your neighbor has 10 pigs. You gain an extra pig; you have 10% more than your neighbor. But if you steal one of his pigs, you now have 22% more. There's a reason why "envy" is considered a "deadly sin" by Christians. It opens the door to destructive win-lose deals and undermines the basic idea of the whole win-win world.

There are many elements to a civilization – including vernacular patterns of music, architecture, manners, common law, and money. But the most important – as Jesus said himself – was the basic rule of reciprocity that governs all civilized relationships: Do unto others as you would have them do unto you. No one would want his neighbor to attack him or his wealth. And if the neighbor could buy into the win-win myth... to the idea that he shouldn't even want anything bad to happen to his neighbor, even if the SOB was getting rich... the whole community would benefit.

Painfully slowly, and with a lot of backsliding, win-win gained. It was a "myth." But it was one that was well suited to a modern, post-Old Testament world.

✑ — AN AFTERTHOUGHT — ✑

Amor Fati

✝·✝·✝·✝

"AMOR FATI" WAS Nietzsche's famous expression. It is a Latin phrase with connections to the Stoic writings of Epictetus and Marcus Aurelius. Literally translated, it means "love of fate." It is a white shoe yearning for mud. It is a turkey looking forward to Thanksgiving. Or an investor stoically preparing for a bear market.

We use the term to describe the grace and courage you need to meet a complex, unknowable, and uncontrollable future. You don't know whether the Earth is warming or cooling… whether it is good or bad… or whether you can do anything about it. You don't know who's doing "equal work." You don't know what equality is… how to measure it… or what to do about it. You don't know who the bad guy is. It may even be you.

It recognizes that we are all God's fools, living in a world of ignorance, headed towards we don't know where. Using our brains, we can make progress in our physical, material world. Technical thinking yields pyramids and Eiffel Towers.

But there is another part of life, which has a mind of its own. It does not bend readily to our desires or yield to our intelligence. It is the part of life whose purposes are unknown. The first and most important Commandment, according to Jesus, was not to fight it, but to love it.

But ignorance can be a charm. You just have to take it seriously. And appreciate it. Recognizing your own ignorance will inform your newfound modesty. You will be aware of it. And fiercely proud. Nobody will be humbler than you are!

And since you are so chummy with ignorance, you will see it everywhere – in every headline, every public announcement, every speech on the floor of the Senate... and every crackpot comment from every dummy voter in the empire.

In private affairs, you reduce uncertainty by getting as close to the subject as possible. That is, you avoid secondhand "news" and try to find out for yourself. The more you know about a company, for example, the more confident you can be about investing in it. That's why the insiders always have the inside track, an advantage that is increased by the SEC's phony "level playing field" propaganda.

In public affairs – policy discussions, economics, politics – as you get closer, you become less cocksure. That is, the more you know, the more you know you don't know.

In an interesting university study, people were asked to pick out Ukraine on a map... and whether they approved of military intervention in that country. Curiously, the further off they were on the geography (the average guess was 1,800 miles off), the more they favored forceful intervention. In public affairs, ignorance and confidence vary inversely.

When we first moved to Baltimore in the 1980s, we noticed this phenomenon in another context. Baltimore was a disaster. Crime, drugs, poverty, venereal disease, broken homes, unwed mothers, corruption – name a social problem; Baltimore had it.

And while its leaders had been noticeably unable to solve any of these problems right in their own back yard, the city's politically correct politicians were loud and clear on one issue: apartheid had to end... in South Africa. Had they ever visited South Africa? Could they find it on a map? Probably not. But they were sure they knew how to make it a better place.

"Moral certainty is always a sign of cultural inferiority," wrote Baltimore's own H.L. Mencken. "The more uncivilized the man, the surer he is that he knows precisely what is right and what is wrong. All human progress, even in morals, has been the work of men who have doubted the current moral values, not of men who have whooped them up and tried to enforce them. The truly civilized man is always skeptical and tolerant, in this field as in all others. His culture is based on 'I am not too sure.'"

"I am not too sure," would eliminate many of the world's myth-driven, self-inflicted ills – pointless wars, dumb arguments, pogroms, persecutions, and lynchings. And reckless spending of other people's money. Imagine a wise Hitler entertaining the idea of building Auschwitz as a "final solution" to the "Jewish problem."

"Hmmm… I'm not too sure that would solve it… In fact, I'm not too sure there is a problem!"

Imagine Simon de Montfort readying to attack the town of Albi to exterminate the "heretics." When told that half the people in the town were good Catholics, de Montfort replied: "Kill them all. God will recognize His own."

Suppose he had thought twice…

"Hmmm… Maybe this is not such a good idea… Maybe killing people is not what Christianity is all about… Maybe the heretics aren't so bad… Maybe I'll take the afternoon off."

The barroom blowhard… so sure he is right about everything… is generally the dumbest guy in the place. And the most dangerous. He's the one who will stir up a mob… and get himself elected president. The whole system of modern public policy is built on false knowledge and unwarranted confidence. The elite claims to know what is best for you. That is how every politician can claim his proposals would "benefit the American people." But the only program that would benefit the American people would be to let them decide for themselves what would benefit them. Give them back their money. Stop bossing them around. End the wars. Stop the empire. But who would suggest such a thing?

A book that appeared in 2018, *Psychology of a Superpower: Security and Dominance in U.S. Foreign Policy*, by political scientist Christopher Fettweis, argued that power really does corrupt, and that when a nation or an empire gets too much power, its elite develops new opinions. Rather than seeing itself as one of many nations that must get along with each other, its elites begin to see that they have a special role to play. They become the one, "indispensable" nation, as former Secretary of State Madeleine Albright put it. They are the world's only hope in combatting evil, which they do, as current Secretary of State Mike Pompeo elaborated, with "the righteous knowledge that our cause is just, special, and built upon America's core principles."

Thus endowed with a special mission and special powers, and subject to the special rules of the only nation with a trillion-dollar-per-year military/empire budget, the elite develop, in Fettweis's judgment, a fatal combination of unrestrained hubris, unrealistic paranoia, and unrepentant ignorance. They see danger everywhere, without undertaking any serious study (they assume knowledge comes automatically with raw power). And they think they have not only the right, but the means, to do something about it, even if the danger is largely fantasy.

But people always come to think what they need to think when they need to think it. "All earthly empires die," wrote St. Augustine in 413, a few years before the Vandals destroyed his city and finally brought down the Roman Empire in the West. The elite contribute, by taking up the myths that help it die. Certainty and ignorance vary proportionally, both on the individual and on a national level.

The surer a nation is of its myths… its exceptionalism… its manifest destiny… its policies… and its position at the right hand of God…

…the more it is damned to Hell.

Index